*Joke*lore

*Joke*lore

Jokelore

HUMOROUS FOLKTALES FROM Indiana

Ronald L. Baker

INDIANA UNIVERSITY PRESS

Bloomington & Indianapolis

Library of Congress Cataloging-in-Publication Data

Baker, Ronald L.
  Jokelore : humorous folktales from Indiana.

  1. Tales—Indiana. 2. American wit and humor—
Indiana. I. Title.
GR110.I6B34 1986   398.2′09772   84-43174
ISBN 0-253-33163-3

  2 3 4 5 90 89

Manufactured in the United States of America

"*Is the subject of jokes worth so much trouble?*
There can, I think, be no doubt about it."

—SIGMUND FREUD

CONTENTS

TALL TALES

CATCH TALES AND HOAXES

SHAGGY DOGS

ANIMALS

MARRIED COUPLES

DRUNKS AND SLOTHS

THE WISE

THE FOOLISH

IGNORANCE OF SEX

KENTUCKIANS

IRISH

BLACKS

POLES

JEWS

KENTUCKIANS

IRISH

BLACKS

POLES

JEWS

CATHOLICS

PREACHERS

GOD AND JESUS

SALESMEN AND OTHER TRAVELERS

DOCTORS, NURSES, AND PATIENTS

SCHOOLTEACHERS

FARMERS

POLITICIANS

GOLFERS

Introduction

SINCE 1846 when an English antiquarian, William J. Thoms, coined the "good Saxon compound," *folk-lore,* to replace what was until then called "popular antiquities" or "popular literature," there has been considerable disagreement about what folklore means. The plethora of definitions of folklore is aptly illustrated in the *Funk and Wagnalls Standard Dictionary of Folklore, Mythology, and Legend* (1949–50), which offers nòt one but twenty-one definitions of folklore written by twenty-one scholars from diverse academic disciplines. A representative definition of folklore in that dated dictionary was written by the esteemed American folklorist Archer Taylor, who saw folklore "as materials that are handed down traditionally from generation to generation without a reliable ascription to an inventor or author."[1] Emphasizing folklore as materials (texts, artifacts), Taylor's definition remained a typical one until the 1960s when many American folklorists became disenchanted with comparative studies of traditional texts and turned their attention to other aspects of traditional culture, including function, context, performance, audience, and individual folk artists or craftsmen.

This shift, from defining folklore as simply materials of oral tradition to defining it more broadly, is reflected in the work of Richard M. Dorson. In 1959 Dorson viewed folklore as "the oral traditions channeled across the centuries through human mouths. . . .

In the United States, folklore has customarily meant the spoken and sung traditions."² Nine years later, however, in a brochure entitled *1968 Festival of American Folklore,* published by the Smithsonian Institution, Dorson redefined folklore more holistically as unofficial culture: "Folklore is the culture of the people. It is the hidden submerged culture lying in the shadow of the official civilization about which historians write."³ Dorson's concept of folklore as the unofficial culture of subgroups is an improvement over earlier definitions stressing folklore as merely items extracted from traditional culture; however, it fails to stress the dynamic quality of folklore. What's more, readers unfamiliar with folklore scholarship could read into Dorson's definition their misconception of folklore as simply quaint survivals found among backward people. Consequently, some contemporary folklorists interested in the ethnographic present have defined folklore not narrowly as traditional materials or broadly as unofficial culture but as a communicative event—a process of social interaction involving performer, text (or artifact), audience, and context. Thus, Dan Ben-Amos, sees folklore as "artistic communication in small groups."⁴ Accordingly, a folktale, for instance, is not a text recorded, printed, and read; it is a storyteller's performance of a tale before a specific audience in a natural physical setting.

My own concept of folklore is eclectic, drawing upon older definitions and approaches as well as on more recent ones. *Folklore,* as I view it, is the dynamic process of sharing informal culture within close-knit groups. *Folkloristics* is the study of the patterned verbal, material, and behavioral manifestations of this informal culture within historical, physical, and social contexts. As Dorson observed, the folklorist is especially interested in subcultures within literate societies. Consequently, the folk are not necessarily illiterate peasants or hillbillies, although they may be. *Folk* means people, especially groups of people who have something in common—ethnic, religious, occupational, or geographic backgrounds, for example. Consequently, all of us are folk, generally belonging to several folk groups at the same time. *Lore* consists of traditional mentifacts, artifacts, and pictographs that are informally passed on from one person to another by word of mouth, customary apprenticeship, handwriting, typewriting, xerography or other informal means of communicating. Thus, the forms of lore range from oral genres like legends, jokes, ballads, and proverbs to material traditions like log buildings, household crafts, woodcarvings, and costumes. Some items of lore—like traditional beliefs, customs, dances, and games—combine oral and non-oral elements. Other forms of lore, like folk cartoons and mock letters and memos, are neither oral nor physical but circulate in contemporary society through xerography and other forms of informal communication. In short, the entire traditional way of life is the subject of folklore studies. There is a folklore of the present as well as of the past, a folklore of the city as well as of the country, and a folklore of the educated as well as of the uneducated.

The proliferation of definitions of folklore over the years reflects the various ways that the subject matter of folklore has been viewed as well as the various ways that the study of folklore has been practiced. Folklorists of Archer Taylor's generation who viewed folklore as materials passed on traditionally were interested primarily in studying versions of folkloric products comparatively, while contemporary folklorists who see folklore as a communicative process are mainly interested in studying folkloric events within particular contexts. These two basic approaches were acknowledged as early as 1935 when Ruth Benedict complained that "Folkloristic studies, since the days of Cosquin and the students stimulated by the collections of the Grimm brothers, have been extensive rather than intensive."[5] The extensive approach, as Benedict noted, is a far-flung comparative study of folklore from different cultures. Today this extensive approach is generally considered a literary or humanistic approach and is text-oriented, often dealing with the formal qualities of a traditional genre and the classification of folklore. The intensive approach, on the other hand, is an in-depth study of folklore in a particular culture. It is usually identified as an anthropological or social scientific approach and is context-oriented, often relating the performance of folklore to other cultural traits or to the folk artist and audience. The extensive approach generally stresses the value of folklore for understanding a common humanity, while the intensive approach often stresses the value of folklore for understanding a particular culture.

The debate between proponents of the extensive and intensive approaches continues, although the jargon varies. Some folklorists refer to macro-level and micro-level approaches. Others refer to cross-cultural and culture-specific approaches. Still others refer simply to the text-context controversy. Whatever they are called, there remain two basic approaches to studying folklore: one approach that is interested mainly in formal and thematic elements in folklore genres wherever they may be found, and another approach that is interested more in the function and meaning of folklore performances in specific contexts. In the late 1960s and early 1970s a particular version of the intensive approach, the contextual approach, was advanced, as Roger L. Janelli has observed, "with all the fervor of a new religious movement. Unlike previous approaches which had been content to coexist peacefully with their alternatives, the performance-centered viewpoint challenged the very theoretical foundations of traditional folklore scholarship."[6] In a classic debate on text and context with Dan Ben-Amos in *Western Folklore,* Steven Swann Jones more emphatically argues that the contextualists are dogmatic since they suggest "that their approach is the *only* valid way of examining the phenomena of folklore. This is simply not the case."[7] In folklore scholarship, as Dundes has noted, "theories and methods come and go, often enjoying several years of faddish favor before joining predecessors in the overflowing dustbin of discarded 'new' approaches."[8] Thus, just as the textual approach was challenged by the contextual approach in the late 1960s and early 1970s, today the contextual approach is being challenged anew by the textual approach as well as by other approaches. As Lynwood Montell recently observed:

> In the late 1960s and early '70s, . . . a radical shift, with far-reaching implications, took place. . . . The study of folklore moved toward a closer alignment with the social sciences, especially cultural anthropology and sociolinguistics. The resulting emphasis was on the study of expressive culture in behavioristic terms. Adherents of the contextual school of folkloristic thought believed it was the key to the revitalization of folklore studies. And any student of the history of the discipline knows what valuable contributions and keen, fresh insights their theories offered. It is still unclear why the anticipated impact of the contextual approach never fully materialized. . . .
>
> One might speculate that behavioral, contextual studies have faltered because, as a discipline, folklore has been shifting gradually toward other emphases, one of which is folklife. The early distinction between folklore as verbal arts and folklife as material culture seems to be giving way to a concentration on the totality of human traditional expression—verbal, artifactual, and behavioral—as a patterned system within a group or a region.[9]

Whereas the textual school of folkloristics was influenced by literary history and formal criticism, and the contextual school was influenced by sociolinguistics and the behavioral sciences, the contemporary folklife school (called the "folk-cultural" approach by Dorson[10], seems to be moving toward a closer alignment with cultural geography and oral history. Thus, the concept of folklore will continue to shift as the folk-cultural approach gains momentum in folkloristics and then in its turn gives way to fresher approaches. The fact that folkloristics is dynamic like the culture it studies is not inappropriate. Folklorists utilize a variety of approaches to examine traditional life from every angle, which only gives strength and vitality to their discipline. Particular folklorists may be reductionists, but the discipline of folkloristics is not reductive. Since the Lang-Müller debate in the late nineteenth century, folkloristics has thrived on controversy.[11] In retrospect, the textualists as well as the contextualists have made valuable contributions to the understanding of the traditional way of life, and the contemporary folk-cultural scholars have examined aspects of traditional culture (notably folk objects and their makers and meanings) that literary folklorists and ethnographers of communication barely touched. Other perspectives—such as the philosophy of culture exemplified in the works of Ernst Cassirer, W. M. Urban, and David Bidney—wait quietly in the wings to one day come forth, make their impact, and help folkloristics mature as an academic discipline.

Among contemporary folklorists, only Alan Dundes is moving toward a philosophy of culture, and he is doing this not by uncritically disparaging the work of his fellow students of traditional culture but by being selective in accepting the many good things that have been accomplished by historic-geographers, structuralists, functionalists, contextualists, and psychoanalysts and then moving beyond them toward a comprehensive theory of culture. For one thing, Dundes recognizes the importance of collecting texts, for he rightly asserts that "good data never go out of style."[12] At the same time, however, he acknowledges the limitations of the textual approach:

The 'object-collecting' philosophy is itself a survival of the antiquarian days of folklore studies. Folklore texts without contexts are essentially analogous to the large numbers of exotic musical instruments which adorn the walls of anthropological or folk museums and grace the homes of private individuals. The instrument is authentic as is the folklore text, but the range of the instrument, the tuning of the instrument, the function of the instrument, and the intricacies of performing with the instrument are rarely known.[13]

While Dundes, like most contemporary folklorists, demands contextual evidence, unlike many contemporary folklorists, he also recognizes the limitations of contextual studies:

> The current interest in the collection of context, however, has partially
> obscured the equally necessary and important task of collecting the mean-
> ing(s) of folklore. One must distinguish between *use* and *meaning*. The
> collection of context and preferably a number of different contexts for the
> same item of folklore is certainly helpful in ascertaining the meaning or
> meanings of an item of folklore. But it cannot be assumed that the collec-
> tion of context per se automatically ensures the collection of meaning. . . .
> One cannot always guess the meaning from context. For this reason,
> *folklorists must actively seek to elicit the meaning of folklore from the
> folk.*[14]

Thus, to aid the folklorist in interpreting what folklore means,
Dundes encourages the collector-analyst to record "oral literary criticism," the folk's own interpretation of their folklore.[15] "For each item
of oral literature," Dundes stresses, "there is a variety of oral literary
criticism. . . . There is no one right interpretation of an item of
folklore any more than there is but one right version of a tale or
song. . . . There are multiple meanings and interpretations and they
all ought to be collected. One could ask ten different informants what
each thought a given joke meant and one might obtain ten different
answers."[16] Dundes goes beyond most contextualists in distinguish-
ing between function and meaning and in emphasizing that meaning
cannot always be guessed even when context is described.

The following joke, collected in April 1978, aptly illustrates the
importance of collecting context and recording the commentary of the
participants in the joking event: "What did Helen Keller do when she
fell in the well?" *She screamed her hands off.* This joke was performed
in a women's dormitory room on the Indiana State University campus
in Terre Haute. Normally tidy, the room at this particular time, 9:00
p.m. during a week of heavy exams, was a mess. Both desks were
cluttered with books and papers, and both beds were unmade and
piled with clothing. More clothing and some dirty dishes and a
popcorn popper covered the floor. Soft music from a portable radio
contributed to a relaxed and informal atmosphere. Besides the informant, three other female students, including the informant's room-
mate, were in the room. All of the girls were approximately the same
age as the informant, and all were good friends. One member of the

audience reported that "we were all finishing up our homework for the evening. The atmosphere was perfect for telling a few jokes and acting silly. It helped us relieve the tensions we were experiencing from our school work."

The informant was a nineteen-year-old female college junior majoring in communication disorders (speech-hearing pathology). Friends of the informant described her as serious, intelligent, and mature for her age. One member of the audience said that the informant "is a friend of mine, but at times I feel a little uneasy goofing off and acting silly around her. . . . She is normally quite sober and serious when it comes to her school work, especially when the subject is her major. Very seldom would one ever hear her making fun of a deaf person, let alone one of the most famous and respected deaf persons of our history. This subject is very dear to everyone, but especially to her."

Members of the audience agreed that the informant was not an active bearer of jokes and that it was out of character for her to tell a joke about a handicapped person. One member of the audience said that "it was shocking but very funny when she [the informant] started telling a Helen Keller joke. It was an old joke I had heard many times before, but it suddenly became funny again. She . . . had trouble even getting through the joke without cracking up. Each time she was about to give the punch line, she would burst into laughter. It was really funny to hear her giggle over such a serious topic. If anyone else had told that joke, it wouldn't have been half as funny." The joke was well received by the audience and served to change the group's attitude toward the informant, as one member of the audience observed:

> It [the performance of the joke] showed us a side of her [the informant] we had never seen. When she told us that joke, it not only lightened up her personality, but it lightened up our feelings about her. Instead of looking at her as a mother figure, someone we all came to with our problems, we now thought of her as a good friend. We will now feel more at ease when it comes to having a good time around her. If she can joke about something that means that much to her, she can relax about other things.

Information about the physical and social contexts and interviews with members of the audience clearly reveal much more about the use and meaning of this Helen Keller joke than the brief text alone does, but the informant's own comments about why the joke was performed in this particular context are equally enlightening:

COLLECTOR: What types of jokes do you like?

INFORMANT: I can tell you some I don't like: dead baby jokes. I hate them. What kind of jokes do I like? I like jokes that . . . that turn out completely different from what everybody thinks they're going to turn out. You know, right to the end. As far as subject matter, I usually don't like jokes on handicapped people unless . . . unless a handicapped person could hear that joke and laugh at it.

COLLECTOR: Why did you choose speech and hearing as your major?

INFORMANT: When I was in high school, a sophomore, I had to get a retainer, and that gives you a very bad lisp for at least the first two to three weeks till you learn to compensate for this thing in your mouth. It changed the way you talked completely. You have to almost learn to say half your phonemes all over again, and it really bothered me because people just . . . I'd say one word, and they knew something was different, and it really made you self-conscious, you know. You didn't want to say anything in class. I remember I was in my English class; and my professor always had me read, and, oh, I refused. It was a week before I would read in that class. It made me understand what these people are going through when they're learning to talk—not necessarily the deaf, just speech problems and, you know, the deaf too.

COLLECTOR: Do you have a special concern for deaf people over other handicapped people?

INFORMANT: I'm more interested in deaf people. I think that their problems are very hard to overcome. What they can accomplish in just . . . it's fantastic what they can accomplish. It's really amazing how someone that has never heard before in their life can learn to speak and learn to get along in the world, can learn to be a normal person.

COLLECTOR: Since this subject is so serious to you, why did you joke about one of the most famous deaf persons of our time?

INFORMANT: I think mainly because she is known to be a deaf person. There are probably a lot of people you would know that are deaf. It wouldn't be funny if you just said a deaf person. You know, it wouldn't be as funny; but Helen Keller is known to be deaf, and she's known to have accomplished. She was known to be a great person, and that's the thing. That's the way society is. We make fun of great people.

COLLECTOR: And so it wasn't just because she was a deaf person.

INFORMANT: It was because of her status, what she had accomplished.

COLLECTOR: So you wouldn't make fun of a normal deaf person. It's just that it was Helen Keller, who was famous.

INFORMANT: I don't think it would be as humorous if you just said a deaf person.

COLLECTOR: Why did you tell this joke in this particular situation?

INFORMANT: Well, I had been studying for a really big test, one that's really important . . . to pass a really important class that's required for my major. And I heard the joke in class, or in, you know, within a bunch of kids that are in my major. But I thought it was really crude, really crude. I didn't think it was funny at the time, but after studying all that time and working so hard that I just needed to get away, you know. So I just . . . that joke just happened to pop in my head, and since you guys were just sitting around here, I don't know, it seemed funny then. It was funny when I wanted it to be funny.

COLLECTOR: What did you hope to gain by telling that joke?

INFORMANT: Relieve tension and relax, just break away from studying.

COLLECTOR: Do you have any other comments on why you told that particular joke?

INFORMANT: I don't think it would be any different . . . it shouldn't be taken any different for *me* to tell that joke than it would be for anybody else. I mean just because that happens to be something I'm interested in and feel really strongly about, it shouldn't be different. I mean, I should be able to joke about it too, and granted there are some really crude jokes about every subject in the book, but, you know. . . .

Very few folklorists, however, have provided us with oral literary criticism of jokelore or, for that matter, of any kind of lore.[17] Instead, folklorists generally rely solely on existing theories pillaged from various disciplines to explain what jokes mean. Theories about the nature and meaning of humor go back to antiquity and range from broad speculative interpretations by early humanists to narrow behavioristic interpretations by contemporary social scientists, with psychologists contributing most abundantly to humor research. Most of these theories, as Christopher Wilson notes, "seem to echo each other in substance as well as in their apparent weakness."[18] Surveys of the various humor theories are readily available. For example, Patricia Keith-Spiegel reviews eight varieties of humor theory: (1) biological, instinct, and evolution theories; (2) superiority theories; (3) incongruity theories; (4) surprise theories; (5) ambivalence theories; (6) release and relief theories; (7) configurational theories; and (8) psychoanalytic theories.[19] Three of these theories (surprise, ambivalence, and configurational) are related to the incongruity theory; and the others generally deal with conflict or relief; consequently, one may, following Levine, generalize a bit and reduce the number of theory families to three:

These are: (1) cognitive-perceptual theory, which stresses the successful and surprising resolution of an incongruity, paradox, or double entendre; (2) behavior theory, with its emphasis on reduction of base drives and stimulus-response learning; and (3) psychoanalytic theory, which emphasizes the gratification of the primary unconscious drives of sex and aggression in conjunction with the pleasures of mental activity, sometimes involving regression to infantile modes of thinking. Experimental evidence thus far has neither confirmed nor disproved any theory, and apparently the supporters of each model remain unmoved.[20]

Most theories of humor, though reductionist in approach and interpretation, deal broadly with humor, which is not a folk genre but operates within a variety of folk, popular, and elite forms; consequently, none of the general humor theories has any wholesale application to the wide range of humorous folktales in the oral tradition. One would guess that folklorists and anthropologists might have contributed to a more pointed theory of jokelore; however, they have contributed virtually nothing to humor theory and very little to humor research beyond the sporadic collection of joke texts, the uneven documentation of joking contexts, and the various explanations of the social functions of joking relationships. Most of the functional explanations of joking offered by anthropologists and repeated by folklorists reflect earlier theories of humor. For instance, Radcliffe-Brown suggests that in reducing hostility, releasing tensions, and avoiding conflict, humor contributes to social harmony and stability. Other anthropologists have proposed that, among other functions, joking offers entertainment, releases sexual and aggressive impulses, serves as a form of social control, releases work-related tensions, provides for catharsis and communication, and contributes to group identity.[21]

In spite of Richard M. Dorson's pronouncement that the speculative psychoanalytic theory is "the school of interpretation most abhorrent to orthodox folklorists,"[22] the psychoanalytic theory has had a considerable influence on the interpretation of jokes by contemporary folklorists. One reason for the popularity of the psychoanalytic theory is that it is the most comprehensive of the various humor theories. At the same time—in the seminal study of jokes by Freud and two later studies of jokes by his disciples, Wolfenstein and Legman—the psychoanalytic theory is the only humor theory that has dealt specifically with jokes.[23] What's more, while Freud's psychoanalytic theory is complex, the psycho-functional approach in its popular application to jokelore is selective, simplistic, and reductionistic, giving the interpreter of jokes pat answers to the meaning and function of jokes. As a matter of fact, Freud, himself, contributed to the reductionism of the psycho-functional approach when he wrote, "The purposes of jokes can easily be reviewed. Where a joke is not an aim in itself—that is, where it is not an innocent one—there are only two purposes that it may serve, and these two can themselves be subsummed under a single heading. It is either a *hostile* joke (serving the purpose of aggressiveness, satire, or defence) or an *obscene* joke (serving the purpose of exposure)."[24] Contemporary psycho-functionalists, however, are even more reductionist than Freud since they have disregarded Freud's allowance for a purely entertainment function of jokes and interpret jokes mainly as an outlet for aggressions. While admittedly the psychoanalytic theory is reductionist, the theory remains one, although only one, legitimate approach to understanding the meaning and use of jokes. Some jokes do entertain, and some jokes no doubt express repressed sexual and aggressive impulses. Jokes may have a cathartic function in alleviating fears and anxieties by bringing them to consciousness and giving them expression. Jokes, however, are too complex for any single reductionist theory to explain everything about them. Moreover, even a single tale may not have the same meaning and same function for all who tell and listen to it in different contexts or even in the same context.

The short Helen Keller joke cited above aptly illustrates that often very little can be learned about the use and meaning of a joke from content analysis. With only the text to examine, one can merely guess how the joke functioned and only generalize about what the joke might have meant to the participants in the joking event. None of the various humor theories seem to have any immediate application to the subject matter alone. With some contextual data—biographical information, and reactions of the joke teller and her audience—however, several of the humor theories may be relevant. First of all, the joke obviously entertained, but the enjoyment resulted more from the situation and performance of the joke than from its content. As one member of the audience observed, "The atmosphere was perfect for telling a few jokes and acting silly." The joke teller said that when she first heard the joke in a classroom with fellow students majoring in communication disorders, she found the joke "really crude," not at all funny; however, relaxing in a dormitory room with a few friends after the day's work was done, the joke teller "had trouble getting through the joke without cracking up. Each time she was about to give the punch line, she would burst into laughter." Thus, as the joke teller stressed, the joke "was funny when I wanted it to be funny"; and as a member of the audience noted, "It was an old joke I had heard many times before, but it suddenly became funny again."

Besides amusement, the Helen Keller joke also served to relieve schoolwork-related tensions. The joke teller said that by telling the joke she hoped to "relieve tension and relax, just break away from studying." A member of the audience agreed that the joke "helped us relieve the tensions we were experiencing from our school work." For the joke teller, the joke apparently had a deeper meaning, too, in providing a psychological outlet for repressions engendered by the frustrations of studying communication disorders. Both deaf and blind, Helen Keller symbolizes everything a speech and hearing pathologist could ever hope to accomplish. In childhood she learned to read Braille, write with a special typewriter, and speak. After graduating with honors from Radcliffe College, she became a famous lecturer and author. The joke teller said she joked about Helen Keller because she "is known to be deaf, and she's known to have accomplished. That's the way society is. We make fun of great people." In other words, by joking about a still mute Helen Keller who communicates only in sign language, the joke teller relieves herself of the pressures of working with physically handicapped students who probably will never measure up to the too ideal model, Helen Keller, who overcame her handicaps and became "accomplished."

The incongruity theory also contributes to an understanding of the Helen Keller joke. The joke teller stated that she likes jokes "that turn out completely different from what everybody thinks they're going to turn out." A member of the audience, however, pointed out that the Helen Keller joke was an old one that she had heard a number of times; consequently, the humor arising from incongruity was not so much in the content of the familiar joke as it was, again, in the situation and performance. Members of the audience considered the joke teller a very sober and serious student of communication disorders who would rarely make fun of a deaf person, especially a respected and famous deaf person. As one member of the audience explained, "It was really funny to hear her giggle over such a serious topic. If anyone else had told that joke, it wouldn't have been half as funny." Since the joke teller did joke about a subject very dear to her, it changed the group's feelings about her and contributed to group stability and social harmony. A member of the audience noted, for instance, that the performance of the joke showed a side of the informant that they had not seen before. The joke, she said, "lightened up our feelings about her. . . . We will now feel more at ease when it comes to having a good time around her."

Text and context are interdependent in a folkloric performance; and, as the Helen Keller joking event suggests, jokes, especially, are context based. Variation, however, is an essential quality of folk literature. Texts change, contexts change, and meanings change. What the folk generally remember and pass along to others, though, are versions of texts and not versions of contexts, although features from an especially memorable context may be incorporated into subsequent performances of a particular story. As Steven Swann Jones has argued, "To my mind, the most convincing argument in favor of acknowledging the value of texts is the point that while the social context of a folklore item may change, the folklore itself remains the same. In other words, a particular item of folklore (for example, a proverb, joke, or story) can appear in many different situations."[25] While Jones probably overstates his case in his defense of textual studies, the fact remains that items of folklore often are widely diffused. While sociocultural factors obviously influence the nature of humor, people from different cultures nevertheless relate versions of the same jokes in many different contexts. As Kenneth Burke suggests, jokes, like Aesop's fables, operate on a high level of abstraction and apply to various situations:

> The situations and strategies framed in Aesop's Fables, for instance, apply to human relations now just as fully as they applied in ancient Greece. They are, like philosophy, sufficiently "generalized" to extend far beyond the particular combination of events named by them in any one instance. They name an "essence." Or, we could say that they are on a "high level of abstraction." One doesn't usually think of them as "abstract," since they are usually so concrete in their stylistic expression. But they invariably aim to discern the "general behind the particular." . . .
>
> . . . A given human relationship may be at one time named in terms of foxes and lions, if there are foxes and lions about; or it may now be named in terms of salesmanship, advertising, the tactics of politicians, etc. But beneath the change in particulars, we may often discern the naming of the one situation.
>
> So sociological criticism, as here understood, would seek to assemble and codify this lore. It might occasionally lead us to outrage good taste, as we sometimes found exemplified in some great sermon or tragedy or abstruse work of philosophy the same strategy as we found exemplified in a

dirty joke. At this point, we'd put the sermon and the dirty joke together, thus "grouping by situation" and showing the range of possible particularizations. . . . First genus, then differentia. The strategy in common is genus. The *range* or *scale* or *spectrum* of particularizations is the differentia.[26]

Since "an item of folklore may be everywhere the same and everywhere different,"[27] the student of traditional jokes must be sympathetic to both the comparative approach and the in-depth approach and equipped to perform either or both; for, suggestive of Burke, Dundes points out that "there are only two basic steps in the study of folklore. . . . The first might be termed identification and the second interpretation. Identification essentially consists of a search for similarities; interpretation depends upon the delineation of differences."[28] A model joke study utilizing both comparative and in-depth approaches is Thomas A. and Inger H. Burns's book *Doing the Wash: An Expressive Culture and Personality Study of a Joke and Its Tellers* (Norwood, Pa.: Norwood Editions, 1976).[29] This empirical study examines versions of a popular joke told by eleven joke tellers and relates each individual's variant to his personality. However, a broad topic like the humorous folktale—even when limited to a single state, as this book is—lends itself better to an extensive approach than to an intensive one since it covers a large geographical area (36,291 square miles) and includes several varieties of jokelore collected in numerous physical and social contexts from many informants. Moreover, Indiana is an artificial political entity, not really a distinct cultural area. The state is not regionally isolated, and there is no other particular cohesiveness found throughout the state. Consequently, there is no single Hoosier folk culture but a number of folk cultures in Indiana. Intensive, or in-depth, studies would have to focus on function, meaning, and/or performance of jokelore of individual storytellers within some context much more specific than Indiana—for instance, within a particular ethnic, occupational, regional, or other folk group in Indiana. This book, then, is a collection of texts. More precisely, it is a collection of humorous folktales from Indiana.

The humorous folktale—also called the jocular folktale, humorous anecdote, merry tale, farcical tale, joke, jest, and *Schwank* in folklore studies—is the humble genre of traditional prose narrative. Simple in form and earthy in content, the humorous folktale has taken a backseat in folktale research since the beginning of serious folklore scholarship in the nineteenth century. As Alexander H. Krappe noted in 1930, "the merry tale," as he called this genre, "was not among the first of the creations of popular genius to attract the attention of scholars contemporary with the Romantic Movement. To be sure, the reason was not that the materials were lacking. . . . It was evidently a feeling of prudishness which inclined the Romanticists to consider this type as rather an inferior genre."[30] Forty-two years later, Jan Harold Brunvand echoed Krappe's observation about the lowly status of humorous folktales in folklore scholarship when he wrote, "Everyone knows jokes, everyone tells them at one time or another, a few gifted people become expert joke tellers with extensive repertoires, and yet jokes remain one of the least collected and least understood forms of folklore."[31]

Though often neglected in folklore scholarship, the humorous folktale is ancient in origin, ubiquitous in distribution, and endless in variety. As Stith Thompson, the eminent folktale scholar from Indiana University, wrote, jokes "are easily remembered and universally liked, so that they travel with great ease. Some of the funny stories heard today have lived three or four thousand years and have been carried all over the earth."[32] Thus, even though the joke is an ancient genre of folk literature, it remains one of the most viable forms of folktales in Western civilization, with only the legend as a close rival. As a matter of fact, in contemporary Indiana, as in the United States generally, the joke is the preeminent form of folktale. There are several reasons for the popularity of the joke in the modern industrial world. For instance, as Will-Erich Peuckert noted nearly fifty years ago, the joke fits very well into the world view of contemporary folk living in urban and industrial societies since it deals with concrete events and rational, rather than supernatural, explanations.[33] Jokes fit very well, too, into the fast pace of contemporary life since they generally consist of only a brief episode and may be told any time during the day, either on or off the job. Moreover, since jokes touch on every aspect of human life, they appear spontaneously in almost any social context.

Since the humorous folktale has been a neglected form of folk literature, folklorists have not developed an adequate universal system for classifying jokes. The tales in this collection, however, have been arranged under twenty-three headings corresponding to several general categories of humorous narratives suggested by either Antti Aarne and Stith Thompson's *The Types of the Folktale* (Helsinki:

Suomalainen Tiedeakatemia, 1964) or Stith Thompson's *Motif-Index of Folk-Literature* (Bloomington: Indiana University Press, 1966). The general categories suggested by these two indexes of international folk literature are: tales of lying, catch tales, humorous animal tales, jokes about married couples, jokes about drunks and lazy people, stories about the wise and foolish, jokes about the clergy and religious figures, and jokes about professional or occupational groups. Although several of these broad categories have been subdivided, still a number of tales could very well appear under more than one of the twenty-three more specific headings used in this collection. The jokes about golfers clearly show how arbitrary systems of joke classification are since virtually all of them could have appeared in other sections of this book. What's more, some entire groups of tales in particular categories could be placed under other headings. For example, Brunvand's classification of shaggy dog stories[34] includes hoax stories that appear in this collection with catch tales, while the section on "Shaggy Dogs" includes only tales with punning punch lines.

Regardless of how they are classified, the jokes in this collection are not unique to Indiana or even to the United States. They are familiar forms of international humorous folktales. While the sociocultural contexts of the humorous folktales in this collection may reflect some traits indigenous to the state, an examination of the texts of these jokes reveals that there isn't much that is distinctively Hoosier in either the forms or thematic content of most of these stories. Hoosiers live in the middle of a dominant American civilization permeated with popular culture spread by mass media. This pervasive popular culture certainly influences Hoosier jokelore, as popular culture nourishes and is nourished by folklore generally. This influence of popular culture on joke telling is not a recent development in only the United States, though. Examining the humorous folktale from antiquity to modern times and from Ireland to India, Stith Thompson concludes that "one gets the very definite impression, in surveying a large number of such anecdotes, that for most countries they belong to a semi-literary tradition, that they are likely to be preserved in cheap jestbooks even today, and that one is more likely to have learned his story by reading it than by hearing it."[35] If Professor Thompson were writing today, rather than in 1946, he no doubt would observe an even greater impact of popular culture on humorous folktales, for now electronic media as well as an expanded print media spread a much larger variety of jokes, including bawdy material once taboo in mainstream popular culture but fairly common now in popular collections of humor and slick magazines that are readily available on drugstore and supermarket newstands and in shopping mall bookstores. This influence of popular culture on modern jokelore gives a certain uniformity to the form, content, and theme of humorous folktales in the oral tradition throughout the United States.

Moreover, many of the jokes told in Indiana are versions of migratory folktales known throughout Europe as well as the United States. For example, "Mighty Good Policy" (Tale 138) is a variant of "The Lazy Boy Eats Breakfast, Dinner, and Supper One after the Other without Working," a folktale that, according to Stith Thompson, "is well known all over eastern Europe."[36] "Dividing Souls" (Tale 218), included here as a tale about blacks, actually is a variant of an international tale type, "The Sexton Carries the Parson." As Thompson points out, this folktale "is certainly as old as the *Thousand and One Nights,* and appears in nearly every medieval and Renaissance tale collection. But it is widely told by oral story-tellers all over Europe and, for some reason, is about the best known of all anecdotes collected in America."[37] As the notes at the end of this collection of tales suggest, innumerable examples could be given to illustrate the widespread diffusion of most of these jokes throughout Europe and the United States. Still, though most of the humorous tales told in Indiana are ubiquitous, changes in locale, changes in folk tradition, and changes made by individual joke tellers lead to regional, local, and ethnic variations, or oikotypes. Consequently, while the *types* of these humorous tales illustrate that folklore is everywhere the same, the *oikotypes* sometimes illustrate that folklore is everywhere different.

Some forms of humorous folktales collected in Indiana, however, show little, if any, localization. For example, the tales classified as shaggy dog stories in this collection[38] have either a vague setting or are set in such non-Hoosier places as Greenwich Village, the Amazon, and Cape Kennedy. These shaggy dog tales often begin like *Märchen* (commonly called "fairy tales"): "Once upon a time there was an old man . . ."; "There was once a knight . . ."; "Once there was a buffalo . . ."; "Once there were two crows . . ."; "Once upon a time there was an old man . . ."; "Once there was this head. . . ." Similarly, humorous animal tales in Indiana are not localized and have a vague setting. Although some of the animals (rabbit, buzzard, turtle, mouse, pig, horse, and rooster) in these tales are common in the Hoosier state, they are by no means unique to or characteristic of Indiana. What's more, humorous animal tales often are about animals like the giraffe, elephant, and camel that aren't even native to the United States. The parrot, a familiar figure in international folktales since antiquity, appears in a number of migratory jokes told in Indiana, and in Hoosier versions of these tales the parrot plays the same role as it generally does in modern parrot jokes. As Rosenberg notes, "The wise parrot of Indian folklore has become, in contemporary jokes, a figure whose primary role is that of taboo-breaker."[39]

Hoosier versions of tales of married couples also are vaguely set and deal with universal themes of this sub-genre: seduction and adultery, competition between husband and wife, the mean wife, and sexual anxieties. A classical example of this kind of tale is Type 901, "The Taming of the Shrew," which has been reported in well over 300 versions from around 25 countries and goes back to at least the Middle Ages. The Hoosier variant of this international folktale in this collection (Tale 110), collected in North Vernon in 1969, shares its major motif, "Wife becomes obedient on seeing husband slay a recalcitrant horse," with other modern versions of the tale. Tales dealing with seduction and adultery, as Thompson points out, "are very old, and they were especially popular with the writers of fabliaux, novelle, and jestbooks."[40] Also extreme laziness—sometimes in wives, though not always, as two tales (Tales 138 and 139) in this collection suggest—is an extremely old theme in humorous folktales found in many literary collections of tales.

Jokes about Catholic and Protestant clergy, jokes about religious figures and orders, jokes about Jews and rabbis, and jokes about occupational and professional groups generally are not localized in Hoosier versions either and deal with timeless themes. As Krappe notes, "Humour shares with its kinfolk Wit and Satire the important fact, regrettable no doubt, but a fact all the same, that the ensuing laughter must of necessity be at someone's expense. Now all ages and all societies have known certain groups of people which for one reason or another furnished material for both humour and satire."[41] Since the Middle Ages tradesmen, lawyers, physicians, and clergymen have been the butt of satirical humor. Especially popular were medieval anticlerical tales of lecherous and hypocritical priests. With the advent of Protestantism in Europe, the preacher assumed the role of the amorous priest in humorous folktales; however, with the end of celibacy among Protestant clerics these tales apparently lost some of their appeal. Although modern tales still deal with the preacher's lust for women, they deal as well with his desire for worldly pleasures and thirst for liquor. Legman maintains that jokes dealing with the immorality of the clergy are now rare, indicating "the very great decay into which religion has fallen in the last half century."[42] As the tales in this collection suggest, however, religion has not disappeared as an important theme in folk humor in Indiana, for a number of Hoosier jokes still deal with such universal themes as the duped preacher and the woman-chasing priest. Likewise, widespread stereotypic traits attributed to Jews—for example, a preoccupation with money, business, professionalism and pro-Semiticism[43]—are found in Hoosier jokes about rabbis and Jews.

Shaggy dog tales, humorous animal tales, jokes about married couples, jokes about drunks and sloths, jokes about occupational and professional groups, jokes about Christian clergy and religious figures, and jokes about rabbis and Jews generally lack localization and other qualities that may be considered Hoosier because, like the *Märchen,* they are not bound to reality. As Lüthi notes, unlike the legend, the fairy tale does not "cling to individual events or experiences."[44] That is not to say, however, that there is never localization in these tales, but only that we find a lesser degree of localization in these tales than in legends, which are set in the real world and generally passed along as true stories. Thus, as Jacob Grimm pointed out, "Looser, less fettered than legend, the folktale [*Märchen*] lacks that local habitation which hampers legend, but makes it more home-like. The folktale flies, the legend walks, knocks at your door."[45] A century later Krappe said about the same thing when he observed that the humorous tale "is not bound to any definite society but floats freely from country to country."[46]

Some kinds of humorous folktales collected in Indiana are localized more than the varieties of tales just discussed; for up to a certain point, at least, tall tales, catch tales, and some tales of the wise and foolish are realistic. Some of these stories share qualities with the anecdote, a short realistic tale about an actual person; and some, like the stories about the hoop snake (Tales 24, 25, 26, 27), share motifs with legends. Tall tales, for example, though tales of lying and exaggeration, often are realistic up to the end, where they turn into fantasy because they are intended to deceive the listener. Moreover, sometimes tall tales are found in a cycle about a local character who perhaps once told the whoppers about himself and subsequently became the subject of versions of the same tales told by others. Good examples are the tales about Rufe in this collection. Rufe, who died in 1955 when he was 80, was born in Illinois but lived most of his life in a shack about three miles east of Farmersburg. He farmed a little with mules, hunted more for meat than for sport, and worked part time in a coal mine. Rufe was well known in his part of Sullivan County for his big feet and tall tales. In fact, one informant claims that "Rufe was such a good liar that he had to have someone else call the hogs for him." The tall tales about Rufe are typical of the genre since they are bound to reality. That is, they incorporate details about local history (such as, "They put the waterworks in here 'bout 1924"), and they are about an actual person who lived near Farmersburg for many years.

Catch tales and hoax stories also begin realistically and are localized. They frequently occur within the framework of ordinary conversation and are told as true stories; however, they end abruptly with a punch line that tricks the reader. "The Two Bumps" (Tale 79), for instance, was collected in Terre Haute from a 20-year-old female student from Indianapolis. To give the tale credibility, the informant refers to two stores that were located in downtown Terre Haute in 1970: "I went downtown today and after walking around for a while stopped into Woolworth's for a Coke. . . . Later I was in Meis walking around." As the informant herself pointed out, "This is a story I have told many times, but details have changed each time according to where I happened to be. It must be told as a true story to get the proper effect."

Some migratory tales of the wise and foolish also have made themselves at home in Indiana. In fact, one tale of cleverness (Tale 144) is an anecdote about a real person, Rufe, discussed above, and is specifically set in Sullivan County. Stories about the foolish collected in Indiana sometimes are general numskull tales dealing with absurd ignorance or absurd misunderstandings and are not about any particular place or group; however, frequently these tales attribute absurd ignorance or other unfavorable qualities to some specific ethnic or regional group. Such tales are popular nearly everywhere. In England numskull tales are told about the Wise Men of Gotham, in Denmark about the Fools of Molbos, and in Germany about the Citizens of Schilda. In Texas the same or very similar tales are told about Aggies (students at Texas A&M University) or Mexicans, and in other parts of the United States tales of absurd ignorance may be told about Italians, Puerto Ricans, or any ethnic, racial, religious, or regional group. Although many of the numskull tales collected in Indiana are reworkings of older material, settlement history and geography help determine the butt of these tales in the Hoosier state.

In northern Indiana, ethnic jokes generally stereotype Polish-Americans as stupid, inept, poor, dirty, and vulgar—typical traits attributed to Poles in the American cycle of Polack jokes.[47] In southern Indiana, especially around Evansville, Kentuckians assume these same qualities in versions of the same jokes. Earlier in Indiana, as in the eastern part of the United States generally, the Irishman was the subject of similar numskull tales, as the few examples of tales about Irishmen in this collection suggest. Clements maintains that such jokes "represent an attempt for joketeller and audience to unite against threats from the Outsider,"[48] who may be anyone who is different from the group doing the stereotyping. One threat, according to Clements, is economic competition, which he says "has joined with other aspects of the American environment to create a climate where stereotyping is an almost necessary factor in human interaction."[49] Thus, just as more established Hoosiers viewed the Irish as a threat to jobs and wage scales in nineteenth-century Indiana, in this century Poles working in the steel mills of Gary and Kentuckians working in the Whirlpool plant in Evansville are similarly viewed.

For most Hoosiers, however, response to Polish jokes or even Kentuckian jokes does not necessarily depend on a familiarity with Poles or Kentuckians, just as response to numskull tales about the Wise Men of Gotham does not depend on a familiarity with Gothamites. As Brunvand discovered, "Among my student collectors of Polack jokes at Indiana University in 1965, several remarked that they personally did not even know any Polish people. Some of them professed not to have known, until I told them, that the term 'Polack' refers to Polish-Americans."[50] The response to Kentuckian jokes may be a different matter, though, since most Hoosiers know what a Kentuckian is. What's more, while only Hoosiers living in southern Indiana compete directly on a socio-economic level with Kentuckians, Hoosiers throughout the state compete vicariously with Kentuckians for basketball supremacy in annual games between the Indiana and Kentucky high school all star teams and between the Indiana University Hoosiers and the University of Kentucky Wildcats. Still, informants' attitudes vary about Kentuckians. An 18-year-old male informant from Evansville said, "I don't believe Kentuckians are truly stupid. They [the jokes] are mostly just for kiddin' and all." Another 18-year-old male informant from Evansville said, "I think that they [Kentuckians] are kinda strange and backward, you know. I've got a lot of relatives down there; and, boy, some of them are pretty weird, you know." Yet another 18-year-old male informant from Evansville said, "I'm indifferent to them [Kentuckians]. I mean, you know, I can take 'em or leave 'em."

Naturally, Kentuckians also tell jokes about Hoosiers for most of the same reasons that Hoosiers tell jokes about Kentuckians. One joke about a Hoosier, for example, was reported in *The Evansville Press* on May 1, 1984 (p. 22). A native of Kentucky, now living in Evansville, phoned a columnist and complained that she gets tired hearing jokes about Kentuckians. "But," she said, "I have one I'd like you to put in the newspaper." Then she related a tale about a Kentucky farmer who gave his son his first rifle. After spending most of a day hunting in the woods, the boy returned home with a puzzled look. "Did you shoot anything?" his father asked. The teenager said he did, but he wasn't sure what he had hit. "It had hair all over its face, and its eyes and nose were running," the son said, "and it smelled awful." . . . The father gave the situation just a minute of thought. "Boy, you know what you've done?" he said. "You've shot a Hoosier."

Hoosiers tell jokes about themselves, too. For instance, one informant claimed a Hoosier is a Kentuckian who ran out of money on his way to Michigan. Other jokes are directed toward particular groups of Hoosiers, such as the well-to-do residents of Carmel: "What did the Carmel housewife wear to her husband's funeral?" *A black tennis dress.* "How many Carmel housewives does it take to change a lightbulb?" *Two: one to make the martinis, and one to call the electrician.* In another joke told by a native of Indiana, a Hoosier visiting Harvard University met a Harvard man on Harvard Yard and asked, "Can you tell me where the library's at?" The Harvard man was shocked. "At Harvard we don't end our sentences with prepositions," he said. "Oh," replied the Hoosier. "Can you tell me where the library's at, asshole?"

Most jokes told about Hoosiers are adaptations of the same jokes told about Kentuckians, Poles, Aggies, and other Outsiders. One of the most popular jokes about Hoosiers, though, does not readily transfer to other groups, for it defines a Hoosier as "a person dribbling a basketball around the Indianapolis 500 race track looking for mushrooms." As a matter of fact, basketball, the Indy 500, and mushrooms appear in other Hoosier jokes. For example, in this collection one story (Tale 299) emphasizes the Hoosier penchant for basketball and esteem for Indiana University basketball coach Bobby Knight. A Polish joke (Tale 235) is about the Indianapolis 500 mile race. A tall tale (Tale 36) concerns a real Hoosier prize, a dog that can find mushrooms. While these jokes may appear to be Hoosier through and through, they illustrate very well what Hoosier folk humor generally is: localization of migratory folklore. The joke about basketball and Bobby Knight has analogues about other sports and sports heroes—for example, golf and either Arnold Palmer or Lee Trevino in some versions, and auto racing and A. J. Foyt in other versions. The migratory tale about the Polish race driver who made several pit stops during a race to ask directions has been adapted to the Indianapolis 500. Even the story about the mushroom dog has as its core a familiar tall tale motif about a dog with remarkable scent, though in Indiana the motif is associated with a traditional Hoosier delicacy, the mushroom. Folklore, indeed, is everywhere the same, yet everywhere different.

This book covers a wide range of humorous folktales from older tall tales to contemporary ethnic and sick jokes. In some contexts and to all readers a number of the jokes may not be funny. Some readers, for example, may find the bawdy tales offensive; however, since bawdry is so very common in the oral tradition, a general collection of humorous folktales, such as this one, would not be honest without a representative sample of obscene tales. As Rayna Green has pointed out, "Obscenity occurs everywhere in traditional expression. Young, old, male, female, rich, poor, urban, and rural tradition-bearers use the bawdy in songs, stories, games, gestures, and artifacts."[51] Some readers also might find the jokes about ethnic and religious groups objectionable, but these tales, too, are quite common in folk tradition. One way of combating the folkloristic stereotypes in such tales is showing through comparative folklore studies that throughout the years many of the same tales have been told about diverse groups. Comparative studies will show that some of the same jokes told about Poles and Kentuckians, for instance, have been told about the Little Moron, Confucius, political leaders, blacks, Italians, Mexicans, and even Hoosiers. In his study of stereotypes of Jews and Poles in American jokes, Dundes concludes:

> No doubt some will argue that the study of ethnic slurs may serve no other purpose than to increase the circulation of such slurs and by so doing unwittingly assist the rise of further ethnic and racial prejudice. However, a more realistic view would be that the slurs are used by the folk whether the folklorist studies them or not. Most children in the United States hear these slurs fairly early in their public school careers. I would maintain therefore that an open discussion of the slurs and an objective analysis of the stereotypes contained therein could do no harm and might possibly do a great deal of good in fighting bigotry and prejudice. Only by knowing and recognizing folk stereotypes can children be taught to guard against them so that they may have a better chance of succeeding in judging individuals on an individual basis.[52]

Thirty-four of the tales in this book are from the collection made in the 1930s by the Federal Writers' Project of the Works Progress Administration for the State of Indiana. All the other tales are from the Indiana State University Folklore Archives, established in 1967. Although folklorists will find the annotated tales from these sources useful in comparative folktale studies, this book is intended mainly for the general reader, who will find it interesting and enlightening to compare the tales from the WPA collection with those from the ISU Folklore Archives. The tales from the WPA collection have been reworked considerably by the collectors, while at least some of the tales from the ISU Folklore Archives have been transcribed from tape recordings. The reader might compare, for example, "The New Harness" (Tale 68) from the WPA files with "Irishman Takes Turtle for a Gourd" (Tale 212) from the ISU Folklore Archives to see the big difference between a rewritten folktale that the collector has tried to make "literary" and a traditional text from the oral tradition that the collector has tried to present accurately. In several instances, versions of the same tale from the WPA collection and the ISU Folklore Archives have been included to illustrate changes in Hoosier storytelling since the 1930s.

A comparison of the tales from the WPA collection with those from the ISU Folklore Archives also will reveal a shift in the kinds of humorous folktales told in Indiana. The older tales from the WPA collection generally reflect a rural culture with a fairly homogeneous population. The WPA stories, predominantly tall tales, deal with hunting, fishing, fertile soil, big crops, rough weather, strong men, and fabulous animals. The more contemporary jokes from the ISU Folklore Archives reflect as well an urban culture consisting of diverse ethnic and religious subcultures and express the tensions of modern life.[53] Even the tales about golfers reflect anxieties and tensions on the golf course, perhaps a microcosm of the modern world, and serve to relieve pressures created by the competition in this popular pastime. While changing social conditions have altered storytelling in Indiana over the years, the variety of the jokes still told in Indiana shows that storytelling is alive and well in the Hoosier state in spite of the rise of literacy and the competition from mass media.

NOTES TO THE INTRODUCTION

1. Archer Taylor's definition is in Maria Leach, ed., *Funk and Wagnalls Standard Dictionary of Folklore, Mythology, and Legend* (New York: Funk and Wagnalls, 1949), I, 402–403. When William J. Thoms coined *folklore* in a letter to *The Athenaeum* (August 22, 1846), he defined folklore as "manners, customs, observances, superstitions, ballads, proverbs, etc. of the olden time." Thoms's letter has been reprinted in Alan Dundes, ed., *The Study of Folklore* (Englewood Cliffs, N.J.: Prentice-Hall, 1965), pp. 4–6.

2. Richard M. Dorson, *American Folklore* (Chicago: The University of Chicago Press, 1959), p. 2.

3. Dorson's revised definition of folklore is reprinted in *Folklore Forum*, 1 (1968): 37.

4. Dan Ben-Amos, "Toward a Definition of Folklore in Context," *Journal of American Folklore*, 84 (January–March 1971): 13.

5. Ruth Benedict, "Introduction to Zuni Mythology," in *Studies on Mythology*, ed. Robert A. Georges (Homewood, Ill.: Dorsey, 1968), p. 102.

6. Roger L. Janelli, "Toward a Reconciliation of Micro- and Macro-Level Analyses of Folklore," *Folklore Forum*, 9 (1976): 59.

7. Steven Jones, "Dogmatism in the Cultural Revolution," *Western Folklore*, 38 (January 1979): 53.

8. Alan Dundes and Carl R. Pagter, *Work Hard and You Shall Be Rewarded* (Bloomington: Indiana University Press, 1978), p. xiii.

9. Lynwood Montell, "Academic and Applied Folklore: Partners for the Future," *Folklore Forum*, 16 (1983): 161–62.

10. Richard M. Dorson, ed., *Folklore and Folklife: An Introduction* (Chicago: University of Chicago Press, 1972), pp. 40–41.

11. For an account of the Lang-Müller debate, see Richard M. Dorson,

"The Eclipse of Solar Mythology," in *Myth: A Symposium*, ed. Thomas A. Sebeok (Bloomington: Indiana University Press, 1958), pp. 15–38.

12. Dundes and Pagter, p. xiii.

13. Alan Dundes, "Metafolklore and Oral Literary Criticism," in *Readings in American Folklore*, ed. Jan Harold Brunvand (New York: Norton, 1979), pp. 405–06.

14. Ibid., pp. 406–07.

15. Alan Dundes, "Texture, Text, and Context," in *Interpreting Folklore* (Bloomington: Indiana University Press, 1980), p. 30.

16. Dundes, "Metafolklore and Oral Literary Criticism," pp. 407–08.

17. For one notable exception, see Paulette Cross, "Jokes and Black Consciousness: A Collection with Interviews," in *Mother Wit from the Laughing Barrel*, ed. Alan Dundes (Englewood Cliffs, N.J.: Prentice-Hall, 1973), pp. 649–69.

18. Christopher Wilson, *Jokes: Form, Content, Use and Function* (London: Academic Press, 1969), p. 9.

19. Patricia Keith-Spiegel, "Early Conceptions of Humor," in *The Psychology of Humor*, ed. Jeffrey Goldstein and Paul E. McGhee (New York: Academic Press, 1972), pp. 3–13. For other reviews of humor theory, see D. H. Monro, *Argument of Laughter* (Melbourne: Melbourne University Press, 1951), and D. E. Berlyne, "Laughter, Humor, and Play," In *The Handbook of Social Psychology*, ed. Gardner Lindzey and Elliot Aronson (Reading, Mass.: Addison-Wesley, 1969), III, 795–852.

20. Jacob Levine, ed., *Motivation in Humor* (New York: Atherton Press, 1969), p. 2.

21. Mahadev L. Apte, *Humor and Laughter: An Anthropological Approach* (Ithaca: Cornell University Press, 1985), pp. 60–61.

22. Dorson, *Folklore and Folklife*, p. 25.

23. See Sigmund Freud, *Jokes and Their Relation to the Unconscious*, trans. James Strachey (New York: Norton, 1960); Martha Wolfenstein, *Children's Humor: A Psychological Analysis* (Bloomington: Indiana University Press, 1978); G. Legman, *No Laughing Matter: An Analysis of Sexual Humor*, 2 vols. (Bloomington: Indiana University Press, 1968).

24. Freud, pp. 96–97.

25. Steven Jones, "Slouching Towards Ethnography: The Text/Context Controversy Reconsidered," *Western Folklore*, 38 (January 1979): 45.

26. Kenneth Burke, "Literature as Equipment for Living," in *The Philosophy of Literary Form* (New York: Vintage, 1961), pp. 260–61.

27. Dundes, *The Study of Folklore*, p. 339.

28. Alan Dundes, "The Study of Folklore in Literature and Culture: Identification and Interpretation," *Journal of American Folklore*, 78 (April–June 1965): 136.

29. This book is a revised and abridged version of Tom Burns, "A Joke and Its Tellers: A Study of the Functional Variation of a Folklore Item at a Psychological Level," 6 vols. (Ph.D. diss. Indiana University, 1972).

30. Alexander H. Krappe, *The Science of Folklore* (1930; reprint, New York: Norton, 1964), p. 45.

31. Jan Harold Brunvand, "The Study of Contemporary Folklore: Jokes," *Fabula*, 13 (1972): 10.

32. Stith Thompson, *The Folktale* (New York: Holt, Rinehart and Winston, 1946), p. 10.

33. Peuckert's observation about jokes is briefly discussed by Seppo Knuuttila in "Jests and Research into Joking," in *Adaptation, Change and Decline in Oral Tradition*, ed. Lauri Honko and Vilmos Voight (Helsinki: Finnish Literary Society, 1981), p. 92.

34. Jan Harold Brunvand, "A Classification for Shaggy Dog Stories," *Journal of American Folklore*, 76 (January–March 1963): 42–68.

35. Thompson, p. 216.

36. Ibid., pp. 210–11.

37. Ibid., p. 214.

38. In "A Classification for Shaggy Dog Stories," Brunvand includes the hoax story, which often is realistic up to a point before absolving into absurdity, as a form of the shaggy dog story; however, in this collection hoax stories appear with catch tales since both of these kinds of tales frequently are told as true stories and tend to be realistic in setting or tone. The tales classified as shaggy dog stories in this collection are not realistic in setting or tone and have punning punch lines.

39. Neil V. Rosenberg, "An Annotated Collection of Parrot Jokes," (M.A. thesis, Indiana University, 1964), p. 18.

40. Thompson, p. 202.

41. Krappe, p. 54.

42. Legman, vol. I, p. 417.

43. For a discussion of stereotypic traits attributed to Jews, see Alan Dundes, "A Study of Ethnic Slurs: The Jew and the Polack in the United States," *Journal of American Folklore*, 84 (April–June 1971): 193-99.

44. Max Lüthi, *The European Folktale: Form and Nature*, trans. John D. Niles (Philadelphia: Institute for the Study of Human Issues, 1982), p. 84.

45. Quoted in William Bascom, "The Forms of Folklore: Prose Narratives," *Journal of American Folklore*, 78 (January–March 1965): 18.

46. Krappe, p. 47.

47. See Dundes, "A Study of Ethnic Slurs," pp. 199–202, for a discussion of the traits attributed to Polish people in ethnic jokes.

48. William M. Clements, "Cueing the Stereotype: The Verbal Strategy of the Ethnic Joke," *New York Folklore*, 5 (Summer 1979): 61.

49. Clements, p. 56.

50. Jan Harold Brunvand, "Some Thoughts on the Ethnic-Regional Riddle Jokes," *Indiana Folklore*, 3, no. 1 (1970): 137.

51. Rayna Green, "Folk Is a Four-Letter Word: Dealing with Traditional **** in Fieldwork, Analysis, and Presentations," *Handbook of American Folklore*, ed. Richard M. Dorson (Bloomington: Indiana University Press, 1983), p. 525.

52. Dundes, "A Study of Ethnic Slurs," p. 203.

53. Some differences between older rural jokes and more recent urban jokes are discussed by Francis Lee Utley and Dudley Flamm in "The Urban and the Rural Jest (with an Excursus on the Shaggy Dog)," *Journal of Popular Culture*, 2 (1969): 563–77.

*Joke*lore

 *Tall Tales*

TALL TALES (sometimes called whoppers, windies, and lies) are an ancient form of folk literature, for in his *Lives,* Plutarch (c. A.D. 42–102) reported a version of Type 1889F, "Frozen Words (Music) Thaw." Thus, the tall tale is not a unique form of American oral humor, as several writers have claimed, but a European genre that became very popular in the United States, especially on the frontier. As Mody Boatright noted in *Folk Laughter on the American Frontier* (New York: MacMillan, 1949), "The frontiersman lied in order to satirize his betters; he lied to cure others of the swell head; he lied in order to initiate the recruits to his way of life. He lied to amuse himself and his fellows" (p. 87). Since many tall tales deal with the outdoors (hunting, fishing, rough weather, fertile soil, big crops, fabulous animals), they were more appealing to Hoosiers living in a rural society than they are to those living in urban and suburban areas, as the tall tales from the WPA files suggest. Tall tales, however, are far from forgotten in Indiana; for only about one-third of the whoppers in this collection are from the WPA files, and the others are from the contemporary oral tradition.

Printed texts fail to capture the art of the tall tale since its art lies in the performance or manner of telling and not especially in its content. Since the art of storytelling depends on situation as well as on text, the best way of preserving oral performances of tall tales today is on film

1

or video tape and not in print. For a general reading audience, creative writers thus far have had far more success in socializing texts and depicting performance features of storytelling than folklorists have. As Richard M. Dorson noted in "Print and American Folk Tales" (*California Folklore Quarterly*, 4 [1945]: 209), "The rendition of a popular tale by a *Spirit of the Times* correspondent or a local-color writer like Rowland Robinson reproduces the tones and emphases and settings of narrative art more faithfully than the literal transcript divorced from mood and audience, so that the freer translation becomes the more realistic." Folklorists now are attempting to perfect performance-centered texts that can be used by folklorists in stylistic and performance studies as well as in comparative studies (see, for example, Elizabeth C. Fine's recent book, *The Folklore Text: From Performance to Print* [Bloomington: Indiana University Press, 1984]); however, for most readers even performance-centered texts do not capture the art of oral storytelling any more than a libretto captures the art of an opera.

Until folklorists become cinematographers and make folklore performances readily available on film or video tape, or unless they become creative writers and recreate contexts of performance for reading audiences, they are stuck with publishing texts that capture only content for a general audience. Preserving the content of folktales, though, is much better than having no record at all of some good stories. A hundred years ago, George Laurence Gomme deplored Andrew Lang's collections of texts in Lang's multicolored fairy book series aimed at a popular audience, but Lang's *Blue Fairy Book* has given thousands of people infinitely more reading pleasure than Gomme's *Folk-Lore as an Historical Science*. As a boy, Andrew Lang was raised among Scottish oral traditions, and after learning to read, he read every folktale he could lay his hands on. As Lang points out in his introduction to Marian Roalfe Cox's *Cinderella* (London: Publications of the Folk-Lore Society, no. 31, 1893), "Ever since I could read, and long before I ever dreamed that fairy-tales might be a matter of curious discussion, those tales have been my delight. I heard them told by other children as a child, I even rescued one or two versions which seem to have died out of oral tradition in Lowland Scots; I confess that I still have a child-like love of a fairy-story for its own sake" (p. xi). Hopefully, many readers still enjoy folktale texts for their own sake.

1

Bear Chases Man Back to Camp

Once there was three fellas went bear hunting. One of them says he would be the cook and the other two could do the hunting because he wasn't much of a hunter. So the first day out they came in and had a couple of quail, a rabbit. So he asked them where the bear was. They says, "Oh, we didn't see a bear. We don't think there are any bears in the woods." So the next day they went out again. They came back. The had a couple of rabbits, quail, and pheasant. He says, "Where's the bear today?" They says, "Oh, we didn't see a bear. We don't think there are any bear in that woods." So he says, "Let me see the gun; I think I could do better than that."

So he took the gun and went up the path, got tired of walking, and he sat down on a stump to rest and let the gun lean up against a tree. So pretty soon he heard the gun fall over. He looks around. There was this bear nudging the gun. So he didn't know what to do, so he started running down the path toward the cabin, the bear right behind him. So he hollered to his buddies to open the door. They opened the door. He got almost to the door and ran around the side, and the bear ran in the cabin. He reached in and shut the door behind the bear. He yelled in and said, "Boys, when you get that one skinned, I'll bring you another!"

2

The Largest Barn

A man who attended barn raisings was prone to stretch the truth. His brother reminded him one morning when they started to a job not to tell such stories that no one could believe. "All right, when you think I am making the story too big just step on my toes."

They were all telling of the biggest building, and this man said, "The largest barn I ever raised was 300 feet long and three [his brother stepped on his toes] . . . feet wide." The story brought a laugh.

3

Rufe Hasn't Time to Lie

Rufe was walkin' to Farmersburg and come past Cal Ridgeway's. Cal was out choppin' wood, and Cal said, "Rufe, stop and tell me a lie." Rufe said, "No, I haven't got time. Dallie Heck just died (that was one of his neighbors), and I got to go and get the undertaker." He come on to town. Cal Ridgeway and his wife got in the horse and buggy and drove down to Dallie Heck's. When they got up to the front door, why him [Dallie Heck] and his wife and Lee, their son, was settin' there eatin' supper!

4

A Lie without Thinking

John Cox was for years known as the outstanding liar of Harrison County. His neighbors liked to listen to his yarns just for the fun.

Early one morning Tom Jones looked up the road and saw John rushing his horses down the lane. Tom called to his wife, "Jane, here comes John Cox. Wonder which way his mind will run this morning?" By this time Cox's horses were galloping by the house. "John, what's your hurry?" Tom shouted. "Jane and I were just pining to hear one of your lies this morning. Stop and tell us one without even thinking." "Sorry, Tom, but I can't today," John shouted back. "I am in a mighty big hurry. Nick Boley's wife died last night, and I'm on my way to Corydon to buy the coffin." And Cox was gone out of sight.

The Joneses were a good deal excited because Mr. and Mrs. Boley were their nearest neighbors. Mrs. Boley had not even been complaining. Now she was dead. They did their chores in a hurry, dressed in their Sunday best, hitched the horse to the buggy and were driving to the Boleys, as the saying goes, before "the wag of a dead sheep's tail." As they drove into sight of the house, Tom burst out all of a sudden, "Who's that sitting on the porch knitting?" "That's Sarah Boley as sure as I'm alive," said Jane. "Well, I suppose we got what we asked for," Tom Jones said, trying to drive by as if he and Jane were just bound for town.

5
Champion Chopper

One morning the champion chopper of the Eighth District, feeling "mighty fitten," took three axes and went down to the Wabash to fell a three-foot tree before breakfast so as to work up an appetite. He swung so hard and fast that his axe got so hot he had to put it in the river to cool. The water hissed and bubbled where he put it in, naturally enough, and the chopper let the axe set and went back for a go with the next one. Pretty soon that axe heated up too, so he gave it the same dose he did the first. And he kept on that way, spelling axes, till the trunk was cut through and the tree fell kerplunk with the upmost branches in the river—not that it bothered the boats any; the ones they used in that part of the river could float on fog anyhow.

Someone that don't know chopping might think an axe would get spoiled that way, but of course anybody that has to do with such things knows that dousing axes in the water that way when they're hot brings back the temper, and they will sharpen up just as well as before.

Well, folks thereabouts thought things like this were nothing to talk about, and of course, they wouldn't be, maybe, only on this morning it seems a neighbor of the champion chopper had started his hog butchering, and he lived just around the bend below, so he used the water that was heated by the axes to scald his fresh-killed hogs.

6
An Incorrigible Liar

Rufe was such a good liar he had to have someone else call the hogs for him.

7
Shorty

You know these German boys down here in Southern Indiana are really the big ones. All that clean, fresh air and all grows 'em straight and tall. I heard once that there was this six-foot-six guy who was called "Shorty," and he was sent up North because he couldn't hold his own with his brothers. In any other part of the United States this man would be pretty big but not down here years ago.

8

The Skillful Marksman

I love going squirrel hunting, so one morning I got up and went to the woods to see if I could get some. I came up to this tree, and there was a squirrel sitting up on one of the branches. I raised up my rifle, aimed, and shot it. I never did see it fall. And the weeds and grass were high, so I couldn't see it on the ground. I looked up at the branch again, and there was another one. I thought I just must have missed and it was the same squirrel. So I shot at it again, and it was still there. This happened twenty-six times, and no more appeared. I used to be a pretty good shot, but I thought I must have lost my touch. Twenty-six times at one squirrel isn't too good. So I went up to the tree to get my one squirrel, when much to my surprise there on the ground laid twenty-six squirrels. So I guess I must have come upon a den tree.

9

Hot Marksmanship

Here is a kind of story which gives an idea of what crack shots the old settlers were in the days when folks depended a deal on their rifles and naturally took pains to practice whenever they could.

It seems two oldtimers had some trouble with each other that couldn't get settled no matter what, so to make it quick and no fooling they figured the best way was to get into the woods by themselves and have it out with their guns. So they went out a ways and turned back to back and stepped off twenty paces apiece. It was the rule in such cases to aim at the other man's left eye, the "sight eye," which naturally was the one left in open when he was sighting a rifle, as you can try for yourself.

Well, these two oldtimers counted "three" together and fired, but blamed if either got so much as creased. They felt sort of ashamed at first, of course, but after they got to remembering how they hated each other and how there was no one looking on anyhow they went to loading up again, holding their place.

Well, they fired again, but no luck. There wasn't even the riffle of a hair to show for the powder and lead they'd used up trying to stir up the material for an obituary. But they were obstinate and determined, so they shot and shot until a dozen charges had been used up apiece. By that time they got worrying what might happen if they run short of powder and ball for the next rumpus with the Indians, so they figured it would be best to call the show off.

Naturally this kind of weighed on them, calling the thing off on such account, but anyhow and someway they walked back midway and shook hands, still wondering what in Tophet had come over their shooting. All at once one of them felt something hot under his boot and jumped. They both looked down. And darned if there wasn't a lump of hot lead! Those two old buzzards had shot so straight at each other's left eye that every pair of bullets had met midbetween, and they had loaded and fired so fast that the next pair had met and melted into the ones next before, so that in the end there was just one lump of lead that hadn't time to cool when they called off the show!

10

Rufe Shoots a Ramrod Full of Quail

Rufe had this old cap-'n'-ball rifle of his. He went out quail huntin'. He put the ball in there and tamped it down with the ramrod, and he forgot to take the ramrod out. These quail flew up, and there was ten of 'em. He shot, and he strung the ten of 'em on that ramrod.

11

The Last of the Wild Turkeys

When wild turkeys were plentiful in the early days in St. Joseph County, a hunter who had never killed one in his life, to anyone's knowledge, told this story:

"I'd been squirrel-shooting late one afternoon just a little before dark, and when dusk came on I hadn't bagged a thing. I didn't like staying in the woods any longer, and yet I hated to go back home with nothing to show but my gun and a tired look. Well, moseying along feeling that way, I got to the edge of the woods and stopped to kind of rest myself and figure things out against the soft side of a rail fence. And as I was about to give it up and ramble on, what do you think I saw? Nothing less than as much as a dozen turkeys, roosting on a limb, all in a row, snug as you please!

"I had to think quick. The only guns we had those days were muzzleloaders. So I drew the load I had and wrapped the ramrod with wadding and chucked it back tight in the barrel. Then all I had to do was keep quiet until I found the right spot to shoot from. Pretty sudden I found my spot, took a good careful sight, and *bang!* Darned if I didn't split the whole dozen turkeys right through!

"I carried the lot home on the rod, but when I was sliding them off I noticed the loose ones were coming to, so I had to wring a few necks. We had turkey for days after that, with some to spare for the neighbors. But I guess I must have wiped out all the wild turkeys there were left, for I've never heard of any being seen around here since."

12

Rufe Shoots Hole in Water Tower

They put the waterworks in here 'bout 1924, and Rufe sat there at home, and he had a long rifle. He shot a hole in the tank, and he seen that wasn't gonna do. The water was a-spurtin' out, and it was about four mile out there where it was. He put more lead in his rifle and shot and plugged the hole up with the next shot.

13

Rufe Wouldn't Lie for a Trifle

One day, while in the barbershop, Rufe told about duck hunting. He said he was sitting by a pond, and 99 ducks landed on it in a straight row. He said he took one shot and killed all 99 of them. The barber asked him why he didn't just make it an even hundred, and Rufe replied, "Do you think I'd lie about one little old duck?"

14

The Fox and the Bullet

In the grist of tall tales turned out at one session of the Liar's Bench is the story of the fox and the bullet:

"Ye've heard of Swain's hill over yonder?" began the first comer. "I wouldn't wonder!" came a voice from the end seat.

"Well it's a small moundlike hill where a fox lived that used to worry the settlers right smart. So one morning on rising exceptional early a farmer saw the fox capering around, grabbed his gun, and ran out to the hill—I said it were a mound-shaped hill. So first he wrapped his gun around a tree—getting the circle of the hill—and then he fired at the fox as it disappeared around the curve. He clumb to the top of a tree at this point to look things over. Sure enough, there was old Mr. Fox goin' at top speed around the hill with one ear cocked backwards listening for the whiz of the bullet, which was maybe a hundred foot behind. Around they went, and when the fox got back to the same point, the bullet was only 75 foot behind. The next time it was 25 foot, and on the fourth round the bullet got him. Yep, it got that fox!"

"Ye don't say!" was the amazed response from the sitter whose head had been moving back and forth as he tried to figure how it would look for a fox to race a bullet around Swain's hill.

15

Rufe Shoots off Birds' Feet

Rufe went snipe huntin', and he couldn't hit snipes very well. They was a-flyin'. And so he just shot their feet off, and they flew themselves to death.

16

Rabbits Caught by Making Them Sneeze

If you want to go rabbit hunting and don't have any shells for your gun, just lay some cabbage leaves in front of a big rock and sprinkle pepper on them. When the rabbit comes up to eat the cabbage and he starts to sneeze and butts his head against the rock and knocks himself out, you just pick him up.

17

The Lucky Shot

There was once this man . . . I think his name was Jim Fletcher . . . who had a lot of stories told about him. I can only think of this one. He once went out huntin', and it turned out he got more than he went after. He took his ol' gun and was shootin' at a bear, and when he shot him the bullet went in one side of his head and out the other side. The bullet went on and hit a fox and killed it. The blast from the gun knocked Fletcher off the fence he was sittin' on into a covey of quail, and that killed six. And then, to beat all, the button flew off his pants and hit and killed a rabbit. Animals were dropping dead all over the place.

18

Good Measure

In the vicinity of Coal City, Owen County, lived a man by the name of Joe Crawl, an old settler who made his home in a cabin a short distance from Coal City. One morning when he got up he saw two deer a short distance from the cabin. Taking his muzzle-loading rifle he went out within close range of the game.

The deer were standing side by side on a little hill some distance from his cabin. He took aim and fired. One of the deer dropped, and the other appeared to scamper away. He went over to the one that he had killed and saw blood leading from the dead one along the trail of the one that had fled. When he followed this trail for a short distance, he found the other deer dead from the same shot.

Upon examination he found that the bullet had gone through both deer, and had left a trail where it had cut off corn stalks and a small sapling. He followed the course of the bullet for a quarter of a mile and found it had finally entered a beech tree, out of which a trickle of honey was running. So he went home and got a bucket and took half a tub of honey from the bullet hole.

The net returns on one shot, therefore, were two deer and a half a tub of honey, which Joe considered fair enough.

19

June to December

Bill Stafford, who lives alone over west of Centerton in the hills near Gold Creek is known in Morgan County as the oddest citizen. He was never known to speak the truth. Bill says he could make $10 a day panning gold out of Gold Creek if he could take time off from his cordwood cutting to work at it. But he just had to cut cordwood. Several years ago it was Bill's custom to go to Martinsville, get a big crowd around him and roar out his yarns.

"I ran across this here bear I was tellin' you about—a fierce one, mind you—while I was picking raspberries in June," one of his stories begins. "Well, I was unarmed, so I turn to run for dear life. But the bear came ripping along, right on my trail. On and on we run up hill and down dale, till finally we came to White River, and I crossed over on the ice." "But, Bill, how could you have crossed the river on the ice in June?" asked one of his listeners. "Why, you see," drawled Bill, "we did a heap of runnin', and by this time it was the middle of December."

20

Old Squirrelly

"Reminds me of Old Squirrelly, an Indian chief." The silence which means consent fell on the listening liars. So the narrator continued:

"Well, a mile west of the bridge crossing Pipe Creek northwest of Bunker Hill was an Indian Village. Squirrel Village it were called, for the Old Pottawatomi Indian chief, Old Squirrelly. Now this here Old Squirrelly were a capital hunter and near always brought home his game. 'Ceptin' one day. This here day he had hunted, 'thout even finding any game till he was on his way home, when he saw a flock of 17 geese sitting in a row on a limb of a tree overhanging Pipe Creek. 'Thout a sound he snuck along a ravine opening out onto the crick until he got his range—and then he drew back his bow and let an arrow go! The arrow hit the limb the geese was sittin' on—splittin' it wide open and clean through the tree into the bargain. Then the opening in the limb closed, and every goose was caught just as it was sittin' on the limb. Yes, sir, it shore was!"

And so convincing was the tale that not a voice was raised to question it. "Re-markable, re-markable, I say!" came a voice from the group, putting the stamp of truth on the story.

21
Fisherman Catches a Lighted Lantern

There was these two guys fishing, and one was telling the other about the fish he had caught that weighed 150 pounds. The other guy shook his head a little and said something funny had happened to him one day. He had throwed out his line, and when he started to pull it back he could tell there was something heavy on the other end. He pulled it all the way in, and there was a lantern, and it was still lit. The other boy said, "That's a pretty good tale." He said, "Yeah, but I'll tell you what. If you'll take a 100 pounds off of that fish, I'll blow out the lantern!"

22
Old Rip Snorter

Old Rip Snorter was the biggest yellow perch that had lived in the Wabash for a good many years. He had lived so long that his teeth had all fallen out, and he had gotten as gaunt and peaked as a grass-fed carp. It was a sad case, and it seemed as though the days of Old Rip were numbered.

One day Mrs. Browne was talking with a neighbor on the river bridge. Mrs. Browne was the proud possessor of a set of teeth which were like the lady villain in the old-fashioned story—beautiful but false.

The brisk breeze blowing over the river struck square between the shoulder blades of Mrs. Browne and made a ticklish sensation to stir in her nose. "Ker-Bizz!" she sneezed, and those lovely teeth sailed out into the air and dropped into the water with a mellow plunk.

Whenever Old Rip Snorter was seen after that, folks were surprised to see him so fat and flourishing. And just to add insult to injury, one day while Mrs. Browne was taking a boat ride, she saw Old Rip Snorter rise to the surface and grin at her, sassy as you please. And right then she recognized in his mouth her very own teeth that she had dropped when she sneezed long, long before.

23

Rufe Shoots Fish

Rufe was a great fisherman. He went fishin' in a canoe, and they had a .22 rifle in there. Aw, the fish wasn't a-bitin', so all the fish he got . . . he got, I believe, twenty-two . . . he shot them, as they hopped up out of the water, with a .22 rifle.

24

Hoop Snake Strikes Tree

Well, let's see. One time a feller had a . . . He's down on a hillside, and they's a snake, what they call a hoop snake. It'd put its tail in its mouth and come a-rollin' down the hill and rolled towards him. And he jumped round behind a small saplin' just as it struck, and said it hit the tree and commenced to growin' and swellin' and got big. And he cut the tree down and made him a . . . oh, I don't know, two- or three-bedroom house out of it. Two or three years later after they'd lived in it awhile, they decided to paint it, and then the turpentine in the paint killed the poison, and it drawed up. And they had to make a birdhouse out of it.

25

Hoop Snake Strikes Wagon Tongue

From Warren County comes the account of a hoop snake, the existence of which has been held in doubt by many people. Once upon a time, a team and wagon was seen going down the road at a leisurely pace. All was going well, and the driver especially was in a mellow mood. Not far along the way the driver noticed a hoop snake rolling down the road towards him at considerable speed. He tried to detour from the path of the oncoming reptile, but it was no go. In spite of all the detours, the snake struck the wagon tongue and buried its poisonous fangs in the shaft. The result was amazing. The wagon tongue swelled up, and when it was sawed they say it yielded 350 foot of lumber.

26

Snakebite Causes Tree to Swell

My uncle lived out on Mahalasville Road and was real poor—had about six kids. There was a farmer that lived down the road that had a little shack and five acres that he wasn't using and told my uncle that him and the kids could have it and make what they could out of it. The next spring he was out in the field hoeing. There was a lot of snakes out there around Mahalasville, you know; and he could just tell there was a snake around him. He looked down and seen a copperhead just getting ready to strike, and he stuck the hoe out and the copperhead bounced off and hit that big poplar tree, and the tree swelled up and pushed his little shack plumb off the five acres. So he decided to build a new house out of the tree. The tree was so big that he was able to build a seven-room modern home out of that one big tree that the snake had bit. Then about two years later he got enough money to buy some paint. Don't you know that the paint had turpentine in it and cured the snake bite! The house shrunk up, and there was just enough room for a bathtub and water bucket—had to hang the dipper outside.

27

Snakebite Causes Yoke to Swell

One day back when they still used mule teams to pull wagons, this old guy was driving his team through the Patoka bottoms. A big ol' water mocassin came along and was just about ready to strike when the old guy got a stick and hit it. This blow just knocked the snake off target. Instead of bitin' the mule, he hit the yoke.

After he got home the old guy noticed that the yoke was swelling. It just kept getting bigger and bigger. Pretty soon it was way too big for a yoke. So he decided to saw it up into logs and build a barn. He worked the rest of the day and got his new barn all built. The next day he was busy all morning and didn't go out back till afternoon. When he started out he noticed it was extra hot. When he got out to his new barn he saw that the swelled up logs had withered and all that was left was a pile of toothpicks.

28

Crippled Cat Kills Rabbits with Peg Leg

The cat got his leg cut off when a train went by one time. So Grandpa and his brothers and sisters fixed the cat up with a peg leg. They lived by a railroad track. Then after that the cat was healed and doing fine. Everyday they would come out and find a dead rabbit on the doorstep. The rabbit had a big bump on its head! "Where did the rabbit come from? How did it get there?" they wondered. So Grandpa followed the cat and watched it. That old cat would sneak out from behind a tree and clobber the rabbit over the head with its peg leg and drag it home. That's the story of the peg leg cat.

29

The Cat Fight

You know, right down there by the covered bridge . . . well, I was goin' down the road, and two cats got in a fight—right in the middle of the road. They were scratchin' and hissin' and clawin', and pretty soon they started climbin' up and up, higher and higher. Why, I watched till they were clear out of sight. I went by there about a week later, and the fur was still a-fallin'.

30

Hair Raising

In the settlement of Penn Township, St. Joseph County, the settlers had a lot of trouble with panthers and other animals that in the early days just about had the run of the place. One night, according to his story, a settler was in the woods at sugartime. He had plenty of sap on hand and was anxious to get it boiled down to syrup to make room for more. Sitting by the fire, with the sap boiling in his big kettle, he dozed off a little until all at once he was wakened by a heavy splash in his kettle of syrup. Whatever made the splash jumped from the kettle as fast as it had got in and made for the woods screaming. The settler, frightened about stiff by the rumpus, made tracks for home.

Next morning the syrup in the kettle was covered with thick scum, and when the settler skimmed it off he found that most of it was hair. The day after that a hunter came into camp with a queer carcass in tow. It looked like a panther, except that it was bald all over. The settler and the hunter got together and agreed that the panther must have been scalded in the syrup. It had misjudged its spring when it leaped for the settler and had come down in the boiling mass, and then had run out to die in the woods. This was the last time a panther was seen in those parts, and it was also the last time that the settler ever kept a fire going under a sugar kettle all night.

31

Dog Skins Coon and Digs Graves

Yeah, Browny's a pretty good dog, but he's kind of slow. Last winter we was huntin' a few miles north with . . . I suppose there was six of us altogether. Started out at nine o'clock and took the dogs out to a good-sized woods and just turned them loose, you know. We trailed them a couple miles and then set up camp until we heard one of my buddy's dogs pitchin' his howl. So we followed the howlin', and it seemed like the dogs was takin' turns barkin', 'cause only one was a-barkin' at a time. Then there was a quiet spell, and then Browny started yelping real loud. By the time we got to him, it was too late. There laid five dead durn good coon hounds and a bloody coon carcass. Browny must have got there late and got mad, 'cause he had that coon skinned and had started diggin' graves.

32

The Intelligent Bird Dog

Me and my buddy went out hunting one day. We used his bird dog because he said it could point, count how many birds were in a covey, and come back and tell him. Well, I just couldn't hardly believe that. So we were out in the field walking along, and the dog was up ahead of us. We saw him come running back, scratch on the ground five times, and then take off running. So we followed him, and sure enough there were five birds in the covey. So we worked them, and the dog took off again. Well, I mean to tell you, I had never seen anything like this in all my years of hunting, and there have been several. The dog came back and scratched on the ground ten times. So we followed him, and sure enough there was ten birds. Well, I just couldn't believe this. The guy said, "Yeah, he does this all the time." We worked these birds, and the dog took off. He was gone and gone. And when he came back, I looked down, and instead of scratching the ground he was hunching his owner's leg. I said, "See, I told you he couldn't count worth a darn. What's he doing that for?" He said, "Yeah, he's a smart dog. The covey was just too friggin' big; he couldn't count all of them."

33

The Intelligent Coon Dog

They was sittin' up there at the store tellin' about their coon dogs. Old Jim said he didn't know if he had the best coon dog or not, but he sure had a good one. He said whatever size coon he'd want, he'd just set the board out on the back porch, and his dog would go bring it in. He said it was a pretty good dog, but the only thing that went wrong was that one day his wife forgot and set the ironing board out there, and the dog left and never did come back.

34

Intelligent and Not So Intelligent Bird Dogs

This guy I know had an old bird dog named Ol' Blue. Instead of pointing quails he would jump on the covey, and when his owner would say "pull," Ol' Blue would lift up his leg and let one go. Another guy I know had the litter mate to Ol' Blue, but it wasn't as good. Sometimes when he yelled "pull," the dog would let two birds go.

35

The Long Hunt

Ol' Jake was the best hunting dog in this part of the country. He would point a quail and hold and hold and hold. One January morning it was so cold. The wind was blowing, and it was really snowing. Me and Ol' Jake went out to the woods to see if we could scare up a few quail. Jake hit upon a big cast in the woods, and I looked and looked for him. But I couldn't find him, so I gave up for the night. I was cold and hungry, and it was getting dark. I went back the next morning looking for him, but I couldn't find him. I did this for two days, but it was no use. The snow was too deep now, so I gave up. When I went back in March after the weather warmed I found Ol' Jake. The only thing standing was his skeleton where he had frozen to death, and in front of him was a covey of twelve birds.

36
The Mushroom Dog

I remember I had a dog once that was a mushroom dog, but nobody knew it for a long time. He never was around much, but in the spring we hardly ever saw him. One spring I got ambitious and decided to train him to hunt birds to make it easier to hunt quail in the fall. I cornered him and put a rope collar on him so he couldn't get away, and off we went to the big woods. We flushed out bird after bird, but that damn dog was more interested in rooting around in the leaves. I knew it was too early for snakes, so I wondered what the hell he was after. That damn dog was digging up mushrooms as fast as he could find them. I wised up pretty quick and let him have his head, only I got the mushrooms before he did. I didn't have any sack, so I tied up the neck and sleeves of my coat and filled that thing clear full. Well, sir, word got out quick, and I mean quick! Everybody in the country wanted to buy that dog. I was even offered a new corn planter in trade for him. I kept him, though, more out of novelty than anything else. He finally died, though. Caught cold one spring, and it ruined his nose. He ate a toadstool and died. Never did have a dog before or since with the same talent.

37
The Split Dog

There was a farmer from Shoals that was chopping wood with an axe. His dog ran under the axe just as the man was chopping down and cut the dog in two long-ways. The man got the two halves and sewed them together. The only problem was he put it together wrong, with two legs up and two legs down. But the dog liked it this way and ran on two legs for a while, then flipped over and ran on the other two.

38
Fox Eludes Dogs

There was always one fox that evaded the hounds and the hunters. It seems that the scent was always lost near a building used for storing pelts. One day the fox managed to evade the entire pack of hounds again, right by the pelt shanty, and when all the hunters were standing around and discussing the feat, the oldest dog of the bunch went inside the shanty where he set up a violent barking. When the hunters went into the pelt house, they found the sly old fox suspended by his tail from a nail in the wall, keeping perfectly still and looking exactly like all the rest of the pelts.

39
Foxes Spell One Another

Well, these farmers were discussing their fox hunting dogs. And one of them said he had some real good hounds, but sometimes the fox would outsmart them. He said that usually the hounds could run the fox until he got tired, and he would go in a hole or someplace where the dogs would tree him. This one time the fox kept running and running. He would make this big circle, and he would go through a hollow log and run some more. And it seemed like everytime he came out of that log he would run faster than before. And that went on until he began to wonder just what was going on. His hounds were about to give out. So finally he went over, and he looked in the hollow log. And he said there was another fox in the log. What they was, they were taking turns. When one fox ran in one end of the log, the other went out the other end. And that way they were running his dogs to death.

40
The Racing Fox

Floyd County has been the fox hunter's Mecca for many years. Here in the neighborhood of Georgetown was the fastest fox that was ever known anywhere. The fox hunters sat around the stove of Jim Harmon's or John Baylor's general store, chewed their tobacco, spat in the box of sawdust, and bragged of how they challenged anyone from anywhere to bring his fastest dog to see really how slow it ran in comparison to this remarkable fox. Several years passed—men came, bringing their dogs from all neighboring counties and even from different parts of Kentucky, but no dog could catch the renowned fox. Often the race kept on for several days. The question was how could any animal run such a terrible race and go on without fagging for so long a time? Different opinions were formed. Some said the fox was a spirit; others said it was a super animal. One of the strange things about the race was that now and again the fox would cross a certain place in the trail where there was a large badly bent tree with numerous branches that almost touched the ground. The fox always ran up this tree and jumped into the woods on the other side.

His fame grew, and with the bragging of the hunters—the Keithlays, Harmons, Johnsons, Cases, Shirleys and others—the race became so famous that it seemed time to investigate. Men were stationed at several points along the trail to look on, and one was set to watch at the leaning tree. After the fox had jumped into the woods, a movement was seen among the branches, and two small bright points of light were discerned. Could there be another animal crouched high up among the limbs of the tree?

Yes, there really was; the puzzle was solved. Two foxes and not one had kept the hunters busy. One ran until it was tired and returned to the leaning tree. As it ran up the trunk, its companion jumped from the branches and the race continued, with one fox always running while the other rested.

The tale is still told around the hunters' fires at night, especially when someone happens to bring up the subject of dumb animals. "Dumb animals!" someone is sure to snort fiercely. "Them two foxes that had sense enough to fool people from all over southern Indiana and Kentucky for years on end wasn't so dumb!"

41

Thomas Pucket and His Bear Story

Thomas Pucket, "the man what fit the Injuns and druv the bear," became a good and loyal native of Vigo County in the year 1816. Any old citizen or the descendant of any of the early settlers will tell you there is no mistake about it.

Pucket was hunting bear one day about 20 miles south of Terre

Haute. He had been hunting cows the day before when a bear had come along. Having no gun, he left the bear until he could go to the house for his rifle. But the bear did not stay put and moved on. Pucket took up his trail. He finally came across a bear lying on the sunny side of a hill, sleeping. He got close enough to examine it and was amazed at its size. He reflected that if he killed it where it lay, he could not get it home, and it was doubtful if he could even carry the hide. But since he was a man of quick conclusions and trusted his own judgment, he approached the sleeping monster and woke him up with some general observation about the weather. The bear raised his head, gaped widely, winked at Tom with his off eye, licked out his tongue in a friendly way, and lay down for another snooze.

Pucket now spoke in a deep, stern, bass voice and ordered bruin to arise and start for town, and backed this language by a punch with the muzzle of his gun. The bear was soon on his feet, but was perverse or else didn't know the way to Terre Haute, and started off waddling toward Vincennes. Pucket headed him off and made him reverse ends, but there was much zigzagging on the way, although the general direction was about right. These byplays of the animal made him travel nearer 40 miles than the 20 he could have made it in if he had gone as the crow flies. The result was that, within seven or eight miles of town, the bear lay down for a rest; and neither moral nor any other persuasion could make him budge. Tom then shot and skinned him, and the immense hide was shown to nearly everyone in Vigo County to prove the story.

42

Squirrels Steal Rufe's Corn

Rufe said he could remember when he and his son lived back on the farm. There were these two squirrels who lived in a hollow tree, and every day they'd come down, go into the corn crib and get corn and store it in the tree. One day while the squirrels were in the crib, Rufe and his son sawed down the tree and carried it off. Then Rufe shot into the corn crib with his 12-gauge. Rufe said, "Those squirrels came out so fast and climbed eighty feet up that tree before they realized it wasn't there!"

43
The Intelligent Sow

Once there was a farmer had a sow that kept getting out of its field. He couldn't figger out how it was getting out. She would get out, but she couldn't get back in. He lived in hilly country. One day he followed her. So she went back in the field up on the edge of a hill in the woods. She chewed off a grape vine. She kept this grape vine in her mouth, and she'd back up on the edge of the hill and swing over the fence and drop off on the lower side, but she couldn't get back in. Every night he had to turn her back in the field. So he decided he would outsmart the old sow. So he cuts the grape vine off.

And she found another way to get out. There was an old log he had put in a washout, and the log had rotted out, and there was a hollow in it. She was crawling through this hollow log. So that went on for a while, and he discovered that. The log was really crooked, almost U-shaped. So he turned the log around and put the other end back in the field and covered it up with some brush. So she would go down every day and go through this hollow log and come back into the same field she was in and not know she had done it, and she thought she was outside. And from then on he never had any trouble with her.

44
The Cow That Drowned
in Her Own Milk

I had this ol' cow that stayed out in the woods one night and missed milking. I didn't miss her till the next morning, and then I went out looking for her. I found her laid down in this big sink hole. The milk had all run out of her tits, and she had drowned. When she was drowning she kicked around and churned the milk and made butter, and there was a fifteen pound block laying on her!

45
A Whopper

Preparing for the siege at Vicksburg, General Grant's men were plowing the channel of a mortar boat canal [not motor boat] some eight feet deep and 15 feet wide to be used as a waterway to float the mortar into position. Such a task was Herculean and demanded the use of 24 yoke of oxen, a total of 48 animals. Handling the plow was a mean struggle for the strongest and required the efforts of a number of men.

An onlooker remarked that if he couldn't do a better job by himself than they were doing, he wouldn't touch the plow handles. General Grant, hearing the remark, and thinking the fellow a braggart, told the bystander to take over the job and plow the canal.

Before the astonished eyes of the soldiers, as the story goes, this boastful fellow commanded the oxen to move on, and, grasping the plow handles, went on to complete the canal. Only one obstacle confronted his efforts and that was a large sycamore stump which completely blocked the path of the waterway. But on coming to the stump the fellow hastened the oxen to more speed, and, firmly grasping the plow handles, cleft it apart and passed through.

But, alas, the stump closed again, catching the coattails of the braggart. The water in the canal was advancing rapidly, with the mortar boats following close behind. With great speed the fellow turned the ox team around, snipping short his coattails, and plowed out the stump before the bow of the foremost boat could touch him.

46

The Surefooted Horse

My bottom land was so flooded one time I had to ride the ol' hoss back to the back because he was the only one of the two of us that could swim, and I had to check the hogs. Well, we walked back there several foot, and I just didn't see any of the hogs. Well, the water in this spot where the horse was standing wasn't too deep, so I jumped off, and the water went up over my head. You know, that horse had been walkin' on the barbed wire fence the whole time!

47

The Well-Trained Mule

I had an ol' mule down in the eastern part of Kentucky, and one day we were out in the log woods. I had that ol' mule trained to pulling logs that when he came to a rough place he would sit down on the log and slide down. When it would quit sliding, he would get up and start working again. There was this bluff where you dumped the logs over, and when that mule got there I'd pull off the gear and shove 'em over. Well, one day I wasn't looking, and the mule went right on over. When I saw him he was about twenty foot from the ground. I hollered "whoa" real loud, and he stopped, and that's the only thing that saved him!

48
The Ferocious Mosquito

John was a-takin' his girl to the dance one Saturday night, and this mosquito kept buzzin' around and around the ol' mule pullin' the wagon. Pretty soon the mosquito flew up and started to dive down on the ol' mule's rump. Just as he was about to make contact, the mule jumped sideways. The mosquito missed the mule, but he split the wagon tongue clear in two.

49
Old Tunnel Mills

"Back in 1840 in the State of Arkansas when I was a mere lad," said an oldtimer, owner of Tunnel Mills outside of Old Vernon, who was born and bred in the hills of Jennings County and had never been out of the state, "I was the best fisherman for miles and miles around. Back in those days we really gigged. I had made for myself, out of an old hickory limb, a gig eight foot long. Now in the next county there was a bottomless pit and in the bottomless pit was a whale, for we had seen it swimming around many a time. There was a drought, and the streams were all dried up except the bottomless pit; and with the water so low somebody measured the pit and found it was only 30 foot deep. It was a rare chance to get the big fish, and several of the boys walked miles and miles to come and tell me about it. I told them I could get it, so they said I should take my eight-foot gig and go over. We all went over and paddled in a canoe to the mouth of the pit."

At this point the oldtimer always stopped and waited for someone to ask what happened next. He would reply, "Well, boys, it was just like this. I leaned over the side of the boat and gigged the fish." "Well," the question would be asked, "did you get it?" "No, boys," would be the reply, "that fish got away, but I speared him so close to the bottom that there was enough meat left on that gig to last my family for the next two weeks."

50

A Historic Fish Story

Moody Dustin, a potter who went south every fall to sell his wares, is best remembered by the people of Jeffersonville as one of the outstanding Falls pilots of the time when some persons were licensed to pilot boats around the Falls, before the canal was built there between Louisville and Jeffersonville.

One of the most remarkable fish stories ever heard of was told on Moody Dustin, by Capt. W. B. Carter, another pilot. Dustin had sold all his goods and had considerable money. The boys on his boat had been fishing and had caught several small fish, which they strung on a line and tied to the stern of the boat. During the night the craft began to rock. All on board were more or less filled with fear of a visit from a highwayman. It was not long before everybody was awake and whispering that pirates were about ready to do some scuttling. All hands arose, buckled on weapons and sallied forth. The boat continued to rock. No one was in sight. A thoughtful man started to lift up the string of fish, but it was so heavy he called for assistance. A big catfish was drawn up. It had swallowed the string of fish, but the last one had stuck in the throat of the big fish, and its efforts to free itself had rocked the boat causing the commotion and alarm of those on board.

51

Tragic End of Tame Fish

Once there was these two men, and they decided to go fishin' in the pond by the creek. Well, they hadn't been fishin' long, and they caught this big fish, about two feet long. That's the biggest one they'd ever seen. Well, they put the fish . . . they decided to take the fish home and eat it for breakfast the next mornin'. And they put it in this ol' tin tub. Well, the next mornin' they got up, but they didn't have fish for breakfast. The fish was out of the tub and chasin' the cats and dogs around the house.

Well, this went on for about a month; and they said since they were going to have this dumb fish around anyway they might as well name it. So they named the fish Charlie. And Charlie became almost human. He went huntin' with 'em, every . . . everywhere else they went. Well, finally snow came, and when the snow came they went huntin'. And when they went, Charlie went with 'em. Well, they went across a stream, and when they got across the stream, they yelled for Charlie to come across. Well, Charlie missed the log and slipped and fell in the stream. Before they could get Charlie out of the stream he drowned.

52

Tom, the Catfish

The story is told around Marion that when old Obidildock Manring of Grant County was young he caught a catfish in the Mississinewa River. It was too small to fry, so he put it in a horse trough. Every day he stopped to feed the fish, and before long it was quite a pet and so tame it would swim to the edge to be fed. One day, Tom—that's what Obe called his fish—jumped out of the horse trough and flopped along beside his master. After that Tom followed along all summer as Obidildock did his farm chores and was good company.

When school started, Tom followed Obidildock to school, for all the world like Mary's little lamb, but one day as they were crossing a foot log over a creek, Tom slipped off and fell in. "Yep," the narrator usually concludes, "it were too bad about that catfish. Might o' been livin' today if he hadn't got drownded thataway!"

53

Large Snake Thought To Be a Log

Old Murphy said one time that he was talking about snakes. He said, "I seen the biggest snake I ever seen in my life. I was comin' up here to the store, and a big black snake come across the road, and I didn't know which way it was goin'. That snake was clear across the road. I ran over him, and it felt just like a rock." Jim said, "I know there is snakes around here in this country that are monsters." He said, "Here 'while back I was over there in the woods a-cuttin' props, and it got to be about noontime and time to eat my dinner. Well, I sit down on an old log and ate a couple sandwiches and drank a cup of coffee, and then I got an apple out." He said, "My teeth are kinda bad anymore, so I have to peel my apples. So I took my knife out and peeled it. I never thought nothing about it, but I stuck my knife in the log, and it run off with me!"

54

Who Was Drunk?

It was on Pipe Creek that Tom Moore took rod and tackle one warm day in July and went to fish. As he had a thirsty nature and feared he would have nothing but creek water to drink, Tom took along a bottle of John Barleycorn.

He found a nice shady place along the stream to sit, baited his hook and cast his line far out into the water. He had sat there for some time before he thought of the bottle in his pocket, took it out and quenched his thirst, which had suddenly become middling sharp. He put the bottle back in his pocket and in a little while fell asleep. On waking up, he found the pole had been dragged from his hand down to the water's edge where a snake was coiled, looking at the fisherman with more than ordinary interest for a snake.

Tom "sot agin," baited the hook and threw it into the water. Again his thirst took possession of him, and he took another drink. He felt something nudging him in the side. As he looked down he saw the snake with mouth open and tongue extended suggestively. The fisherman poured some of the contents of the bottle into the snake's mouth, and it went scurrying off into the water. Soon it appeared with a catfish in its mouth and laid the fish down beside Tom. It nudged him again and opened its mouth, and Tom gave it another drink. Again it disappeared into the stream and this time came up with a bass in its mouth. Tom kept up the game, giving it a drink and in return receiving a fish each time. He finally stopped fishing and just watched the snake, which now approached the bank with considerable difficulty. It proceeded in this wandering fashion for some time, getting more and more off its course, when suddenly two other snakes appeared on the scene. They slipped along on either side of their boon companion, one wrapping a tail around the neck and the other around its middle, and the three snakes disappeared among the weeds at the side of the stream.

55
Frog Churns Butter

We used to live at a place where in the summertime we would run out of water. We would have to go to the spring to get water and carry it back to the house. Well, Mom used to take a crock of milk down to the spring to keep it cool. This one time she had this lid on this crock of milk when she took it down there. And a frog jumped up there and knocked this lid off and fell in this crock and he couldn't get out. He jumped up and down so much that he churned a big ball of butter. When Mom went down there to get the milk, there that old frog was, sitting on that ball of butter.

56
Fertile Soil

John Oswald, crossing watchman at Decatur, Indiana, recalls some of the experiences of early days in Indiana:

"When our folks settled in Adams County, Indiana, they were so late getting the first field cleared that it was too late to plant corn, so my father planted pumpkins and turnips in the new ground. He sowed the turnips first and then planted pumpkin seed. As he left the field he noticed that the turnip seed was up and good-sized turnips were growing.

"Then he saw that the pumpkin vines were growing so fast that he ran for the rail fence to get out of the tangle, but they twined around his legs and held him fast on the fence. Quick as a lick he out with his Barlow knife to cut himself loose, but he was too late. A big pumpkin had grown over his pocket, and he could not get at his knife.

"Just then my grandfather came out to the field and, seeing the plight of my father, pulled up a large turnip and, swinging it by its leaves, hit the pumpkin, bursting it into bits. He then cut my father loose, and they returned to the house to boast of their luck in getting such fertile land. It took just three of the turnips to fill a bushel basket, so when they sold a half bushel they had to cut one turnip in two."

57

Cornstalk Yields Shelled Corn

This was my first experience with that newfangled hybrid corn . . . and my last. I wouldn't have that crazy stuff planted on my ground ever again. What happened was the durn stuff didn't sprout no ears. Oh, the stalks got good and big. They were about six feet high and four inches thick when they first tasseled. It just kept on a-growing and a-growing and getting taller and taller, and still there weren't no ears.

One day I was out looking at it. It was almost fall, and the stalks were beginning to fire, but there still wasn't any ears to be seen. Them cornstalks was the biggest ones anybody had ever seen. They were 15 feet tall and seven or eight inches through. While I was out there in the field, Jake came along and got out of his truck and started inspecting the corn hisself. We looked at stalk after stalk, but there just wasn't any ears on any of it. Ol' Jake, he got to laughing 'bout how I'd been skinned and how all I had was stalks in my field. I got so blame mad that I just hauled off and kicked one of them cornstalks. I kicked it so hard it broke over, and, lo and behold, shelled corn rolled out of that stalk all over the ground! It had been inside the stalk all along and didn't need no ears.

58

Crops Produced from Stakes

There was a farmer who was always experimenting with all kinds of fertilizer. He would always put a broomstick handle in the ground at the spots where he used a different kind of chemical so he would know which chemical he used. His crops never seemed to get any improvements, but he found that two broomsticks yielded several large ears of corn and that the other stick developed into a very healthy potato vine and that the two others sprouted new brooms.

59

Wind Blows Rooster into Jug

These old men always sat around the filling station talking. They always tried to see who could be the windiest and all that stuff. There was a tornado come through out there in Horseshoe one day. It done a lot of damage and blowed a lot of trees down and everything. And this one guy who lives in Bethel, he said, "Remember that old shack out in the back, Jim?" Jim said, "That little smoke shed?" He said, "Yes, it blew that shed down over the hill, and I have looked all up and down the creek and everywhere, and I can't find even a board." Jim said, "I know it blowed awful hard. It blowed the front glass out of my house and scared my wife to death. But the funniest part of it is that little red rooster. You remember that little rooster, don't you? It used to sit on the back porch all the time. Well, we couldn't find that little rooster anywhere after that storm. But you know we kept hearing him crow. So we looked and looked. And you know where we finally found him?" The old guy said, "No, Jim, where?" And Jim said, "You know that old jug we got sittin' out back? Well, the wind blew so hard it blew that little rooster clean into the neck of that jug."

60

Indiana Winters Are Rough

We were down there in Louisiana, and it was kinda chilly down there. We was tellin' about how cold it was. This one guy he been down there in Louisiana; he was born down there; he was a Louisiana person. And he said, "Well, one year it was so cold down here," he said, "the mosquitoes hijacked a semi, took the tires off of it, and was burning them to keep warm." And another guy said, "Oh, I don't know." Said, "I'm from up there in Montana." Said, "Now, we really get cold up there." Said, "One year it was so cold up there we couldn't even light our cigarettes outside." Said, "We'd strike the match, and we'd have to run inside to thaw the flame out so we could light our cigarettes." I told 'em they ain't been anywhere until they been to Indiana in the winter. Said, "Them Indiana winter's are rough!" Said, "It got so cold there one winter you could set a steaming tea kettle of water out on your front porch, and it would freeze solid before it quit steaming."

61

The Thick Smog

Pollution isn't any new thing. A long time ago my grandad was workin' in an oil field down near Petersburg. The smog was really thick one day when Grandad was supposed to climb up a piling and tie a rope on the top. He kept climbin' and climbin' higher and higher. Finally, the guy at the bottom yelled, "How high you gonna climb, anyway? The bottom of this rope left the ground five minutes ago!" So Grandad looked down and saw the top of the piling two feet below! He'd climbed the rest of the way in smog!

62

He Roofed the Fog

Years ago there lived in Waukarusa a carpenter renowned for the size of the stories he told. One time during damp and foggy weather this carpenter was shingling a house. It was so foggy that he could hardly see to do his work, but he continued nevertheless working hard, and went home finally in the fog.

During the night the fog cleared, and he went back to the job in the morning. "Imagine my surprise," he related afterwards, "when I arrived at my place of work, to find that I had finished the yon side of the roof and shingled two feet beyond the eaves in the fog."

63
Fish Swim in Thick Fog

One morning a man was driving to work when something hit the windshield of his car with a very heavy thud. When he stopped the car and got out to see what hit it, he saw a big catfish lying on the hood of his car. Then all of a sudden some catfish and perch and suckers were swimming through the air about three or four feet above the creek. So this man picked up some of these fish and put them in the car so he would have a fresh fish supper. The fog was so thick the fish swam right from the water into the fog and didn't know the difference.

64
Hail, Hail!

"I mind the time," an oldtimer started with his customary signal for a tall tale, "when it hailed so hard in July near Camden that it killed 500 chickens for one farmer." "You don't say," commented the most interested listener. "Yep, it did. And that farmer and his wife dressed the chickens, put them in barrels, scooped the hailstones over the chickens and they had chicken the rest of the summer."

"Humph," the interested listener began again. "Reminds me of the time it hailed out home and one hailstone was so large that it hit the top of my silo, bounced around some, and then fell off and killed a calf below." Oldtimer looked sternly at his companion. Then he spoke: "Only, ye see, I wasn't lyin' about the chickens."

65
Some Rain!

Clem Watkins, the father of Tom, used to live in the vicinity of Indian Hill in Tippecanoe County. So this story might be credited to that locality.

Clem had heard that you could raise cucumbers in the driest season by simply taking out the head and bottom of a whiskey barrel, setting it upright in rich soil, filling it halfway to the top with well-rotted manure, and planting the cucumber seed; every day thereafter water could be poured into this barrel to supply moisture and fertility. By this process, vines throve exceedingly and brought forth a hundred-fold.

Clem thought he would try it. He obtained the barrel at Lafayette (no hard task) and had taken out the bottom and head when a tremendous storm came up from the southwest. The rain fell in torrents and no one dared go out to get the barrel under cover.

So the barrel lay out in the yard on its side, with the bunghole up. And, believe it or not, it rained so hard through the bunghole that the flood couldn't pour out fast enough at the ends, and it burst the barrel.

66

Hard Man—Hardpan

This story was told by George Mitchell, a river rat who lived years ago in the vicinity of Black Rock. He may have heard of George Washington and his legendary reputation for truth telling, but the information evidently made little impression upon him.

Mitchell was engaged in the job of digging a well. All early wells were dug wells, the work being started with spade, shovel, and pick, and the dirt shoveled out at the top. This continued until a depth of eight or ten feet was reached, when it became necessary to resort to a windlass to remove the dirt.

The bucket was usually made of half a barrel furnished with a bail of heavy wrought iron. This bucket was filled with dirt and then drawn up and emptied by two men at the top. It was a tedious job, and a dangerous one for the digger, should the bucket come loose.

Mitchell had dug to the depth of 20 feet or more and had struck a hardpan, a thin stratum of gravelly rock which usually overlies gravel. The bucket, full of wet clay and gravel, weighing 200 pounds, broke loose at the top of the well. A horrified cry from the men above warned Mitchell that he was in danger. He could not dodge—the well was too narrow. So he braced his legs and bowed his back to the descending bucket. It fell right on his back and drove his feet into the hardpan up to his knees.

67

The Stretching and Shrinking Harness

There was a guy in Martin County that was pulling logs with his team of horses. The harness was made out of rawhide leather. It started, and the harness began to stretch. The man led the horses to the house, but the logs stayed because the leather was stretching too much. When he got to the house he took the harness off the horses and put it over a fence post. When it stopped raining and the sun came out, the harness started shrinking back to its normal size, and finally the logs came over the hill and down to the house.

68

The New Harness

"Did I ever tell ye the one about the new set of harness the feller got my father knowed onct?" began Lemuel Snodgrass at one of the opening sessions of the Liar's Bench. "By gum, ye never!" "Tell it!" came the response from the other sitters.

"Well, this feller's harness was plumb wore out, so he set to work to make hisself a new set of harness out of raw buffalo hide. It were sure a beauty—broad traces an inch thick, and three or four inches wide. So one morning he set out to haul in a load of wood he'd cut the day afore. He felt middling good, and as he loaded he sang, and on his way home he warbled like a lark."

"Don't you mean he hummed like a hum-bird?" put in one of his listeners. "Who's tellin' this story anyhow? You or me?" "Why, you air. Go ahead. Nobody's stoppin' you."

"Well, 'like a lark,' I said. And it had been purty dry hereabouts for quite a spell, so this feller, he'd been prayin' for rain. When all of a sudden like, his prayers was answered. And a storm come up that started him along towards home at a right smart clip. When he reached the bottom of the steep hill, the rawhide traces had been soaked and began to stretch. So he got down and walked beside his team. But the wet traces jest kept on a-stretchin'. When he reached the top, the wagon, by gum, was still down to the bottom. By then he were plum disgusted. So he stripped the harness from the horses, hung it over a stump, and went home."

"Humph! And then what happened?" urged one of the sitters. "Why, the sun come out, and the harness begun to dry, and the traces begun to shrink." A pause here while Lem took a good draw on his corncob pipe. "So the next time he looked out, the wagon was up to the top of the hill! Wet rawhide's the stretchinist stuff!" he wound up, looking wise.

69

Rufe's Horse Keeps Ahead of Storm

The best one was when Rufe told about having the fastest horse around. He said one day his wife sent him into town with a hen and some eggs. She told him that it looked like rain so to hurry and be sure not to let the eggs get wet or the people wouldn't buy them. Now the eggs were right behind the seat, and the hen was on the end of the wagon. Well, Rufe took off for town. The rain kept getting closer and closer, so Rufe made that horse get up and go. Rufe said, "Well, when I got to town, there wasn't a drop on the eggs, but that hen was drowned."

Catch Tales And Hoaxes

THE CATCH TALE or hoax story generally is told as a true story, but it ends abruptly and humorously by tricking the audience with either a punch line or by forcing a listener to ask the storyteller a question to which he gives a foolish answer. Many kinds of jokes are swapped within joking sessions; however, the catch tale is most effective when it appears spontaneously within the framework of ordinary conversation—that is, within a non-joking context. Children and adolescents, especially, have appreciated this kind of story.

Most of the tales in this section have been classified as shaggy dog stories by Brunvand (see the headnote to the following section on shaggy dog tales), and some have been called anti-legends by other folklorists. Writing on one of the tales (Tale 73) in this section, William M. Clements says that "it seems possible to consider 'The Walking Coffin' a discredited legend, a story which possesses the characteristics of a legend but substitutes something incongruous for a supernatural climax. . . . Ranke especially sees this phenomenon as a manifestation of the process of disintegration of one type of traditional narratives [*sic*] and the transition into other forms. Bausinger, on the other hand, uses similar examples to prove the close relationship between legends and outlandish jokes" (*Indiana Folklore*, 2:2 [1969]: 9). Likewise, in "The Belief Legend in Modern Society: Form, Function, and Relationship to Other Genres," Linda Dégh claims that

"The Walking Coffin" is erroneously listed in Baughman's index as a catch tale (*American Folk Legend,* ed. Wayland D. Hand [Berkeley: University of California Press, 1971], p. 68). John M. Vlach, who calls these kinds of tales "humorous anti-legends," agrees that these stories "should not be placed within the genre of the joke" (*Indiana Folklore,* 4:2 [1971]: 122).

While it is true that skeptical legend tellers discredit legends or belief tales with rational explanations, and while it is also true that some legends are transformed into jokes (see, for example, the note to Tale 111, "The Surpriser Surprised"), there is no firm evidence that most catch tales are disintegrated legends that have lost their credence. Catch tales and hoax stories, I feel, never were legends and are not now anti-legends. They may contain legend motifs and, if effectively told, may at first sound like legends. Most certainly, for their special effect, catch tales require the audience's familiarity with formal qualities and performance features of legends, but this is precisely the appeal of catch tales. The humor in them arises from the disjointed pairing of a seriously told legend-like beginning with an obviously ridiculous conclusion. As such, catch tales support the incongruity theory of humor. While the incongruity results from the mocking of the legend, this does not presuppose that the catch tale is a discredited legend or an anti-legend. If anything, the catch tale is a sham legend and consequently a particular kind of joke.

70

The Golden Arm

There was a man who lived in a small house in the woods. He had one arm which he had lost just up past the elbow, but instead of a regular artificial arm he had a golden arm to replace it. Each night he took it off and put it in a box beside his bed. A man heard about it and decided to steal it one night while the man was asleep. He made his way carefully through the woods and waited a long time after the lights went out. He tiptoed into the house and took the golden arm from its case as quietly as he could and left the house. He then thought he was safe, so he took his time leaving the woods. When he was about half way out of the woods he heard a low voice behind him in the darkness which said, "Who stole my golden arm?" He got a little scared, so he walked a little faster. Soon he heard the same thing again: "Who stole my golden arm?" And it was getting closer! He tried to go faster, but it kept getting closer. "Who stole my golden arm?" Closer and closer it came. "Who stole my golden arm?" Then it was right behind him and a lot louder, "Who stole my golden arm?" "Who stole my golden arm?" "You stole it!" [Storyteller grabs the listener.]

71

The Dog's Cigar

A man one time was going to build a fireplace out of bricks, so he figured it out to the last detail in blueprints and everything on how many bricks he needed—499 bricks. So he went to the brick company and asked for 499 bricks, and the guy said that they only sold them in lots of 500. He said, "Look, I don't need 500; I only need 499." The guy said, "Well, you can take it or leave it 'cause we won't split 'em up." So the guy took 500 bricks, and he went home and started building his fireplace. And, sure enough, with all his blueprints and everything, it only took 499 bricks, and you know what he did with the last brick? He threw it up in the air!

I'll tell you another one if you don't like that one. There was this man one time, and he had to get to this certain city on time, and he was going to take a plane. So he went to the ticket counter, and he said he had to be in this certain other city by such and such a time. And the lady said that all the tickets on that flight had been sold already. And he kept explaining to her how urgent it was, and she finally said, "Well, there's a real fat lady on the plane, and I had to sell her two tickets, but I'll go ahead and sell one to you, and maybe you can squeeze in." So he gets on the plane and finds his seat, squeezes in between this fat lady and the window, and what does she have but a goddamn lap dog. So the dog is panting, and he simply just detests lap dogs, and he detests airplane rides, too. So he finally decides that he's gonna have to make the best of it. So he takes out a cigar and starts smoking it. The lady goes, "I simply detest cigar smoke." And he looks at her and goes, "Well, I simply detest lap dogs." She goes, "Well, look, we'll make a deal. We'll open the window, and if you'll throw the cigar out, I'll throw the lap dog out." He goes, "Fine." So they open the window and threw the dog out and threw the cigar out. So they're gettin' off the plane . . . he got through the trip okay . . . and as he's goin' down the steps, he glances down the side of the airplane, and there's the dog hanging on with one paw to the window. And you know what he had in the other paw? [The listener usually thinks it's the cigar.] That brick that guy threw up in the air a little while ago.

72

It Floats!

There was this ghost story, or joke really, about a man and his wife who were taking an ocean voyage on this ship. And when they were, oh, way out in the middle of the ocean, the woman died. And the man was just crushed, but he knew that he had to see to her funeral and burial, you know. So he talked to the captain, and the captain said that they were too far away from land to give her a decent burial on land, so they'd have to give her a burial at sea—you know, where they wrap the body and throw it into the ocean.

So, anyway, the man wasn't happy about it, but there was really nothing he could do except that, you know. And he knew his wife wouldn't have liked it, but he just couldn't help it. So they had the burial, and they threw her body into the ocean. And the man went back to his cabin to mourn for his wife. After a little while he went to bed, and he heard this strange voice saying, "It floats! It floats!" Well, you know, he thought he was just hearing things because he was so upset, and he went to sleep.

The next day he heard the voice again: "It floats! It floats! It floats!" Well, he was beginning to get worried. He knew he wasn't imagining the voice. The next day he heard it again: "It floats! It floats!" He couldn't stand it. He was thinking, "Oh, my gosh, my wife is following me. The ship . . . her body is floating after the ship because I threw her out into the ocean!" Well, he just couldn't stand it. He had to find out what was floating. He had to be sure. So he heard the voice again: "It floats! It floats!" So the man screamed out, "Voice, what floats? *What* floats?" And the voice said, "Ivory soap!"

73
The Walking Coffin

This one guy went into a bar one day and heard a man talking about a coffin. The man said that a man hasn't been born yet that could sleep one night in the same room with this certain coffin. Hearing this, he went over and asked the guy if he wanted to make a little bet that he couldn't do it. The man said that he would bet him, but he had to warn him that three men had tried it and all three were found the next day dead and that their hair had turned white with fright. He said that he didn't care, that no coffin could ever scare him to death. They made a bet of one thousand dollars and made the arrangement that if he walked out of the room the next day at twelve noon he would win the money.

That night at twelve midnight he went into the room with this average looking coffin and decided that he would just go to sleep and get up the next day and get his money. He was sure that it was only a matter of mind over matter. He locked the door and shoved it [the key] under the door so even if he wanted to get out he couldn't. He went to sleep with the lights on, and everything went well, until about three o'clock in the morning a strange noise woke him up. He opened his eyes and looked around and then rolled over and tried going back to sleep, thinkng that he had just imagined it.

He had just got to sleep again when the same noise woke him up again. He looked up, and the coffin seemed to have moved. He decided that he was seeing things and rolled over when he heard the same noise again. This time the lights in the room started flickering, and he jumped up. He decided that he couldn't get any sleep, so he figured that he would look around the room to find something to do. All of a sudden he saw out the corner of his eye that the coffin was moving, and he knew that it was really moving this time. He started to panic, but caught himself, remembering what had happened to the other three men. He slowly started edging over to the door till he almost got there, and then made a mad dash for it. It was locked; he had locked it and threw the key under the door. He tried getting the key back, but he couldn't get near it.

Then he started shouting for help. All the time the coffin is getting closer and closer. He started panicking and screamed at the top of his voice. It was no good; there was nobody around to hear him. The coffin kept getting closer and closer, and still nobody came to help him. Now it was almost touching him, and he jumped out of the way. The coffin changed its course and started coming towards him again, closer and closer. He started thinking, "I can't panic; I can't panic; remember those other three guys." He started looking around thinking, "What will stop the coffin?" Then he saw a sturdy well-built chair and thought, "That will stop the coffin." He picked up the chair and threw it at the coffin, and it splintered into a million pieces, and the coffin kept coming. Then he saw another chair, but this one was better built. "This will stop the coffin." He threw the chair, and it splintered. The coffin kept coming closer and closer and closer. "I got to stop that coffin!"

By now the coffin had him trapped in the corner. He thought desperately of how to stop the coffin, but couldn't think of anything. The coffin kept coming closer, inch by inch. "I got to stop the coffin!" Now he was up against a dresser, and he only had a few more minutes to stop the coffin or it would get him. Frantically he started ripping at the dresser drawers trying to find something to stop the coffin. He ripped out the bottom drawer, and there was nothing. He threw the drawer at the coffin, and it splintered. And the coffin kept getting closer. He ripped out the next drawer. Nothing! So he threw it at the coffin. Almost insane with fear, he kept thinking, "I've got to stop the coffin! I've got to stop the coffin!"

Only two drawers left, and the coffin was almost on him. He ripped one of the drawers out, and all there was in it was a small dirty box. He knew that wouldn't stop the coffin. The coffin was touching him by now, so he broke the drawer over it and kept swinging until there was nothing left to swing with. He jumped up on the dresser now, and he wasn't able to get to the last drawer. Maybe that was the one. The dresser started crunching from under him, and he started crying like a crazy man, screaming, "I've got to stop the coffin! I've got to stop the coffin!" It was almost all over; the dresser started giving way under his feet. And he kept screaming, "I've got to stop the coffin! I've got to stop the coffin!" This was it; the dresser was going down. And he threw his hands in front of his face, and as he did he saw the little dirty box in his hand from the drawer. He started to throw it at the coffin as a last try, when he saw the label on it: *Smith Brothers Wild Cherry Cough Drops.* "That'll stop the coffin!"

74

The Rapping Paper

I heard it from my brother before, and I heard it from Betty just last week. It's kind of sick. There's a man and a woman who hadn't been married very long. One night they were sleeping, and the woman heard a noise: rap, rap, rap, rap. She didn't know what it was, and she got kind of scared 'cause she thought it might be a burglar or something. And she woke up her husband and told him to listen, and he heard it too. So he got a baseball bat or some kind of club to defend himself, and they went lookin' for this noise.

And they got out in the hall; and it sounded louder, sounded like it was coming from upstairs. And they went upstairs, and they heard it: rap, rap, rap, rap, rap. And they walked down the hall; and behind the door that led to the stairs to the attic, it sounded even louder. So they went up to the attic, and it sounded even louder up there—*real* loud: rap, rap, rap, rap, rap, rap, rap, rap, rap, rap, rap, rap, rap. And he couldn't imagine what it was. And it was coming from a box over at the corner of the attic. So the woman said to her husband, "Go see what it is and kill it." And he said, "Well, you're comin' with me." And they went over to the box, and he lifted the lid and was ready to hit it. And there was a box of wrapping paper!

75

The Encounter with a Horrible Monster

There was a traveling salesman who got caught in a terrible thunderstorm. It was really a bad storm, and he couldn't find any house to stop at for the night. Finally he came upon an old, huge, three-story house that had lights on, so he decided to stop. He parked the car in front of the house and ran up to the porch and knocked on the door. Finally a little old man came to the door and asked him in. The salesman asked if he could spend the night because of the storm, and the old man said yes. He said he lived there all alone and was glad for the company. He showed him to a room on the second floor; then they went downstairs to the library to have coffee and talk.

After they had talked for a while the old man asked the salesman if he had ever seen a blue gorilla. The salesman said that he hadn't, so the old man said he would show him one. The old man went to the bookshelf and reached up to the fourth shelf and took down the book *Mutiny on the Bounty*. He opened the book to page 104 and went down to the eighth line and pushed on the word *An*. The bookcase swung open and revealed a long dark hall. The old man picked up a lantern and lit it and motioned for the salesman to follow him. They went down the long dark hall, then down a long steep staircase. Then they went through an iron gate, which the old man unlocked, then through a heavy wooden door, then through another dark passage, and finally came to a heavy metal door. Inside the small room the old man held the lantern high, and in the center on a wooden stand was a small cage which held a small two-inch-high blue gorilla. The salesman was really shocked because he had never seen one before, and he reached out to touch it. The old man yelled and told him not to touch it. The salesman asked why, and the old man wouldn't tell him, and they went back upstairs—back through the heavy metal door, through the dark passage, the heavy wooden door, the iron gate, up the steep staircase, down the long dark hall, and back into the library, where the old man closed the bookcase and said it was time to go to bed. The salesman tried again to find out why he couldn't touch the blue gorilla, but the old man wouldn't say, so they both went upstairs to bed.

Later when the salesman thought the old man was asleep he tiptoed back downstairs to the library. He went to the bookcase and from the fourth shelf took the book *Mutiny on the Bounty* and opened it to page 104. He pushed on the word *An* in the eighth line. As the bookcase swung open, he lit the lamp and walked down the long dark hall. He went down the steep staircase, unlocked the iron gate, through the heavy wooden door and finally the metal door and held up the light to see the blue gorilla again. Then he reached out and touched the two-inch-high blue gorilla. The blue gorilla started to grow and broke the small cage open. He continued to grow, and the salesman got scared and ran. He went through the heavy metal door, the dark passage, and the blue gorilla was still coming and getting bigger. The salesman ran as fast as he could through the heavy wooden door, the iron gate. By this time the blue gorilla was as big as he was, and the salesman kept going. He went upstairs, down the dark hall to the library and shut the bookcase, but he still heard the blue gorilla coming.

He decided to get out of there, so he ran to his car. As he got in the car and started it, the blue gorilla came out the front door . . . now almost two times the size of the salesman. The salesman took off down the road with the blue gorilla still after him, growing bigger with every step. Soon the salesman came to a bridge which had been washed out by the storm, and he couldn't go any farther. The blue gorilla was getting closer and closer. He got out of the car and tried to find someplace to hide, while the blue gorilla got closer and bigger, because now he was almost the size of the three-story house the salesman had just come from. Closer and closer the blue gorilla got until he could reach down and touch the salesman. He backed away, but the blue gorilla touched him and said, "YOU'RE IT!" [Storyteller tags the listener]—then shrank back down to a two-inch-high blue gorilla.

76

Pulling the Leg

I was downtown shopping in the dime store and had an awful lot of things in my arms. Finally I had so much I just put a few of the smaller items in my coat pocket. Just then, a man came up from behind and said, "I saw you!" Man, was I shocked. So he took me back to the office and told me to wait while he got the manager. There was a little old lady sitting there crying. She told me she had been caught three times for shoplifting and they would really get her this time. She said I had to help her. I didn't really know how; I was pretty scared myself. After a while, she said she wanted me to help her out the window. It was rather small and led out into the alley. So I helped her. Man, what a squeeze! I sat down again to wait and decided I could make it out the window, too. So I started to climb out just as the man came back in. He ran over to the window and started pulling my leg . . . just as I'm pulling yours!

77
Feeding Baloney

I was in McDonald's one day paying for my meal when I dropped five dollars on the floor. Before I could bend and pick it up, this little crumbsnatcher ran and took my money. He ran to his mother, and when I went over there to tell her that her son took my five dollars, she said, "No, my son doesn't have your money." I said, "The hell he doesn't; he picked my money up off the floor." She said, "The money doesn't belong to you. Anything that touches the floor belongs to no one." I noticed she had been shopping, and her bag was on the floor. I picked up her bag and headed for the door. She said, "Where are you going with my bag?" I said, "This isn't your bag; anything that touches the floor belongs to no one." I went on out the door, and she followed me. I didn't give her the bag until I got my five dollars worth out of it. Guess what was in it. Baloney, just like I'm feeding you!

78
The Dog That Drank Gasoline

You know, one day this farmer was out in the barnyard, and he had a pan of gas laying on the ground. All of a sudden that farmer's dog came up and lapped up that pan of gas before the farmer could stop him. All of a sudden that dog took off just a-running to beat hell. He ran as fast as he could around that barn, just a-yelping and carrying on. Then all of a sudden that dog just dropped over on its side. That old farmer thought, "Well, that old dog is dead." So he walks over to see. And you know that dog wasn't dead at all; he had just run out of gas!

79
The Two Bumps

I went downtown today and after walking around for a while stopped into Woolworth's for a Coke. After I finished, the lady brought me two bills and said that the man who had been sitting near me said he

was my father and I would pay for his lunch. I had noticed him vaguely and thought he was fairly old and looked rather nice. He had white hair and carried a cane. Since I didn't know him, I insisted that I didn't and said I wouldn't pay his bill. The lady was mad. Well, so was I. Finally I left and paid for only mine.

Later I was in Meis walking around, and I thought I saw the old man who played that stupid trick. So I went around the corner and walked up to him. I said, "That was pretty dirty of you pulling a stunt like you did 'while ago." He said, "What are you talking about?" I said, "You said I was your daughter to get out of paying your bill." He said, "I did not!" I said, "Yes, you did; I saw you!" He was really getting violent, and he picked up his cane and started hitting me right across the chest. How else do you think I got these bumps?

80

The Cushman

There was a young man, and he didn't have any trade that he could do well. Since he couldn't get a job, he decided to try and join the service. He went to the Army, Marines, and Air Force and asked if he could join. They all asked him what he could do. And when he replied, "Nothing," they all said they had no need for him. So he thought he would try the Navy, but he knew that he had to come up with a trade. So when he went to the Navy and they asked him what he could do, he said he was a cushman. The induction officer, not wanting to appear stupid, said, "Okay," and he was inducted. He was assigned to a ship.

One day, while out at sea, he was laying on the deck sunbathing when the captain walked by and said, "What are you doing, sailor?" He said, "I am sunbathing, sir." The captain said, "What is your job?" He said, "Cushman First Class, sir." This captain, not wanting to appear stupid because he didn't know what a cushman was, said, "Carry on, sailor." This went on for some time while he did nothing.

Finally the fleet was going to have an inspection by the admiral. While the admiral was inspecting men, he was asking them what they did. The admiral finally came to this fellow and said, "What do you do, sailor?" And he said, "Cushman First Class, sir." The admiral, not wanting to appear stupid because he didn't know what a cushman was, but being a little smarter than the rest, he said, "Okay, sailor, I am going to be inspecting this ship again in one month, and at that time I want a demonstration of your trade." Then he turned to the captain and said, "Give this man everything he needs in order to perform this task." So the captain asked the fellow what he needed. The fellow said, "I need a big room at the bottom of the ship and two other sailors to aid me. I want these two men to bring in a two-by-four twice a day, with two cases of Miller's beer each time they come." The captain said, "Okay." This went on for the whole month.

Then finally it came time for the admiral's inspection, and when the admiral saw this fellow, he said, "Are you ready to give the demonstration?" The fellow replied, "Yes, send four men down to my room to get it and have them bring it up and set it on the railing." When the men did this, the admiral said, "I still don't understand." So the fellow pushed the raft he had made, which had all the empty cases of Miller's beer on it, over the railing. When it hit the water, it went, "CUSH!" Then the fellow turned to the admiral and said, "See, I told you I was a *cush*-man."

81

The Purple Passion

There was this little kid in the classroom one day. He had heard a new word and didn't know what it meant. So he asked his teacher. "Teacher, I heard a new word, and I don't know what it means." "Well, what is the word? If I know it, I will help you." "It's purple passion." "Purple passion! Don't you ever say that again, or I will send you to the principal." So the boy was out on the playground, and he decided he'd ask some of the older guys. "Can you tell me what purple passion means?" "Purple passion! Don't you ever say that again, or we'll turn you in."

So the boy thought about this new word for many years. Then when he was in the Army, he decided the Sergeant might be able to tell him because he was older now. "Can you tell me what purple passion means?" "Purple passion! Don't you ever say that again, or I'll have you court martialed." So when he got older, he got married. One day he asked his wife, "Do you know what purple passion means?" "Purple passion! How could you say such a thing? I'm getting a divorce."

Finally the guy was real old, and he still didn't know what purple passion meant. One day he was in a tavern, and a woman sat down next to him. He decided he'd ask her if she knew what it meant. He just had to know before he died. "Can you tell me what purple passion means?" "Purple passion! Oh, I can't tell you here. Why don't you come to my apartment this evening at eight? I live on the top floor, and I will have a green light in the window. Wait for me to turn it on. When I do, that will be a signal for you to come up." That night the old man stood across the street on the sidewalk. Soon he saw the light. He started across the street, but just then a car came around the corner and killed him. And he never found out what purple passion meant.

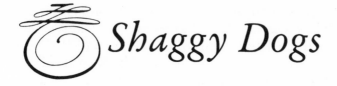# Shaggy Dogs

According to Jan Harold Brunvand in his valuable index, "Classification for Shaggy Dog Stories" (*Journal of American Folklore*, 76 [January–March 1963]: 44), a shaggy dog story is "a nonsensical joke that employs in the punch line a psychological non sequitur, a punning variation of a familiar saying, or a hoax, to trick the listener who expects conventional wit or humor." After collecting and classifying around 700 texts from oral and printed sources, Brunvand observed that shaggy dog tales generally "describe ridiculous characters and actions and often are told (to heighten the effect of the final letdown) in a long drawn-out style with minute details, repetitions and elaborations" (p. 44).

In *The "Shaggy Dog" Story: Its Origin, Development and Nature* (1953; reprint, Freeport, N.Y.: Books for Library Press, 1970), Eric Partridge sees an "age-long evolution" of the shaggy dog story, "beginning with 'the sudden unexpectedness' of the Greeks, passing into the epigram and the catch-poem or the catch-story, gathering strength from the limerick, the clerihew and the tall story, and emerging finally as the 'shaggy dog', finest flower of a noble tradition, and acme of the storyteller's art" (p. 51). While Partridge recognizes a relationship between catch tales and shaggy dog stories, he views the shaggy dog as a story "usually told in a leisurely manner," one that "is inconsequent and, in some instances, absurd." According to Partridge, "The final touch—a sudden and unexpected conclusion—contains a striking *non sequitur* that, in the purest form of the genre, is psychological" (p. 104).

Most shaggy dog tales are not about shaggy dogs or even about dogs. Partridge traces the name *shaggy dog* to a particular tale that has been popular, he says, since only 1942 or 1943, although the genre certainly is older than the name for it. The tale that supposedly gave the genre its name is about an Englishman who lost his valuable and rather shaggy dog. After repeatedly advertising for the dog in *The Times* without success, he gave up hope of ever seeing his dog again. A New Yorker read the ads in *The Times*, though, and appreciated the Englishman's concern for his lost dog. Since he had to go to England anyway on a business trip, he found a shaggy dog that matched the description in the ads and took it with him across the Atlantic. On arriving in England, he phoned the missing dog's owner and arranged to deliver the dog the following morning to the butler, as the owner had to be away from home on business. The next day when the American delivered the shaggy dog he had brought all the way from the United States, the butler looked at the dog, and shutting the door in the American's face, exclaimed, "But not so shaggy as *that,* sir!" (Partridge, pp. 54–56).

The shaggy dog tales included in this section are not realistic in setting or tone and have punning punch lines. Seven hoax stories (Tales 75–81) and two tales with punning punch lines (Tales 73, 74) that Brunvand classifies as shaggy dogs appear in the previous section with catch tales since they share the quality of beginning realistically before dissolving into absurdity. The final story (Tale 352) in this collection also is a shaggy dog tale, an unusual one in that it is moderately obscene.

For a rare content analysis of shaggy dog tales, see Martha Wolfenstein, *Children's Humor: A Psychological Analysis* (1954; reprint, Bloomington: Indiana University Press, 1978), pp. 150–56. After a brief general discussion of shaggy dog tales, Wolfenstein gives a detailed Freudian analysis of "The Guilty Moth" (Tale 89).

82

A Benny Shaved

It was in Greenwich Village, and these two beatniks met. The boy's name was Benny, and the girl's was Suzie. Benny had real long hair and naturally quite a long beard. Suzie had long, stringy hair, too. After a while they decided to get married. They got an apartment in the Village and moved in. After some time she became pregnant, and they decided they had better go straight and get a job. Benny decided that he'd best shave off the beard so he could get a job. So he locked himself in the bathroom early in the morning. By afternoon he still hadn't come out. Suzie began to worry. She knocked on the bathroom door, but he didn't answer. A couple more hours went by, and finally she knocked the door in. All she found was a vase with some ashes in it.

Moral: A Benny shaved is a Benny urned.

83

The Foo Bird

Did you hear about the Foo bird? Well, the Foo bird lives in the deepest Amazon, in this one region. There was this old Indian temple, and these archaeologists, about three of them, went down to explore this Indian temple. They recruited native help, and as they were going through the jungle they came upon this one section, and the native guides wouldn't go any further. And the three archaeologists asked them why not, and they said, "Well, that is the domain of the Foo bird." And they said, "What is the Foo bird?" And the Indians said it was a powerful bird that flies by very dangerous, and the archaeologists didn't believe it. They started to go in, and this great big bird flies over, and they can hear the natives say, "The Foo bird, the Foo bird!" And the Foo bird shits, and it lands on one of the archaeologists. The archaeologist wipes it off, as any person would wipe off shit from a bird, you know. As soon as the last bit is off, he falls down dead. So this kind of upsets the two archaeologists, but they are determined to go on and explore these temples.

After a couple of days of thorough exploring of the temple, they start on their way back, and at about a quarter of the way back, they hear the flapping of wings and see this same kind of bird, a Foo bird, fly overhead. It shits, and it lands on one of the archaeologists. He jumps right into a river which is right next to where they are walking. He washes all the Foo shit off, and as soon as the last bit of it is all off, he keels over dead.

Well, this really upsets the third archaeologist, and he is determined to get out of that jungle as fast as he can. So he starts running and running. He is almost out of the area where the bird lives when one flies over and shits on him. And he thinks back what happened to his two friends when they washed and wiped off all the shit and cleaned it off. So he decides just to leave it. So he has what he wanted: films and documents and all this other stuff from the temple. And he goes back still worrying of the Foo shit that landed on his head, and he takes back, everything back, to New York where he was situated. And he lives a normal life, as normal a life as anyone can live with a pile of Foo shit on your head. And gradually, you know, the Foo shit wears away. About ten years later, he has got just a very little speck of Foo shit left on his head, and he is kinda old, so he decides just the hell with it; he is going to brush it off. So he brushes that last bit of the Foo shit off, and as soon as he does that, he falls dead. You know what the moral of that is? If the Foo shits, wear it.

84

The Knight and His Mount

There was once a knight that was a very strong and brave soldier, but also this knight was a little strange. Instead of riding a horse, he always rode a Great Dane. One night after coming back from a battle in the rain, he decided to spend the night at a nearby inn. The innkeeper hated knights and refused him a room. But then he changed his mind and said he couldn't turn a knight out on a dog like this.

85

A Pit to Hiss In

There was a mother snake and three baby snakes hissing in a pit. The mother couldn't take all the hissing, so she sent the baby snakes over to Mrs. Pot's pit while she went for a walk. So the baby snakes hissed over to Mrs. Pot's pit. Mrs. Pot came home and found the baby snakes hissing in her pit. She sent the baby snakes home. When the mother snake returned she found her baby snakes hissing in their own pit. She asked them why they were home. They said, "Mrs. Pot sent us home." The mother snake said, "Why, that ungrateful woman! I remember when the Pots didn't have a pit to hiss in!"

86
The Head

Once there was this head, and all he was was a head. He was a pretty smart head, and he went to school like the other kids did. Every day his mom would drive up in front of the school, and the teacher would open the window. And she would toss her the head, and the teacher would put the head on the desk.

So one day a new girl came to class, and she was really pretty. He was going to ask this girl to the dance. So he goes up to her at lunch, and he goes, "Will you go to the dance with me?" She gets real mad and says, "I wouldn't go to the dance with you even if you were a grape." So he turns around and walks away. So he's thinking, "Maybe she'll go with me if I'm a grape." So he goes to this witch doctor's hut and gets him to turn him into a grape. The next day he goes back to school and says to her, "Now will you go with me?" This time she gets really mad and stomps on him and squishes him all over the floor. The moral of this story is: Quit while you're a head.

87
Shoot the Bear

There were two fellas out in the woods hunting, and they only had one shell left. They looked up the path one way and saw a bear coming. They looked down the path the other way and saw a bull coming. So one of them says, "Hey, Joe, what are we going to do, shoot the bear or shoot the bull?" He says, "Well, Mike, why don't you shoot the bear; we can shoot the bull anytime."

88

The Hardy Sailor

This is the story of a young man who had nothing but hardships from the day he was born. Right from the start his parents didn't want him, and nobody would adopt him. All he had was hardship after hardship. He grew up in an orphanage that didn't even want to take him in. More hardships followed; he couldn't keep a job or amount to anything. The only thing he accomplished was more hardships.

Finally he decided to try and join the services. Here again he ran into many hardships. The Army, Marines, and Air Force didn't want him because he was not able to do anything right. Finally the Navy accepted him, and he was assigned to a naval station. At the station only hardships followed him from one job to another. As a last resort they assigned him to a ship. He held every job but one, and always the hardships followed him. The last job on the ship was a lookout man. One day while on the job a storm arose, and the boat began to rock. He fell from the top of the lookout point to the deck of the ship. The captain ran up and said, "Are you okay, sailor?" He looked up at the captain and said, "Yes, sir, I'm okay. It was just another hard ship."

89

The Guilty Moth

This boy was going off to college, and his dad made a bargain with him. If he could keep a fur coat all year and not lose any hairs out of it, his dad promised to buy him a new sports car in the spring. The boy took the coat to school and packed it into a trunk so none of the hairs would be lost. Two moths were in the trunk, but they knew the deal, so they didn't eat any of the hairs. In the spring the boy went home. His dad counted the hairs in the coat, congratulated the boy, and gave him the keys to the new sports car.

The second year the father made the deal again, but this time promised him a new speed boat if no hairs were lost from the coat. The moths knew the story again, so they didn't eat any hairs off the coat. In the spring, the boy went home. Sure enough, all the hairs were there, and he got his speed boat.

The third year the father promised the boy he would put $10,000 in a checking account for the boy if he lost no hairs off the coat. The moths knew the story again, so they didn't eat any hair off the coat, but they were getting awfully hungry. In the spring the boy got his $10,000.

For his final year, the boy's father promised to duplicate all he had given him before if he could make it this last year without losing a hair off the coat. This year the moths were so hungry that they decided to split one hair off the coat. Surely no one would know they even did it. In the spring the boy went home. His father threw a big party for him and was bragging about how his son went four years and took such good care of the coat that he didn't lose a single hair off it. One guy wouldn't believe it and challenged him to count those hairs again. Sure enough, one was missing. The father was embarrassed. He even took away all the things he had given his son. The moths heard what happened and were sorry. Have you ever seen a moth bawl?

90

The Missile Shot

Once there was a buffalo named Bernard. His friends called him Bernie the Buffalo. He decided to take his herd across the U.S. They finally ended up at Cape Kennedy in Florida. They saw a great rocket ship, and Bernie said, "I'll go check this out." So he went inside the ship and came back to his herd. "It looks safe," he said. So the herd entered the ship. And behind them the door closed, and the ship blasted off and started in orbit around the earth. They were the first herd shot around the world.

91

Don't Fly Off the Handle

Once there were two crows who always sat on a pump handle outside a farmhouse. One day the farmer left a bushel basket of prunes on his back porch. One crow flew to the porch and ate half the prunes in the basket and flew back to the handle. Then the other crow flew to the porch, ate the other half of the prunes, and flew back to the handle. They decided it was time to fly south for the winter, so they took off, flew about a hundred feet, and fell to the ground and died. The moral of this story: Don't fly off the handle when you're full of prunes.

92
Don't Lose Your Head

It is said that one day a cat was beginning to cross a railroad track when all of a sudden a train came through. After the train had gone past, the cat discovered about two inches of its tail had been cut off. After finding this out, the cat went back to the tracks to get his tail. And another train was coming, and it ran over the cat's head.

Moral: Don't lose your head over a piece of tail.

93
You Can't Please Everyone

Once upon a time there was an old man, a donkey, and a young boy. They were traveling across the country. As they started out, the boy was riding the donkey, and the old man was leading the animal. Soon they came to a town, and the people there saw them and began to whisper among themselves, "Look at that nasty young boy making that poor old man walk while he relaxes on the donkey." Well, the boy heard this, so when they got out of town he asked the old man if he could lead the donkey while the old man rode. So they traded positions and continued.

Soon they came to another town. As they passed the local pub some men were standing around and shooting the bull. The old man heard them say, "Look at that dirty old man making that poor boy walk while he relaxes." This kind of hurt the old man's feelings so that when they got out of town he told the boy what he had heard, and the boy told him what he heard in the first town. They decided to both get on the donkey for the next town. And they continued on.

When they came to the next town they saw a man point at them and say, "Look at that nasty old man and that nasty boy causing such a

heavy burden on that poor donkey." They were both very dis-
couraged and decided to bypass the next town, but to do this they had
to cross a river. The boy and the old man swam it easily, but the
donkey was washed downstream and drowned, which goes to show
you that if you try to please everyone you lose your ass.

# Animals

FOLKTALES IN WHICH animals talk and behave like human beings are ubiquitous and among the oldest forms of literary expression. In ancient and tribal cultures, animal tales often were etiological, frequently explaining some characteristic of an animal, such as the rabbit's long ears or the bear's short tail. In European folklore, since at least the Middle Ages, the most popular animal tales almost always have been about a clever animal tricking a stupid one. While the European animal tale was a short narrative, usually a single episode, there was a tendency to string together several of these short tales into a longer narrative with a favorite animal as the central character. This practice reached epic proportion in the medieval European cycle of Reynard, which consists of a number of animal tales in which a clever fox always comes out on top.

From the ancient collections of animal fables, through the medieval beast epic of Reynard the Fox, to the modern renderings of some old animal tales by Joel Chandler Harris, many familiar animal tales have been passed along in literary works. Even today in Europe and North America, many animal tales survive as children's entertainment in storybooks and cartoons. Animal tales are far from dead, though, in the contemporary oral tradition, but generally they take the form of indelicate jokes rather than droll tales for children. Many of these animal jokes, as G. Legman notes in *No Laughing Matter* (Bloomington: Indiana University Press, 1968), "are not of the cute, anthropomorphic animal type, but concern the sexual intercourse of human beings with other animals" (vol. I, p. 206). While there are many modern jokes of this sort (Tales 98 and 99, for example), stock characters from ancient Indo-European folklore, such as the parrot, and favorite themes of international folktales, such as the trickster animal, persist in contemporary jokelore. As noted in the Introduction, taboo-breaking is a common theme in some modern animal jokes, especially in those about parrots. Parrots and other animals often do things in jokelore that people refrain from doing. Many of the animal jokes that follow, though, project in the behavior of animals deep-seated male fears of castration (Tale 101), quick orgasms (Tale 95), disparity in the size of male and female organs (Tales 96, 104), and insatiable females (Table 103).

94
Rabbit, Buzzard, and Turtle

Well, there was this rabbit and the buzzard and a turtle. And they decided they was gonna start this farm. So they needed some fertilizer for this field, and they said, "Oh, let's send the buzzard; he can go faster." Then they said, "No, he can't carry enough." Said, "Let's send the turtle; he can carry more. But he's too slow." So they sent the rabbit. And then the rabbit was gone for a few years, and while he was gone they struck oil on the land; and, well, they made a mansion, got maids and butlers and had wells and a big yard and everything. The rabbit come back and said, "Is Mr. Turtle here?" He says, "Mr. Tur-TELL is down by the well." So he says, "Is Mr. Buzzard here?" He says, "Mr. Buz-ZARD is out in the yard." Says, "Well, you tell Mr. Tur-TELL and Mr. Buz-ZARD that Mr. Rab-BIT is back with the shit!"

95
Wham, Bam, Thank You, Ma'am

There was once a bunny who hopped through a cemetery where there were several stone statues of bunnies. One day this male bunny saw a female bunny hopping along the lawn. And he jumped on her back and in a few minutes said, "Wham, bam, thank you, ma'am!" The next day he saw the same bunny and hopped on her back again. Pretty soon he hopped off and said, "Wham, bam, thank you, ma'am!" The next day he saw one of the stone bunnies and ran over to it. He hopped on its back, and in a few minutes, he said, "Wham, bam, goddamn!"

96

The Mouse and the Giraffe

There were these three animals sitting at the bar. One was a lion, one was a tiger, and one was a mouse. A female giraffe walked in, and the lion says, "Wow, look at that! I sure would like to get some of that!" The tiger said he sure would, too. The mouse slammed his drink on the bar and said, "I'm aching to get me some of that tonight!" The lion and tiger both laughed and bet the mouse $100 he couldn't get any. So the little mouse goes down the bar and talks to the giraffe, and then they went upstairs. The lion couldn't believe what he saw, but he still didn't believe that the mouse would get any. About a half hour later, the mouse came back down the stairs, and the lion says, "Well, you didn't get any, did you?" The mouse says he sure did. The lion says, "Well, doesn't sex make you tired?" The mouse says, "No, sex doesn't make me tired, but I must have run fifty miles between kiss, sex, kiss, sex!"

97

The Talking Elephant

There was a circus, and they was a pretty small circus. And they went travelin' all around, and they weren't too famous, you know. So they wanted to have a big promotional event that would really make them famous. So they decided they was gonna do this thing that if anybody could get this elephant to jump ten feet in the air, they were gonna give him $10,000. So, boy, this was a big event. So everybody was out to make the $10,000. They'd go all around to these little cities, you know, and big towns. And people would get in line, thousands of them, trying to get this elephant to jump ten feet. And everybody had a little gadget.

Finally they pulled up to this little bitty town in some small state, and they had this big long line. And finally they had this little kid standin' in line there, you know, and they all just laughed at him, you know. They said, "Well, he can't make an elephant jump ten feet in the air!" And that little kid got up on his turn and said, "Can I try?" And the circus guy said, "Yeah, you can try whatever you want to." And that kid had a little brown bag. He opened it up and took out two bricks. And he walked up to that elephant, and he walked around. And he walked underneath that elephant, took those two bricks, and smacked them together as hard as he could, and that elephant jumped ten feet in the air. So they gave the kid the $10,000.

So they thought, "Oh, we can't have this anymore." They were gonna run out of money, you know. So they became pretty well known for this. This kid became famous over this, you know. But it kind of died out. And so they said, "Well, we'll try something new," you know, "and if anybody can get this elephant to say 'yes' and 'no' we'll give him $100,000." And this prize news just went fantastic all over the world.

They'd travel all around these cities, and finally they got back to that same little town in that same little state. Going through the line, they got to this young man, you know, and he had this little brown bag. And they go, "Hey, we remember you! You can't do the same thing you did last time." And he said, "I'm not planning on it." And he said, "Can I try again?" And they go, "Yeah, you can." So he walked up to the elephant. And he stared him in the eye, and he opened that brown bag, and he took out those two bricks. And he asked the elephant, "Do you remember me?" [The informant nods his head yes.] "Do you want me to smack you with these bricks again?" [The informant nods his head no.]

98

The Colonel and the Camel

A colonel arrived at his new desert command in North Africa. While being shown around, he saw a female camel tied beside a building.

"What's the camel for?" asked the colonel. The sergeant said, "She's a morale builder. We are far from town and girls, so we keep the camel to help the men out." The colonel didn't like it, but he said, "Well, tie her up farther out from the post."

A few months later the colonel got horny and called his sergeant in. The sergeant took the colonel out to the camel. The colonel told the sergeant to make the camel kneel down. Then he proceeded to screw her. When he was finished he asked the sergeant if that was the way his men did it. The sergeant said, "No, sir, they usually ride into town where the girls are."

99

Johnny Ringo's Girl

Well, it just so happens there was this miner, an old-time prospector really beat all to hell. He was a grubby lookin' old man. He'd been up in the mountains for seven, eight months mining his claim, and he came into town with a bag full of gold. And he really looked like a piece of shit. So he went to the hotel, and he did the threes of life—a shit, shower, and shave—and got all cleaned up, bought a new suit of clothes, and he went down and went to the bar. And he said, "Give me a bottle of your best whiskey." So the guy set the bottle on the table, and the prospector paid for it. And he said, "Hey, you got a pretty nice town here, except I noticed one thing. You don't have any women." And the guy said, "Yeah, that's true." And he said, "Well, I just came in, and I been gone for six months. I'm a little horny, and I got myself a good bottle. What do you do for some excitement?" The bartender said, "Well, there is a pig farm about a mile and a quarter down the road, and we go down there and get ourself a pig." And the prospector said, "Well, hell, what can I do?"

So he picked up his bottle of whiskey and headed down the road. He came to the pig farm and knocked on the door and said, "I need a pig." The guy said, "Well, come on back here." And he went back and picked himself out the cutest little pig you ever seen with a nice curly tail and everything, and he thought, "Hell, I'm not going to take it here. I'll take it back to my motel room and really have a good time tonight."

So he put the bottle under one arm and the pig under the other arm and proceeded to go back into town. And just as he got to the outskirts of town, everyone started screaming and locking their doors and windows and everything. He couldn't understand what the hell it was, so he caught this old man who couldn't quite get away, and he said, "What's the deal, buddy? Why's everybody running?" The old man looked at the guy and said, "Listen, no one screws Johnny Ringo's girl and gets away with it!"

100

The Horse That Laughed and Cried

This guy is a prospector and lived in the hills for years. So he goes to his store for supplies. He sees a picture of a horse in the window. The sign in front of the horse says, "If you can make this horse laugh, you get a free meal." The guy asks the owner, and he says, "I wouldn't mind to try." The owner says, "I have had him for years, and no one has ever done it." Guy says, "You mind if I take him behind so we can be alone?" The owner says, "Okay." The guy takes the horse around back and comes back in five minutes. The horse is laughing his ass off. The owner says, "I don't believe you did, but you did."

So the guy goes back up into the hills, and five years later he has to come back in town for supplies. The same horse is in the window, but the sign says, "If you make this horse cry, you get a free meal." So the man walks in and says, "Mind if I take him around back?" The owner says, "Okay." The guy takes him around back and comes back in five minutes, and the horse is crying, tears rolling down his face. Owner says, "Don't I recognize you? Weren't you the one who got this horse to laugh about five years ago? But tell me how you did it." The guy says, "The first time I told him my dick was bigger than his, and the second time I showed him."

101

They're Off!

There was this man who had a real good racehorse, except that in a race it would get behind a filly and just stay there, so it would always come in second. The man said, "This ain't right." And so he took the horse to a vet and had his balls taken off. He said, "This ought to do it!" And the next race he said to the horse, "I've put all the money I have on you, $10,000, so you better win!" And so all the horses were lined up behind their gates, and the man shot his gun and said over the loudspeaker, "They're off!" The horse just folded up his legs and sat down. His owner went over and asked him what was wrong. The horse said, "He just told everybody!"

102
The Insatiable Rooster

This guy had a thousand eggs, and all of them hatched, so he had a thousand hens. He needed a rooster. He was in a bar one night, and he said he was going to buy some roosters. Another man said he would sell him a rooster, Charlie, for $45. The guy said that Charlie would screw every hen he had. The guy paid for the rooster. The next day Charlie was delivered in a crate. He weighed only four ounces and was very puny. The guy was really pissed off about Charlie. He was going to kill the rooster, but his wife said to give him a chance.

He put the rooster in the pen with the other hens, and he charged the hens and proceeded to grab one and then the other. He jumped from hen to hen and really went to town. The wife said to get Charlie out of the pen or else he would kill himself. They let him stay in the pen, and the next day he screwed the 999th hen and finally did the last one. Charlie then laid on his back and closed his eyes, and the farmer thought that he was dead. All this time buzzards were flying around and were getting closer to Charlie. The farmer started to pick up the rooster to bury him. The rooster then opened his eyes and said to the farmer, "Sh! Get out of here; they are about to land!"

103
What's Wrong with the Sows?

There was this farmer who had a bunch of sows that wouldn't get bred. They wouldn't get pregnant. While talking to another farmer, he mentioned this. The other farmer said, "You don't have a boar, do you?" The first farmer said, "No." "Well, there's your problem. I'll tell you what. For a small fee I'll let you bring your sows over, and we'll turn them loose in the lot with my boar."

So the first farmer loaded up his sows, took them over and turned them loose in the lot with the boar. After a while he loaded the sows up, and as he was getting ready to leave, the other farmer told him that this wouldn't have any effect if the sows ate grass. The other farmer said, "Okay."

Well, the next morning he got up, and all the sows were eating grass. So he loaded them up, took them to the boar, then brought them home again. The next morning he awoke to find the sows eating grass. Again he took them back to the boar. Again they ate grass.

After about two weeks of this, the farmer brought his sows back home. The next morning the farmer's wife came running in the house saying, "Harry, Harry, what in the world is wrong with the sows? Two are trying to climb in the back of the truck, and one's in the front honking the horn!"

104

The Oversexed Ant

Well, once there was this little ant who was so oversexed that none of the ants could ever satisfy him. So he decided to go on to bigger and better things. One day he saw a cat, so he went over and screwed the cat. But he still wasn't satisfied. So he found a dog, but no luck there either. Then the little ant screwed a cow, but he still wasn't satisfied. Finally he decided that the only place that had animals big enough to really satisfy him was Africa. When he reached Africa, the little ant looked around and saw this huge elephant standing under a coconut tree minding her own business. The little ant was delighted and rushed right over and started to screw the elephant. Right in the middle of all the action, a coconut fell on the elephant's head, and she let out a shriek. The little ant looked up smugly and said, "Suffer, baby, suffer!"

105

The Old Maid's Parrot

This is the story about the old maid who had a parrot. She had gotten very lonely and had acquired this parrot from a seafaring man. And it cussed, you know, like a trooper, and she was really upset when her friends came to visit because every time somebody strange would come into the room the parrot would start cussing. So finally she found the secret, and she found that if she went to the cage when she saw it was ready to swear and give the cage a whirl that the parrot would immediately be still. So things went along smoothly after that, and her friends would come to see her, and she was always glad to see them because she had no qualms over the fact that the parrot would start cussing.

On this particular Sunday the preacher and his wife were coming by, and she was looking forward to the visit and so forth. And they came in and sat down, and she kind of looked over at the parrot, at the bird cage, to see if it was going to do anything. And he was kind of walking around the cage just about getting ready to say something, so she thought, well, she'd catch it in time. So she went and she gave the cage a big whirl, and the old parrot cocked back and said, "Whee, feel that fucking breeze!"

106

The Conductor's Parrot

There was a conductor who had a pet parrot named Sam. Sam went to work with this conductor whenever he was called to make a trip. In the course of these trips, sometimes they would run into trouble, such as the brakes sticking, burst airhose, etc., and after correcting the trouble, the conductor would give the engineer a highball [the signal to go]. Sometimes the engineer would be going too fast, and the flagman would have to set the air on the train so the conductor could get on cabin. The conductor would be really mad. While getting on cabin, he would tell the flagman, "I gave the engineer a highball, and the dumb son of a bitch never looked back to see if I got on!" Ol' Sam picked all of this up in the course of years.

It came to pass that the conductor retired from the railroad. Knowing that Ol' Sam would miss the railroad, he exacted a promise from the flagman to take care of Ol' Sam so that he could still make trips on the railroad. In time, the flagman retired. None of the new men wanted to take Ol' Sam on the trips. The conductor decided to take Sam to his farm. He thought that along with the chickens and geese, Sam wouldn't get too lonesome.

One day Sam and the gander were sitting on a stump in the barnyard sunning themselves when a horse came right up to the stump and took a shit. A kernal of corn was stuck in the horse's ass, and the gander spied it. He flew up and grabbed it. This being a tender part of the horse's anatomy, he clamped his tail down hard on the gander's head and took off on a dead run. The gander, flapping his wings in a violent manner, tried to get loose. Ol' Sam jumped up and down on the stump, yelling at the gander, "No use in giving him a stop signal. The dumb son of a bitch will never look back anyway!"

107

The Hermit's Parrot

Oh, well, there was this old hermit that lived by himself, with the exception of a parrot. And him and the parrot lived in this house for years. And finally the old hermit passed away, and the parrot just stayed on by himself. The house got the reputation of being haunted, or people thought it was haunted. And a bunch of fellows told this fellow to stay all night in this supposedly haunted house. So he decided that he'd try it, and he went there about dark and nothing. . . . He didn't see anything strange or abnormal, so he stayed awhile and decided he would go to bed.

And shortly after he got in bed, why, he heard this voice. Says, "There's two of us here ain't they?" And he sat up in bed and listened, and he heard it again. And he immediately got his clothes on quick as he could and took off running out the door and just ran and ran until he couldn't go any further. And he stopped and was gasping for breath and panting and going on, and finally in a little bit this voice said, "It was a pretty good race we had, wasn't it?" And the fellow said, "Yes, and we'll have another one just as quick as I can catch my breath!"

108

The Magician's Parrot

Did you hear about the parrot and the magician? There was this magician who always put a parrot out in front of him when he did his act, and when he did a trick the parrot would say, "I saw it! I saw it! I know what you did with it!" Well, the magician got to be pretty famous, and one day he was going over to Europe on a boat to do his shows. But the boat sank, and as it ended up, he and the parrot were drifting around on a raft. The parrot didn't say anything for about three days, and then he looked over at the magician and said, "All right, goddamn it, what did you do with it?"

109

The Preacher's Parrots

There was this guy down the block who had a parrot that could talk. The only thing that the parrot could say was, "I'm Sally the Whore." Well, the guy tried everything to try to get the bird to say something else or not say "I'm Sally the Whore." He worked and worked, but the bird still said, "I'm Sally the Whore."

Well, finally one day the preacher came over, and the guy worried that the bird would say this in front of the preacher. Well, sure enough, the preacher wasn't there five minutes before the parrot said, "I'm Sally the Whore." This embarrassed the owner a lot, so he told the preacher that he was extremely sorry, but he couldn't make the bird say anything else. The preacher said he understood and that he could possibly cure the bird. He told the guy that he had two parrots at home that did nothing put pray all day and that if he took the bird home his parrots might teach the bird some manners.

Well, the preacher took the bird home and put it in the cage with his two parrots. The first thing the bird said was, "I'm Sally the Whore." At this moment one of the parrots looked over at the other one and said, "Well, Charlie, I believe our prayers have finally been answered."

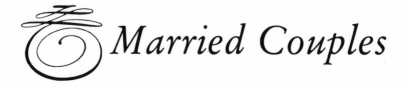 *Married Couples*

HUMOR ABOUT MARRIED COUPLES is very common in international folklore. In Francis James Child's impressive five-volume collection, *The English and Scottish Popular Ballads* (1882–1898; reprint, New York: Dover, 1965), there is only a handful of humorous folk ballads, and virtually all of them deal with incompatible married couples. One of the most popular of the humorous ballads, "Our Goodman" (Child 274), deals with the very common motif of the unfaithful wife. "The Wife Wrapt in Wether's Skin" (Child 277), another favorite humorous ballad in both England and the United States, incorporates a variant of the widespread "Taming the shrew" motif (T251.2), as a husband cures his new bride of her vanity and laziness by beating her. "Get Up and Bar the Door" (Child 275), with both European and Asian analogues, concerns the stereotypical obstinate wife, an extremely popular theme in folktales nearly everywhere. A humorous ballad that has been especially popular in the United States is "The Farmer's Curst Wife" (Child 278), which is about a wife so mean that the devil himself can't tolerate her. These age-old themes and others about married couples abound in modern jokelore. The following jokes deal with, among other things, adulterers and adulteresses, sexually unresponsive husbands and wives, wives outwitting their husbands, retorts between husband and wife, and a wife who withholds intercourse from her husband to get her way.

110
Taming of the Shrew

A couple got married back in the horse-and-buggy days. So they were driving along, and the old horse stopped. The driver got out, went up to the horse. The man said, "That's once!" So he got back in. They went on their way, and before long the old horse took a notion he wanted to stop again. So he stopped. The man got out, looked at the horse, and said, "That's twice!" So he got back in and started up again and went on their way. So finally the horse decided to stop again . . . contrary old cuss . . . and so the man got out and looked the old horse in the eye and said, "That's three!" He pulled out his gun, shot the horse between the eyes. So he got back up on the carriage with his new little bride, and, boy, she started in on the old gent . . . just like a woman! She did all but cuss him out. The guy just sit there and looked at her and said, "That's once!"

111
The Surpriser Surprised

There was this guy who loved baked beans, but these beans had a terrible effect on him. When he started eating baked beans he just didn't know when to stop, and the aftereffects were always the same. He would get gas and fart so bad he'd just have to get out someplace by himself till they work off. As a matter of fact, after this guy got married, he had to give up baked beans because it embarrassed him so much to fart in front of his wife.

Well, this went on about a year, and this guy hadn't touched a baked bean in all this time, but one day on his way home from work he happened to spot a sign in front of a restaurant that said, "Baked Beans—All you can eat for 50¢." Well, this poor guy just couldn't resist temptation, so he stopped and gorged himself on baked beans. Sure enough, he had terrible aftereffects, and he farted all the way home. He drove up in his driveway of his home, got out of his car, and walked up to the front door. There stood his wife waiting for him. "Honey," she said, "I've got a surprise for you. Put this handkerchief over your eyes before you come in." He didn't feel much like playing games because he could feel another fart coming on, but he went along with her and put the blindfold on. Naturally, he was too embarrassed to fart in front of his wife, so he just kept holding it. His wife led him into the dining room and sat him down and proceeded to put dinner on the table. In the meantime the pressure was really building up. The poor guy was squirming and crossing his legs and really fighting to keep from farting in front of his wife.

Well, luckily, the phone rang, and his wife had to go out of the room to answer it. As soon as she left the room and he was sure she was out of hearing distance, he cut one of the worst farts he'd ever let in his life. He sure did feel better. He felt so much better that he started thinking about this surprise that his wife had for him, and he was getting a little impatient wondering what it was, when she finally came into the room. She said, "Well, I've kept you waiting long enough. You can take your blindfold off now." He reached up and took his blindfold off, and he sure was surprised. She had twelve guests for dinner!

112

A Dirty Trick

One day Tom Mount, who belonged to the Old Ox Church, was sprucing up to go to the annual foot-washing service. He had carefully washed his feet. Why he went to all the trouble to wash them when they would get washed anyway is a question, but anyway he did. But his wife, who thought all this foot-washing was "durn foolishness," didn't do a thing but put black soot in his nice clean socks. And Tom innocently put them on and sallied forth to the foot-washing.

When in the solemn part of the ceremony Tom pulled off his sock to let a brother wash his foot, lo and behold, his black foot shone forth in all the glory of the morning!

If some of the elders didn't snicker, they must have had a real serious grip on their religion. History does not record just what Tom said to his wife when he returned home.

113

The Furburger

A lady went into a pet shop to buy a rare exotic animal, one that no one else had. When she told the storekeeper what she wanted, he proceeded to show her everything that he had in the line of rare and exotic animals. After much distress, the lady hadn't found anything quite unusual enough to suit her taste. She made one last plea to the storekeeper. Out of desperation, the storekeeper said, "I do have one animal left that you haven't seen yet; however, I am somewhat reluctant to show it to you." "Oh, please do," cried the lady.

So the storekeeper went back into the backroom of the store, and after a little bit returned with a cage. Putting the cage on the counter, the storekeeper proceeded to open the cage and take out the animal and set it on the counter. The lady looked, but all she saw was a piece of fur, not a head or a tail, no eyes, nothing. "What in the world is that thing?" said the lady. "It's a furburger," said the storekeeper very nonchalantly. "But what does it do?" asked the lady. "Watch very carefully, madam," said the storekeeper. Then the storekeeper looked down at the furburger and said, "Furburger, the wall!" And immediately the animal flew over and hit the wall like a ton of bricks, completely destroying the wall and leaving nothing but dust. Then, just as swiftly as before, the furburger flew back and sat on the counter again. Then the storekeeper said, "Furburger, the door!" And immediately the animal flew over and hit the door like a ton of bricks, completely demolishing the entire door and doorframe. Then, just as quickly as before, the furburger flew back and sat on the counter.

"I'll take it," said the lady. "All right, if you really want it," said the storekeeper. And so, as the lady was leaving the store with her furburger, the storekeeper said, "Pardon me, ma'am, but what are you going to do with your furburger?" And the lady looked back and said, "Well, I've been having trouble with my husband lately, and so tonight when I get home, I'm going to put the furburger in the middle of the kitchen floor. And when my husband comes home from work, he will come in the door and look down and say to me, "What in the hell is that?" And I'm going to say, "Why, dear, that's a furburger." And my husband will look at me and say, "Furburger, my ass!"

114

Who Wears the Pants in the Family?

One day a husband and wife were having an argument. She was getting kind of bossy, so he took his pants off and threw them at her. He says, "Woman, can you fill these pants up?" She says, "You know I can't." He says, "That's right. I wear the pants in this family." She took her pants off and threw them at him and said, "Can you get into these?" He said, "You know I can't get into those pants." She said, "And you won't either until you change your attitude!"

115

She'll Be Mad Anyway

A man always came in drunk, and his wife always raised Cain with him, and he always got mad at her. So she went to the priest and told him about it—how he always came in drunk, and she got mad at him, and he got mad at her—and asked what should she do. He told her, "Next time he comes in drunk, treat him nice. Take his shoes off, offer him coffee, and offer to put him to bed." So she did. The next time her husband came in drunk, she took his shoes off him, offered him some coffee, and asked him if he'd like to go to bed. The man answered, "I might as well, 'cause when my wife finds out, she'll be mad anyway."

116

He Dreamed He Was in Heaven

This fellow, one night, went to bed and went to sleep, and so he dreamed he died and went to heaven. He was standing out at the golden gates by St. Peter when this beautiful redhead walked by, and he looked at St. Peter and said, "Boy, I'd like to have some of that." St. Peter said, "Okay, go ahead." The fellow said, "Where?" And St. Peter said, "Aw, just take her over there behind one of those clouds." So he did, and he came back and was standing there by St. Peter again when this beautiful blonde went walking by, and he said, "Wow, I'd like to have a piece of that, too." So St. Peter said, "Go ahead. Take her over there behind that cloud." So he did and came back and after a bit was standing there by St. Peter again, and this real shapely good-looking brunette walked by, and he said, "Now, I wouldn't mind having a little of that, too!" St. Peter said, "Okay, go take her over there behind that cloud." So he did, and he came back and was standing there beside St. Peter, and he said, "You know, I have to go to the bathroom *bad*." St. Peter said, "Well, go ahead; go over there behind that cloud." So he did, and after a bit he stuck his head out from behind the cloud and said, "What do you use for toilet paper up here?" St. Peter said, "Aw, just tear off a piece of that cloud." About that time he woke up, and his wife was shaking him like crazy. She said, "Wake up, for godsakes, wake up! You've screwed me three times, shit the bed, and now you're tearing up the sheets!"

117

Why Don't You Diet?

A fat housewife went to a doctor and complained that her husband wouldn't have sex relationships with her anymore and wanted to know what she could do to get him to notice her again. The doctor leaned over and said, "Why don't you diet?" The housewife asked, "What color do you think he'd like?"

118

I Want a Man!

The husband goes to the doctor and tells the doctor that his wife isn't doing the thing that a husband and wife should be doing. And so the doctor says, "Okay, I'll give you these pills. Give her two before bedtime, and then in the night she'll want to do what husbands and wives are supposed to do." So the husband slipped and gave her four, so he took two to balance it out. And so in the middle of the night the wife wakes up, and she goes, "I want a man! I want a man!" And he wakes up and goes, "I know just how you feel!"

119

Still Warm after Fifty Years

An old couple was celebrating their fiftieth wedding anniversary, and they decided that they would reenact their first breakfast after they were married. They both came out to the breakfast table, and they were both stark naked. They started to eat. The old man asked his wife to pass the eggs. She leaned over and started to pass them and said, "My boobies are as warm as they were fifty years ago." The old man then replied, "Well, they ought to be. One is hanging in the coffee, and the other is hanging in the oatmeal!"

120

What's Happened to Our Sex Relations?

The old man and the old woman was sitting there in the living room one night. The old man was reading the paper, and the wife was sitting over here knitting. He put his paper down and said, "Ma, what's happened to our sex relations?" Ma said, "I don't know. I didn't get a Christmas card from them last year."

121

The Magic Whistle

A man was in the Far East during the war. While he was there, he bought a magic whistle, which would make any piece of rope or string or anything like that stand straight up in the air.

He came back to the United States after the war and was broke. He really wanted a drink so he went into a bar and asked the bartender if he could get a drink if he'd do a trick with his whistle. The bartender said sure he could, so the man began blowing on the whistle and all the strings and stuff on the bar began to stand straight up. A woman was sitting in the bar and rushed over to the man and offered him $500 for the whistle. Since the guy had no money, he sold it to her.

The woman went straight home and found her husband already in bed. She stood at the door and began to blow on the whistle. Pretty soon the covers began to shake, and they rose in the air. When they were held straight up, the woman rushed over and flung them back . . . to find her husband's pajama strings standing in the air.

122

The Three Beeps

There was this man who just couldn't seem to get it up so he could make love to his wife. After much frustration he finally consulted a doctor, and this doctor gave the man a pill that would make his thing rise. He told him that all he'd have to do was to say "beep" to make it go up and "beep-beep" to make it go down, but he must remember it would only be good for three times.

So on the way home from the doctor's office he decided to test it out to see if it'd work right and everything. So he said "beep" and it went up and "beep-beep" and it went down. And he got really excited and in his hurry he started to cross the street in front of a little sports car. So the sports car went "beep" and it went up, so he quickly said "beep-beep" so it'd go down, and it did. Finally he got home, and he told her to hurry up and get in bed, so she did. He came in and stood in front of the bed and said "beep" and up it went, but she thought he must be going crazy and said, "What's all this beep-beeping about?"

123

Playing Bingo

And you know the one about the lady going out every night and she says she's playing bingo. And one night she asked her husband to . . . you know, she came home with lots of furs and diamonds and everything, and she'd tell her husband she won them at bingo. So one night she said, "Honey, I'm going to play bingo. Would you run my bath water?" And so he ran just a little bit in there, and she says, "What the hell is this? I thought I asked you to run my tub full of water, and you just put like a half an inch in there." And he says, "Well, I wanted to be sure I didn't get your bingo card wet."

124

Why the Sixth Child Has Blond Hair

After twenty years of marriage, a couple decided upon a divorce. To celebrate the granting of the divorce, they dined out together. After the third glass of champagne, the husband confessed, "There's one thing I've always wanted to ask you, but I never had the nerve. Now that we're splitting up, your answer can't possibly hurt me, so please be honest. Why is it that five of our six children have black hair, but little Tommy is a blond? Whose child is Tommy, anyway?" "I can't tell you," said the wife after a long pause. "It would hurt you too much." "Oh, don't be ridiculous," the husband insisted. "I don't care who the father is. I'm just curious." Finally the wife admitted, "Well, if you really want to know, Tommy is your child."

125

Things Could Be Worse

There's this story, and I swear to God it's true. This man goes into this poolroom. There's this man in the poolroom who always was saying, "Things could be worse." He was always saying that to whatever anybody told him. He always said, "Things could be worse." Well, this man goes in to talk to him. He was telling him about this other man. I don't know his name, so I'll call . . . I'll call him Frank. He said, "Did you hear what happened? Frank got home last evening and found this man in bed with his wife, and he shot him." Well, this other man he says, "Well, things could be worse." The other man just looks at him and says, "Now how the hell can you sit there and say things can be worse? He killed the man!" The other guy says, "Well, things *could* be worse. I was there the hour before."

126

The Paramour in the Refrigerator

There was a guy who thought his wife was running around with another man on him. And he decided he was going to find out for sure, so he went to work one day just like he always did, then sneaked back about noon. But his wife saw him coming and was acting like nothing was going on, but he stormed around. But he couldn't find anything. While he was storming around, he picked up the refrigerator and threw it out the window, and then he had a heart attack and died.

When he got up to heaven, St. Peter stopped him at the Pearly Gates and said, "I can't let you in here until you tell me how you got here." The man said he had thought his wife was running around with somebody else, and while he was looking he threw a refrigerator out the window and had a heart attack and died. St. Peter said, "Okay, you can go in." Then the next guy stepped up and said he had been walking along minding his own business when a refrigerator dropped on him. St. Peter told him to go in, too. Then the next man came up and said, "Believe it or not, the last thing I remember is hiding in this refrigerator."

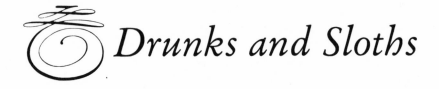 *Drunks and Sloths*

IN MODERN JOKELORE, drunkenness and laziness often are attributed to ethnic minority groups—drunkenness to Irishmen and laziness to blacks, for example. In the tales that follow, however, these negative traits are not attributed to any particular group. Nevertheless, these jokes serve much the same purpose as jokes about ethnic minorities. In these general jokes about drunks and sloths, tellers and listeners compare themselves favorably with those considered less virtuous and thus feel superior. Most of the jokes about drunks in this collection incorporate motifs of absurd misunderstandings: similar sounding words are mistaken for each other, or one thing is mistaken for another. Attributing ignorance to drunks is a way of rationalizing foolish behavior. Something of the same process occurs in some versions of "Our Goodman" (Child 274). In older British versions of this folk ballad a cuckold is simply gullible, but in more recent Irish and American versions, the folk have made the cuckold a drunk in order to rationalize his gullibility.

Jests about extreme laziness are ancient and widespread. As Stith Thompson notes in *The Folktale* (New York: Holt, Rinehart and Winston, 1946), "A thorough exploration of these tales of laziness would take one through most of the literary collections of tales, both in Europe and the Orient, for many of them have considerable antiquity and have been repeated by nearly everyone who has issued a book of anecdotes" (p. 211). The two tales of laziness below (Tales 138 and 139), both from the WPA files, are familiar international tale types.

127

The Unrepentant Drunkard

An old drunk is sitting on a park bench, and a preacher comes by and is gonna reform him. "Man, don't you know you shouldn't be drinkin' that vile liquid? Don't you know what that will do to you?" said the preacher. The drunk said, "No." The preacher said, "Let me give you an example. If you put a worm in a cup of water and a worm in a cup of gin, the worm in the water will live, and the worm in gin will die. Does that prove anything to you?" The drunk says, "Yeah, as long as I drink this stuff I won't have worms."

128

The Thankful Drunk

A drunk came out of the tavern, staggering down the sidewalk, when he stumbled over to the curb and started to walk down the curb with one foot in the gutter and the other foot on the sidewalk. The drunk was walking down the street like that when a policeman stopped him. The policeman told him he was under arrest and had to come down to the station with him. The drunk asked what he was being arrested for. The policeman said for public intoxication. The drunk replied, "Thank God, that's all it is! There for a while I thought I was crippled for life."

129

The Drunk and His Dog

There was this drunk that went into a bar. And he had his dog along, so he tied his dog outside to a parking meter. After a while a cop come in and said, "Is that your dog out there?" And the drunk said, "Yeah."

Says something about "Your dog's in heat." And the drunk says, "Naw, I just watered it awhile ago. It's not hot." Says, "No, I mean it needs bred." Says, "Naw, I just fed it awhile ago. It doesn't need bread." And he goes, "I mean your dog needs screwed." And he says, "Well, go ahead and screw it; I always wanted a police dog."

130
The Drunk in a Bar

There was this guy that went in a bar, and he told the bartender that he could tell when and where and the year that a bottle of wine was made by just tasting it. The bartender bet the guy $20 he couldn't. So he handed him the first bottle, and the guy sniffs it and tastes it and says, "Oh, that's simple. Mogan-David, 1950, Southern California." The bartender says, "That's amazing," and he gives him another bottle to try. The guy sniffs it and says, "That's Sherry, 1942, France." The bartender begins to get worried, being afraid he will have to pay the guy the $20. He hands him a third bottle. The guy tastes it and says, "Well, that's Champagne, 1943, France." The bartender says, "That's amazing," and pays the man the $20. The guy starts to leave, and this drunk at the end of the bar stops him and hands him a bottle and tells him to taste it and tell him what it is. The guy tastes it and says, "Well, that's piss!" And the drunk says, "Yeah, but whose?"

131
The Drunk in the Restaurant

There was this one woman who was real sick and didn't know what was wrong with her. So she went to the doctor. The doctor examined her and said "Well, your problem is that you've been eating too many peas, and they're gettin' you down. Now I don't want you to eat any peas for the next year. Then come back, and we'll see if you're better."

So she went the whole year and didn't have any peas. So she went back to the doctor, and she had just been feeling great. The doctor said, "All right, I think your problem is over with, so you can eat peas now, but don't eat them as often as before."

So that evening she and her husband went out to eat. They were seated beside this drunk. So she got the menu and was ordering, and she says, "I haven't had a pea in a year, so I think I'll have one now." The drunk seated next to them jumped up and yelled, "Those of you who can't swim, grab the chandelier! She's going to flood the place!"

132

The Drunk on an Airplane

A lady got on a plane with her new baby and happened to sit down by a drunk. After they took off, the drunk woke up and took a hard look at the baby. He said, "Lady, that's got to be the ugliest baby I've ever seen. Boy, is it ugly!" The lady got pissed and called the stewardess. "Get this drunk away from me, or I'll sue this airline for a million dollars." So the stewardess took the drunk to the back, then returned and said, "Now don't be upset. Just relax, and I'll get you a cup of coffee. And maybe I can dig up a banana for your monkey."

133

The Drunk on the Elevator

There was this Avon lady in New York who just loved her job and all the Avon products. She was selling her Avon one day in a huge apartment building when she suddenly got gas on her stomach. She didn't know where else to go except into the elevator. After she pushed the button for the lobby she let a fart that smelled so bad that it was peeling the paint off the walls. She hurried and looked through her samples of Avon and found a can of pine-scent air freshener. She sprayed the elevator, and just then the doors open and a drunk comes in. He starts smellin' and sniffin' the air and says, "What's that smell?" The woman was so proud of her Avon that she said, "Well, what does it smell like to you?" The drunk sniffed again and said, "It smells like somebody shit a Christmas tree!"

134

The Drunk in Church

A long time ago a preacher was giving his Sunday sermon. Right in the middle of his preaching an old town drunk came stumbling into the back row with a bottle of rotgut whiskey. Just then a young lady that was standing in the balcony accidentally fell but managed to grab hold of one of the hanging lamps from the ceiling.

Then the preacher said to the crowd, "Any person who looks up that young lady's dress will be struck by the lightning of God, which will in turn blind both of his eyes for the rest of his lifetime." Well, the drunk, who wasn't very religious anyway, covered his left eye and said, "I think I'll chance my right eye just one time."

135

The Drunk in the Whorehouse

A man came into the whorehouse, and he had a hundred dollars. He told the madam there that he'd give the hundred dollars to any girl who would screw him on the roof. That was sort of an odd request, but she knew somebody would do it. So this one girl said she would, so they went up on the roof and went to it. After a while they got carried away and started rolling and rolled off the roof. They hit the sidewalk still hooked together, and it killed them both. A little later this drunk comes by and sees the two lying there on the sidewalk. So he goes into the whorehouse, and the madam sees him and says, "We don't service anyone who comes in drunk." The drunk says, "I didn't come in for that. I just wanted to tell you that your sign fell down."

136

Drunk Falls in an Open Grave

Three drunks were walking through a cemetery, and it just so happened that there was a grave which was dug for a funeral the following day. One of the drunks fell into the grave, and the other two were so drunk that they couldn't get him out. They then decided to let him lay. The next morning at sunrise the drunk woke up and crawled out of the grave and said, "Well, it's Judgment Day, and I am the first one up!"

137

Two Drunks Fall in an Open Grave

There was this drunk going through a cemetery, and he fell into a grave. A few minutes later along came another drunk, and he fell in, too. After a while, the first drunk looked at the second drunk and said, "Gosh, it's cold in here." And the second drunk said, "Well, no wonder, you kicked all the dirt off you!"

138

Mighty Good Policy

W. C. Smith tells of a farmer south of Bloomington who wished to hire a hand. A young fellow came and applied for the job. "Well, I'll tell you," said the farmer, "I want a man who never gets hungry and never gets tired." "I'm the one you want," answered the young man. And so he was hired.

About the middle of the forenoon, the farmer saw the young hand stop work and go to the house. When the farmer went to the house to investigate, there sat the hand eating. "I thought you never got hungry nor tired," said the irate farmer. "Why, I don't. I eat before I get hungry and rest before I get tired," calmly replied the new hand. The farmer kept him four years.

139

Drive On!

Jeff Dawson was said to be the laziest man in Fountain or any other county. His neighbors labored with him on behalf of his family, hard up because he was so lazy, but appeals were of no use. Finally the citizens told him in so many words that there was no need of a dead man walking around on top the ground and he could take his choice of getting down to work or being buried alive. He chose to be buried.

On the way to the cemetery, with Jeff in a coffin on the wagon, they met a man who inquired the reason for such unusual doings, since the "corpse" was calmly puffing a corncob pipe. When it was explained to him, he offered to help Jeff get a start in life by giving him a bushel of corn. Jeff pondered this a moment and finally rose up to ask, "Is the corn shelled?" "Why, no!" replied the Good Samaritan in astonishment. Jeff resignedly lay back again in the coffin. "Drive on, boys," said he, "drive on!"

 *The Wise*

TALES OF THE WISE are not as popular as tales of the foolish in the Hoosier oral tradition. This situation is not unique to contemporary Indiana, for Stith Thompson points out in *The Folktale* (New York: Holt, Rinehart and Winston, 1946) "that tales of cleverness have not appealed especially to the oral story-teller except when such incidents are a part of a series or of a complex tale such as The Clever Peasant Girl." Such tales, however, as Thompson adds, can be found "by the hundreds in the jestbooks of the Renaissance, the large collections of medieval exempla, and the Oriental literary works from which many of these European collections borrowed" (p. 190). Several of the tales of the wise that follow are anecdotes—brief, humorous, oral narratives about local characters. While these anecdotes are attached to real people and have realistic settings, they are versions of common traditional tales told in other locations about other characters.

As Thompson notes in *The Folktale*, the folk do not "always draw a sharp distinction between the fool and the clever man" (p. 196). This is especially true in the universal tales of the trickster, probably the most paradoxical character in folklore, who sometimes is a clever deceiver and other times is a numskull. As in some of the following tales, the trickster often is a lawbreaker or does other things that most people refrain from doing. Such tales frequently serve a cathartic function, providing a socially approved outlet for social repressions.

140

The Clever Gambler

There was a captain of a ship who had a problem with a sailor on board. He was a maniac on gambling. He couldn't go very long without placing some kind of a bet. He constantly bugged someone to challenge him to bet. Well, the captain had just had it, so he put the sailor in for a transfer. Just by chance he was transferred to another captain who was a friend of the first captain. One day in a bar the two captains met. The first captain told the second captain that he should watch out for the sailor, 'cause he was a maniac on betting.

Well, for about a week there was no trouble, but finally the sailor started betting, so the captain decided he would talk to him. He called him to his cabin and told him any time he had to bet to come to his cabin. So a couple of weeks went by . . . no trouble. Then the sailor just had to make a bet. He went to the captain's cabin. He told the captain he just had to make a bet. The captain said, "All right, what do you want to bet?" The sailor thought. Finally, he said, "I bet you $500 that at noon tomorrow it will rain. The captain checked the weather maps, and it said sunshine and nice, so the captain said, "Okay." The next day it was just beautiful. The captain really thought he had the bet won, but right at noon there was the worst storm ever. So the sailor won $500.

Well, after several weeks of betting and the sailor winning, the captain had just had about enough with the sailor. So the next time the sailor came to the captain for a bet, the captain asked him what he wanted to bet. The sailor said, "I bet you $1000 that you have hemorrhoids. The captain just laughed and said, "No, I don't." But to make sure he went to the ship's doctor and had a complete physical. The captain went back to the sailor and said, "Okay, I'll take your bet, but how are you going to find out if I have hemorrhoids or not?" The sailor said, "All you have to do is stick a banana up your ass, and if it comes out red you have them. If it comes out yellow you don't." Sure enough, the captain stuck the banana up his ass, and it came out yellow, so he won.

Well, a few weeks later, the two captains met in the bar again. They got to talking about the sailor. The second captain said, "I think I've finally fixed him." He told the captain about the banana incident and how he had won the bet. Well, the first captain just laughed and laughed. The second captain asked the first captain what was wrong. The first captain said, "That son of a bitch bet me $5000 that he would have you sticking a banana up your ass within six months!"

141

The Clever GI

A GI was always picking up scraps of paper, looking at them, and saying, "This isn't it." This occurred on the drill field, in the barracks, in the mess hall, and in all other areas of the camp. He couldn't pass a piece of paper without picking it up, looking at it and commenting that "This isn't it." This was finally called to the attention of the commanding officer, who after observing this GI for a short time, reached the conclusion that the man was obviously psycho. He called him in his office and handed him his discharge papers. The GI looked at it, and in a soft voice said, "This is it," and calmly walked out of the office.

142

A "Sockdolager"

Sam [the name is fictitious, as the biggest liar is always well known in his community], a hunter famous in the vicinity of Vincennes both for his tall stories and his ability to bag game, was once overtaken and accosted by the game warden. "What luck?" began the game warden's inquiry. "Oh, plenty!" said Sam; and he related his day's experiences and elaborated upon them: "Why, I bagged 17 squirrels (squirrels were out of season at the time) and 23 rabbits and killed 35 birds today." "I see you've been fishing too," urged the game warden. "Did you catch many?" "Oh, not with a line," bragged Sam, "but I have six nets out and do pretty well with them."

"Say, do you know who I am?" asked the game warden suddenly, thinking he had the goods on Sam. "No," truthfully replied our hero. "Well, I'm the game warden," he replied. But Sam, undaunted, asked, "Do you know who I am?" "No," snapped the game warden. "Well," drawled Sam, "I am the biggest damn liar in the county."

143

Rufe Changes His Story

Rufe was tellin' the game warden over here paintin' the town store about huntin' quails, and the fellows in there was tellin' tales about it. Rufe, he up and told 'em a big tale how he shot 20 quails with 20 shots. The game warden said, "You know who you're talkin' to?" Rufe said, "No." He said, "You're talkin' to the game warden." Rufe said, "You know who you're talkin' to?" He said, "No." Rufe said, "You're talkin' to the damndest liar in the whole world."

144

Rufe Changes His Story Again

One day Rufe was coming across a field with a sack of sticks and rocks and things he had found. He met a man who asked him if he'd been hunting. Rufe said he had and that he'd got three squirrels, two rabbits, and a pheasant. The man said, "I guess you don't know who I am, do you?" Rufe said, "No." The man said he was the game warden here in Sullivan County. Rufe said, "I guess you don't know who I am, do you?" The man said, "No." Rufe said, "I'm the biggest damn liar in Sullivan County!"

145

Rufe Outwits the Game Warden

The game warden raided Rufe when he was in a canoe fishin'. They had some dynamite. They was dynamitin' fish, and the game warden got in the canoe with 'em. Rufe took him out where they was dynamitin', and he . . . he lit the fuse on the dynamite. Rufe said, "Now you throw it out." The game warden had to throw it out, you see, and they never got Rufe for dynamitin' fish.

146

"Blue Jeans" Williams, the Commoner

While "Blue Jeans" Williams was campaigning about the state during his race for Congress [1874] he capitalized on his homespun appearance and the fact that he was one of the common people. The nickname "Blue Jeans," with which he had been derisively dubbed while running for Governor, had literally swept him on to victory, as he hoped his common habits and customs might do again.

"Why folks," he exclaimed while making a political speech in Southern Indiana, "I'm jest an ordinary dirt farmer. I jest growed up between two corn rows." "Some punkin!" shouted one of his adversaries in the crowd.

147

Big Bedbugs

One of the Butler Boys of the Carbondale neighborhood told this story of Lem Martin of Independence, now deceased, who once made a visit to Arkansas:

It was Lem's first visit to the Bear State, and naturally, being a Hoosier and up on his hindlegs about it, he was forever braggin' about the place, and naturally that meant running down the other parts of the Union. According to Lem, the crops were heavier, the men braver, the women prettier, and well, to come right down to it, Indiana was so far away and above the rest of the country there was no use discussing the business. Regardless what the Arkansawyers showed Lem, he would have it that Indiana had something to put it in the shade.

Finally the natives got mighty tired of Lem's bragging around and set out to take him down a peg—which is a way of saying that comes of the way people used to have of putting pegs in the side of drinking horns to score your gulp. So the landlord of the place Lem was putting up at had some of the boys catch a lot of the snappingest turtles they could coax onto and bring them to him, and tucked the catch away in Lem's bed. Then he sat down all peaceful to wait for the returns.

He didn't wait long. Pretty sudden after Lem turned in, an awful howl comes down the stairs, fit to raise the roof, and almost as sudden down comes Lem, dragging one of the daddies of the lot that just couldn't let loose of his Indiana underwear, of which Lem was more than considerably proud.

The landlord let on to say nothing while Lem told him about the turtles in his bed. Lem was too excited to remember the one that was hanging onto his heel. But when Lem got him aloft and showed him the bed and floor crawling with turtles—"Why," said the landlord, "those, Mr. Martin, are only Arkansas bedbugs." Lem kind of caught himself, rubbing one Hoosier foot over the reptile worrying his ankle. "Well," he said, after giving a good think, "these're middling big . . . for their size . . . but we got lots bigger ones in Indiana."

148

The Pony Don't Look Too Good

A mangy pony with burrs and tangles, and his hooves were long, you know, was run into a sale ring to be sold. The pony was all rough and malnourished, and the auctioneer says, "I know he don't look very good, but let's sell him." Well, the pony sells finally, and after looking the pony over real well in the back of the barn, the new owner went back to the auctioneer and tells him that the pony is completely blind. The auctioneer replies, "Well, I said he don't look too good."

 *The Foolish*

The tales in this section are general numskull tales, sometimes called noodle tales. Stories about absurdly ignorant individuals or character types are told all over the world—in tribal cultures, in which the trickster is both dupe and duper, as well as in folk cultures. Frequently, numskull tales attribute absurd ignorance to people living in a particular town or region or to people of a particular ethnic or religious group. For instance, such tales are told in Denmark about the Fools of Molbos, in Germany about the Citizens of Schilda, and in England about the Wise Men of Gotham. Tales of Kentuckians, Irish, and Poles, as well as some tales about blacks, in other sections of this collection are examples of Hoosier numskull stories that attribute absurd ignorance to specific groups. The general numskull tales in this section incorporate familiar motifs of absurd misunderstandings: instructions or words are forgotten or misinterpreted; foreign languages are not understood; and people, animals, or objects are mistaken for something else. Numskull tales have appeared in literary collections of tales since the Middle Ages, and they continue to be extremely popular in the contemporary oral tradition.

149

Man Falls in Open Grave

There was this guy who always walked home through the graveyard, and his friends knew it. One night they dug a grave and covered it lightly. One man put a sheet over himself, and they hid and waited for the man to come down the path. He came down the path and fell into the grave. Just then the man with the sheet over him looked down into the grave and asked, "What are you doing in my grave?" The friend replied, "What in the hell are you doing out of it?"

150

Man with Lisp Amazed at High Prices

This guy went into a bar and said to the bartender, who happened to have a humped back, "I'll haff a beer." So the bartender gave him the beer and sat down with him, and they started talking. They were just having a good ol' time. The guy said, "I'll haff anutha beer, pleath." The bartender gave him the beer, and they continued to talk. Finally the man asked for the bill. The bartender gave it to him. He yelled, "Are you thittin' me? Ten dollars!" The bartender said, "I wouldn't shit you. You're a nice guy. I like you." The guy said, "Yeth, you've been nith, too. You didn'th even thay anything abouth my lithp." The bartender replied, "Yeah, and you didn't even say anything about my humped back." The guy said, "Humped back! Hell, I thought it wath your gothdamn assth. Everything elth in this plath is tho high!"

151

Duck Mistaken for Man's Member

A man and his pet duck were walking around downtown when the man decided to go see a movie. He went up to the ticket window to get a ticket, but the ticket lady said he couldn't take the duck inside, so he left. He really wanted to see the movie, so he decided to stick the duck in his pants. He went back and bought a ticket and went in and sat down. He was watching the movie when he remembered the duck was still in his pants, so he unzipped his pants to let the duck get some air. Two little old ladies were sitting next to him, and one looked over to the other one and said, "Sister, the man sitting beside me just unzipped his pants." The other woman said, "Oh, sister, you've seen that before." The other one said, "Yes, but it's eating my popcorn!"

152

Turd Mistaken for Candy Bar

There were these two hoboes walking down the railroad tracks, and they noticed something on the ground. One hobo, he kicks it. He says to the other one, he says, "It's a candy bar." The other guy kicks it. He says, "No, that's a turd." So the first hobo, he picks it up, takes a bite out of it, says, "No, that's a candy bar." The other guy says, "Let me see that." So he takes a bite out of it. He says, "No, no, that's a turd." The first guy takes a bite out of it, says, "Yeah, I think you're right; it is a turd. It's a good thing we didn't step on it."

153

Mail Hook Mistaken for Broken Wiper

There was this man, you see, and he never was on a modern train before, see. So he had to answer a call of nature . . . had to answer the call of nature, so he asked the conductor, says, "Say, I've got to answer the call of nature." So the conductor says, "Just go right back there in the corner; there's a rest room back there," he said. Well, he'd never been on a modern train before, so he didn't know what the place was for. So he walks back there, and the window was open, so he just proceeds to do it out the window. And about the time he gets through, why, they pass one of these stations, you know, where they've got this arm that grabs the mail, you know, and it gets him and knocks him back in the car. He straightens himself up and goes back out. And the conductor comes through and says, "Well, how'd you make it?" He says, "All right, but you better have that wiper fixed." Says, "It's gonna kill somebody!"

154
Buttocks Mistaken for Face

See, there was this guy. He wanted to go on this trip, and so he got on this train, and he started going to New York. And he's goin' down the tracks, and 'bout that time he needs to use the bathroom. So he runs around and asks everybody where the bathroom's at, and they say, "We don't have one." So there was this kid, and he says, "Why don't you just hang it out the window?" So he did, and 'bout that time two hoboes was walkin' down the track, and it smacked one of 'em in the side of the face. He says, "Well wonder what brand of chewin' tobacco that is?" He says, "Well, never mind the tobacco. Did you see them size cheeks he had?"

155
The Forgotten Word

There was this guy who went to the doctor to be castrated. The doctor told him he should think about it for a while. Well, this guy came in to see the doctor a week later, and he still wanted to be castrated. The doctor told him to think for a little longer on it. The guy went back to the doctor and again said that he wanted to be castrated. The doctor told him to think real hard for one more week. The man came back again to see the doctor. He still wanted to have the operation. So the doctor said all right.

Well, the operation was performed, and the doctor went in to see the man after the man was done. Then the doctor asked the man how he felt. The man wanted to know if the operation was a success. It was a success. The doctor then said to the man that he had noticed something about the patient during the operation, that the man was never circumcised. The patient then said to the doctor, "Ah, that's the word!"

156

Words in Foreign Language Misunderstood

This man went to Japan and wanted to go to a whorehouse. He looked all the girls over until he found one he really liked. When he got in bed with her, she started scratching his back and kicking and biting something fierce. She kept saying, "Ooey Tooey!" The guy thought she really liked it.

The next day this man was playing golf . . . the Japanese are great golf fans . . . with two of his Japanese friends. He hit a long drive over the hill, and it went right in the hole, right in the cup. He thought he would show his friends the Japanese he learned the night before, so he started jumping up and down waving his golf clubs in the air and screaming, "Ooey Tooey! Ooey Tooey!" His two friends looked at each other, then looked back at him, and said, "What does he mean, wrong hole?"

157

Owl's Hoot Misunderstood

There's a fella name of Eli Ball goin' on through this patch of wood one night, and there was an old big owl sittin' up in a tree right over top of him. And so old big owl seen him comin' along the road, you know, and said, "Who, who, who are you?" And he said, "Eli Ball." So he went a little bit further, two or three more steps, and the old big owl hollered at him again and said, "Who, who, who are you?" Says, "I told you once! Eli Ball!" And he went ahead a little piece further. He's gittin' purty well worried, and that old big owl hollered at him again. Says, "Who, who, who are you?" "Eli Ball!" So he looked up first one way and then the other. He said, "Well," says, "I told you," says, "Three times who I was." So he started to holler again and didn't make it all the way out. He looked down, and he says, "Feet," he says, "old feet, I'll tell you," he says, "if you carry me in home tonight, I'll get you a new pair of shoes tomorrow."

158
She Does Everything Backwards

These two doctors were standing in the hospital corridor, and one looked over at the other one and said, "You know, I just don't know what I'm going to do with my nurse." The other doctor said, "Well, what about her?" About that time, here came this fellow running down the corridor of the hospital with his gown tail just standing straight out, and here came this nurse behind him with a pan of boiling water. "Well," he said, "You know, if I tell her to give four pills in the morning and two pills at night, she always gives two pills in the morning and four pills at night. She always does everything just backwards." So this guy kept screaming and running down the hall, and the doctor said, "Just look at that, for instance. I told her not ten minutes ago to go in there and prick that man's boil!"

159
The Near-Fatal Initiation

There was a guy trying to get into this exclusive club. Well, the members didn't especially want him in, so they gave the man some tasks to do. They thought that if he did these, then he should get into the club. The first was to go into this tent. There he would find a gallon of wine, and he should drink it. Then they told him to come back when he finished that, and they would tell him the second task. So after a while the man staggered out of the tent and walked up to the head and said, "I've finished the first task. Now what?" So they told him that the next tent had a bear in there that had a sore tooth, and he should pull it. If he did this he could go on to the third tent where a beautiful maiden was who could be satisfied by no one. He went into the second tent, and there was a lot of thrashing and yelling. The tent almost fell down. Soon the man came out all bloody and scratched, and he said, "Okay, now where's the girl with the tooth that needs to be pulled?"

160

Boy Puts the Milk Back

There was this boy who went out to the barn to milk, and he stayed gone a long time. His dad went out to see what had happened. He'd milked but was letting the cow stand there and drink it. His dad said, "Look there, the cow's drinking the milk!" The boy said, "Yeah, I know; there was some chickens up in the loft, and they knocked down some straw in the milk. So I'm running it through again."

161

The Mistaken Entrails

Three ol' boys decided to go out rabbit huntin'. They agreed that the one who got the least rabbits would skin and gut all the rabbits. Well, they got them a jug to drink on and set out to huntin'. They hunted all day. One got 25, one got 18, and the other six. When they got back home the two who got 18 and 25 said they were tired and went to bed. So the other guy started skinning and gutting the rabbits. When he got to the last rabbit he decided to have a little fun. The one who had got 25 was sound asleep, and his big ol' bare ass was sticking out from under the covers. So he just throws them guts from the last rabbits in bed with the other guy.

The next morning the one who got 25 asked the one who got six how he had slept. He said he slept pretty good after he got all those rabbits skinned. "How did you sleep?" "Well, I slept okay till about four o'clock. I woke up then, and my bowels was all hangin' out, and, you know, I had a hell of a time gettin' them all stuffed back in."

162

Bus Driver Forgets His Announcement

The Hotel Astor had hired a new bus driver and instructed him to meet all incoming trains and announce at the depot in a loud voice: "Free bus to the Hotel Astor!" On the way to the station on his first trip he kept repeating to himself, "Free bus to the Hotel Astor!"—until he had it letter perfect. Upon arrival at the station, however, he had become confused at all the noise and hubbub and started shouting as loud as he could: "Free Hotel at the bust your Astor; I mean free ass at the Hotel Buster; I mean freeze your ass at the Hotel Bastard; I mean squeeze your bust at the Hotel Faster; I mean bust your ass at the Hotel Freezer! Oh, shit, take a street car!"

163

Three Wishes

A cowboy was riding along through the desert one day when he spotted a rattlesnake laying on the ground. He pulled out his six-gun to kill the snake, but the snake stopped him saying, "If you'll spare my life, I'll grant you three wishes." The cowboy was a little leery, but he decided he didn't have anything to lose, so he thought he'd just go along with the snake. "Okay, snake," he said, "first of all, I want a brand new ranch house to replace the old beat up one I have now. Second, I want Bridget Bardot lying stark naked in my bed when I get home. Third, I want to be hung like this horse I'm riding. The snake said, "Your three wishes have been granted. When you get home you will find a new ranch house with Bridget Bardot lying stark naked in your bed, and you are now hung like your horse."

The cowboy practically went out of his mind. He tore off across the desert riding as hard as he could till he came to his ranch house. Sure enough, there stood a brand new split-level ranch house. He ran into the house and went straight to his bedroom. There lay Bridget Bardot stark naked smiling at him. he jerked down his pants, and as he looked down at himself he screamed, "Oh, hell, I was riding Maude instead of Claude!"

164

Think Thrice before You Speak

Tell you one 'bout the . . . oh, it was 'bout a little boy. And his dad, mom was all sittin' in the house, and the boy kept gaggin' and goin' on, you know. So the old man says, "Hey, son," he says, "let me tell you something 'fore you git to talkin' so much." Says, "Always think three times before you speak once." And so, well, the little boy says, "All right," says, "I'll do that."

So the next night, why, they was all settin' up before the fire, and his mother wore one of these here old aprons, you know . . . had long strings on it. And so one of them strings was down, and she got around agin the stove, and got that apron string on fire agin the stove. And the little boy seen it, and the boy says, "Dad," says, "I think." And he set there 'bout half a minute. He told him, "I think." "Well," he says, "son, what in the world do you think?" "Well," he says, "you told me to think three times 'fore I spoke once." Says, "I think," says, "my mom's apron string's on fire." "Well, why didn't you tell me sooner?" Says, "You told me to think three times 'fore I spoke once."

165
The Frog-Jumping Experiment

There was this scientist who was conducting scientific experiments about frogs, so he went out and got a frog. And he was going to conduct the experiment, so he put the frog on the floor. And he told the frog to jump, so the frog jumped. And he took a measure, and he measured the distance. And so he wrote down in his book, "Frog jumps 12 feet with both legs." Then he cut off one of the frog's legs, and he put the frog on the floor and told him to jump again. The frog jumped, and the scientist measured the distance. And he wrote in his book, "Frog jumps six feet with one leg." Then he cut off the other leg, and he put the frog on the floor and told him to jump. The frog just sat there, so after about five minutes of telling the frog to jump and the frog just sitting there, the scientist wrote in his book, "Frog can't hear with both legs cut off."

166
Big Enough to Fit a Camel

One day this guy and girl were out parked, and the girl found a box of safes in the glove compartment, so she asked her date what they were.

He said, "Oh, those are covers for your cigarette so that when it rains it won't go out. Being a little gullible, she believed him, and then one day as she was walking down the street smoking a cigarette it started raining. So she dashed in the drugstore and told the man she wanted a safe, and he said, "Okay, but what size do you need?" She said, "Oh, just one big enough to fit a Camel."

 *Ignorance of Sex*

THE JOKES PRESENTED in this section are varieties of the general numskull tales illustrated in the preceding section, but they focus on one kind of absurd ignorance, sexual ignorance. Most of the characters in these tales are innocent children or country bumpkins, who in these tales are themselves childlike in their ignorance of human sexuality. Martha Wolfenstein shows in *Children's Humor: A Psychological Analysis* (1954; reprint, Bloomington: Indiana University Press, 1978), that children's jokes "become more complicated as various devices become necessary to guard sexual and aggressive pleasures from the encroachment of inhibitions. . . . In jokes dealing with sexual exposure we found the series of stages: I expose myself; I expose you; I expose a third person whom you and I can laugh at together" (pp. 190–91). The jokes that follow are especially popular in the folklore of prepubescent children and attribute ignorance about sexual anatomy and sexual intercourse to a third person. As Rosemary Zumwalt notes in "Plain and Fancy: A Content Analysis of Children's Jokes Dealing With Adult Sexuality" (*Western Folklore*, 35 [October 1976]: 267), "Once the child's body matures, the jokes [of this sort] lose their impact, and are discarded and forgotten. As one fourteen year old boy told me, 'Yeah, I used to know a lot of jokes like that. But you sort of grow out of them.'"

103

167

Get Up, Betsy!

Young Zeke was on his way home from the market when he saw a girl from the next farm and offered her a ride. Pretty soon they came to a clump of trees, and she asked him to stop. Seeing that he was bashful she took his face in her hands and kissed him. Then she asked, "Do you want to go a little farther?" He said, "Yep, get up, Betsy!" So they rode a little farther, and she asked him to pull up at another shady spot. Then she took one of his hands and placed it inside her bosom and his other hand on her thigh and asked, "Do you want to go a little farther?" Again he said, "Yep, get up, Betsy!" So when they stopped at the third bushy place, she reached over and opened his fly and took his spider out. She spread herself before him and asked, "Now do you want me to put it in for you?" He replied, "Yep, my pa would kill me if I came home with it hanging out."

168

She Told Him What To Do

There was this young naive kid going out with a girl. It was said that he could get anything he wanted, but he didn't know what to do since this was his first date. So he thought he'd ask his buddies and see what they had to say. So they told him to get in the car and drive to a nice lonely dark road and stop. "Then put your arm around her, kiss her, rub her stomach, and tell her you love her." So the kid said, "That's not so bad, but how do I know what to do next?" His buddies said, "She'll let you know." So the kid has his date and drives to a lonely dark road and stops. Then he put his arm around her and kissed her. Then he began telling her that he loved her and rubbing her stomach. She said, "Lower, lower!" So he says [in low voice], "I love you; I love you."

169

The Country Boy and the Town Boy

This is a story about a country boy who visited his town cousin. Upon arrival, his cousin told him he had a date, but he could also get him a date if he would like one. The country boy said he didn't know what to do with a girl. So the town boy said, "Don't worry; do everything and say everything I say." So they went to the show, and things went fine. Then they took a walk in the park, found a bush with a bench on each side. The town boy said to his girl, "Oh, sweet constellation, your eyes are like a dove. Throw your arms around me, and tell me who you love." Upon hearing this, the country boy thought he could remember this, so a few minutes later he said, "Oh, sweet cock and asshole, your eyes are like a frog. Throw your legs around me, and screw me like a dog."

170

Come Again

There were two boys who lived on a farm. They were brothers, and one was a lot older than the other. The older brother always got to do anything he wanted to and go anywhere he wanted. The younger brother had to do almost all the work around the farm, and he just got fed up with it. Finally he asked his older brother if he could go to town with him. The older brother said yes, so off they went.

They went to bars and nightclubs. At one bar they were approached by two prostitutes. The older brother went into one room with one girl, and the younger brother went into another room with the other girl. The younger brother didn't know anything about sex. The girl started by washing his peter with soap and water, and he came all over the bowl. The girl then said, "I hope you can come again!" The younger brother then said, "Sure, I can come, if my brother will bring me in next Saturday."

171

Just Watch Old Brother

These two hillbillies were so stupid that their pa couldn't make them understand what sex was. So he called Ma in, took off her clothes, spread her out on the bed, and said, "Boys, you see that brown spot? Well, you just watch old Pa!" After a while one boy caught on, but the other one didn't, so the one said, "You see that brown spot between Pa's legs? Well, you just watch old Brother!"

172

The Man Who Couldn't Get Interested in Women

There was this little old German man who was just fabulously wealthy and was getting along in years. He'd always had everything in life except a satisfactory sexual relationship. He just never could seem to get interested enough in a woman to develop a good sex life or anything. So finally one day he goes to this brilliant Swiss doctor. And after the doctor checked him over, he said, "Herman, there's nothing wrong with you that getting yourself a beautiful German mistress won't cure." So Herman goes out and gets this really beautiful German mistress. And she's really something—long blonde hair, a beautiful body, and very affectionate. Anyway, Herman sets her up in this lavish apartment with her own bedroom and everything, but he still can't seem to get over his shyness of women.

So one day she goes into her bedroom and calls to him in this very sultry voice, "Herman, I vant you to come into my bedroom." And Herman goes in. Then she says, "Now, Herman, I vant you to unhook my dress and take it off." So Herman unhooks her dress and takes it off. "Now, Herman," she says, "I vant you to take off my sexy black lace slip." So he does. Next, she says, "Herman, I vant you to unhook my stockings." And he does. Now she says, "Herman, I vant you to take the stockings off." He does this, and she says, "Now, Herman, I vant you to take off my black lace bra." So Herman takes it off. "Now, Herman, I vant you to take off my panties." So Herman takes off the panties. Then she says, "Now, Herman, don't you ever let me catch you wearing my things ever again!"

173

Call Him Houdini

A young girl who just started dating has a discussion with her mother. Her mother tells her the easiest way to stop a guy from having sex is to ask him, "What are we going to name it?" The girl dates around and finally settles down with one guy.

One night they are balling to their hearts' content. Suddenly she remembered what her mother said, so she asks the guy, "What are we going to name it?" He jumps off, takes off his rubber, ties a knot in it, and says, "If he gets out of here, then we will call him Houdini!"

174

It Wasn't Her Belly Button

Little Johnny and Susie were going to go to the show. Johnny was five years old, and Susie was six. Anyway, when they got inside and were sitting down, Johnny decides not to waste any time, see, and he leans over and says, "Hey, Susie, can I put my arm around you?" And Susie is real indignant because she thinks he's trying to get fresh or something and says, "No!" She was really mad. But Johnny begs and pleads, and finally she says, "Okay." So she lets him put his arm around her shoulder.

After about five minutes . . . Johnny doesn't want her to think he's trying to rush her or anything . . . he leaned over and whispers, "Susie, can I put my hand in your hand?" Susie was really shook, and she says, "Oh, no, Johnny, I couldn't let you do that." "Oh, please, Susie, I'll be real good. Please, please." "Oh, all right, Johnny."

So after a while, Johnny leaned over again and said, "Susie, can I put my finger in your belly button?" This time Susie was really upset, and she said, "Oh, no, Johnny!" "Oh, please, Susie, I'll be real good. Please, please, please." So just to get him to shut up she agreed. So after a while, Susie lets out a scream, and yells, "That's not my belly button!" And Johnny says, "Oh, that's all right; that's not my finger, either."

175

Just a Duck

One time there was this man who wanted to get a suntan all over his body. He figured the only way he could do this was to go off somewhere on the beach where nobody could see him. So he decided to go way down the beach. He took off all his clothes and was laying there in the good hot sun when all at once this little girl wandered down where he was. He told her to go away because he didn't want her seeing him naked. She wouldn't leave and started asking him questions. She asked him what that thing was sticking up, and he told her that it was his duck just to get her to leave. She kept hangin' around there, so he decided to get some sleep anyway. The next thing he knew, he was in the hospital. The little girl was standing next to him, and he asked her what had happened. She said, "Your duck wet on me, so I broke its neck, cracked its eggs, and set its nest on fire!"

176
Who Will Pay the Mortgage?

There is this little boy, and it's his birthday, and all he wants for his birthday is a new bicycle. He goes to his daddy and asks for a new bicycle, and his father says no, that he can't have a new bicycle because they just bought a new house and they must pay off the mortgage first. The little boy then goes to his mother and asks her for a new bicycle for his birthday, and she says that he can't have a new bicycle because they just bought a new house and they have to pay off the mortgage first.

Well, that night the little boy is going past his parent's bedroom door and he hears his dad say, "I'm gettin' off! I'm gettin' off!" His mother says, "I'm coming, too! I'm coming, too!" The little boy says, "Goddamn it, they're not leaving me here to pay off the mortgage!"

177
She Would Rather Have a Puppy

There is this little girl and her father walking through the woods. And the little girl sees this dog hunching another dog. The little girl says, "Daddy, what are they doing?" The father says, "They're making puppies." That night the little girl walks in on her parents in the bedroom and says, "What are you doing?" The father says, "We're making you a baby brother." The little girl says, "Well, turn her over because I want a little puppy!"

 *Kentuckians*

DURING THE EARLY DECADES of the nineteenth century, a large percentage of Hoosier settlers came from the south, especially from the upper south. Many of these early settlers, if not born in Kentucky, had at one time or another lived in Kentucky. There is a kernel of truth, then, in the joke that a Hoosier is a Kentuckian who ran out of money on the way to Michigan. According to Raven I. McDavid, Jr. ("Word Magic, Or 'Would You Want Your Daughter to Marry a Hoosier?'" in *Dialects in Culture,* ed. William A. Kretzsmar, Jr. [University: University of Alabama Press, 1979], pp. 255–56), along the Atlantic Seaboard *hoosier* is a derogatory epithet suggesting rusticity and is roughly synonomous with such terms as hillbilly, hayseed, and hick. Thus, as the state nickname for Indiana suggests, early settlers in Indiana were considered extremely backward by their friends and relatives back home in Kentucky and other more established southern states.

Kentuckian jokes are especially popular in southern Indiana, where ties to Kentucky and the upper south are strongest. These jokes told by contemporary Hoosiers permit a reversal of roles, allowing Hoosiers to discount their southern roots and identify more closely with other northerners, who often feel superior to southerners. As John H. Burma observes in "Humor as a Technique in Race Conflict" (*American Sociological Review,* 11 [1946]: 710), often "humor arises from a

109

conception of superiority in ourselves by comparison with the inferiority of others." At any rate, ridicule of other groups is common in regional and ethnic jokes, and the same numskull jokes told about Kentuckians by Hoosiers are told about Hoosiers by Kentuckians, especially those living in cities like Louisville and Henderson that are close to Indiana.

178

A Quart Low

This Kentuckian came to Indiana and went to the doctor. He had a brown line across his forehead. They ran tests and everything on him and told him to come back in a couple of days and they would tell him what it was. Well, he came back, and the doc told him they had figured out what it was. He said that they knew that all Kentuckians were full of shit and that he was a quart low.

179

There Isn't Much Left

It seems that there was these two lions talking in the jungle the other day. One lion was sleek and fat, and the other lion was nothing but skin and bones. The skinny lion asked the fat lion how he got so sleek and fat. The fat lion said that he ate Kentuckians. The skinny lion said that he ate Kentuckians, too, but he sure wasn't putting on much weight. The fat lion asked the skinny lion what his technique was for catching the Kentuckians. The skinny lion told him that he would sit in a tree real still-like till a Kentuckian came along. Then he would jump down behind him and scare him real bad and chase him till he was out of breath. Then he would eat him. The fat lion said, "That's where your trouble is. Once you get the wind and shit out there isn't much left."

"No, you're not lights! Get down here and go to work!" And he said, "No, we're lights. We can't work. We're lights." And the foreman said, "If you're not down here in two seconds, you're gonna be fired." So, of course, the time went by, and the Polacks wouldn't come down. So the foreman said, "Get out! You're fired!" So they got down and walked out. In a little bit these two Kentuckians walked out. And the foreman said, "Where you goin', boys?" And the Kentuckian goes, "Well, we can't work without lights."

188

The Dumbest Kentuckian

Okay, there was these two executives in the office, and they both had office boys—one was a Polack and one was a Kentuckian, the office boys were. This one executive says, "Boy, I must have the dumbest office boy in the world. I just told him to take this two cents and go out and buy me a Cadillac, and he went off and tried to do it!" And this was the Kentuckian. And the other executive said, "I just told my office boy to go upstairs on the third floor and get me."

So these two boys were out, and the Polack said, "Boy, I must have the dumbest boss in the world. He told me to go up on the third floor and get him when all he had to do was get on the phone and call him himself." So this Kentuckian goes, "Well, that's nothing. My boss gave me this two cents and told me to go out and buy him a Cadillac, and he didn't even tell me what color to buy!"

189

Where the Ducks Ford

A Kentuckian was on his side of the Ohio, and an Indiana guy was on the other side. The Indiana guy wanted to get on the Kentucky side, so he asked the Kentuckian where the river was low . . . two feet or lower. The Kentuckian said, "See that rock? It's lower there." So this guy started out, and he came up fussing. The Kentuckian said, "I thought it was low 'cause three ducks have been walking on it for hours."

180

A Case of Diarrhea

There's one about a Kentuckian and an Indianian who are fishing. They are on opposite sides of the river. The Hoosier will fish for a while, and then he'll go back in the woods, and then he'll come back and fish for a while and then go back. And he just kept doing this all afternoon, and finally this Kentuckian just can't stand it any longer, and he goes, "What is that guy doing?" So he yells, "Hey, whatcha doing over there?" And the Hoosier goes, "What do you mean?" And he says, "You keep going back in the woods and then coming back. What are you doing?" And the Hoosier goes, "Well, I got a case of diarrhea." And the Kentuckian goes, "Wait a minute, and I'll be over to help you drink some!"

181

Talk a Little Slower

Three or four guys were sitting around telling jokes. This one started telling a Kentuckian joke. The joke started going against the grain of a Kentuckian in the group. The Kentuckian said, "Hey, wait just a minute. I'm a Kentuckian, you know." So the person telling the joke said, "Oh, I'm sorry. I'll talk a little slower."

182

Kentuckians' Brains Are Expensive

There was a man who was getting a brain transplant. The man who had the brains on display was giving his sales talk. "Now here is a brain that costs $400." "My!" said the buyer, "Whose brain was that?" "Oh, that was the brain of a great mathematician," said the salesman. "And here is a brain which costs $500. Its owner was a great scientist." "And here is a small one marked $700 down here," remarked the buyer. "Why is such a small brain $700?" "Oh, that is a Kentucky brain," said the salesman. "But why the high price on this Kentucky brain?" asked the buyer. The salesman turned to him in dismay and said, "Why, do you realize how many Kentuckians it took to make that little brain?"

183
"My Old Kentucky Home"

There was this guy who wanted to be a Polack more than anything else in the world. So he went to this doctor that performs operations. So they scheduled him for an operation. And the day of the operation he went to the hospital, and they had him on the operating table. And all at once the doctor had a call from outa town that he had to go to a different hospital. So he said to the guy who wanted to be this Polack that he had an able-bodied assistant that could perform the operation just as well and that if he didn't mind that, this assistant would do it. So the guy said, "Okay." So the operation went on as scheduled, and it went pretty good.

And so a couple days later the original doctor came back and was talkin' to the assistant doctor. And he said, "Well, how did the operation go?" And the assistant doctor said, "Well, okay." And he said, "You did do the operation as scheduled? You removed ten percent of his brain?" And the assistant said, "Ten percent of his brain! I took out ninety percent of his brain!" And the original doctor said, "Oh, then that explains why he was singin' 'My Old Kentucky Home'!"

184
The Kentuckian and the Chain Saw

This Kentuckian had this handsaw, and it only cut down four trees a day. Then he saw an ad in the Sears and Roebuck catalog for a chain saw guaranteed to cut down twelve trees a day. So he bought it and took it home, and it only cut down four trees a day, too. So he took it back to the guy he bought it from and told him that it didn't work right. The man took the saw over to a table and pulled the string and started the motor. The Kentuckian said, "What's that noise?"

185
Kentuckians Need a Bigger Truck

These two Kentuckians went in business and were buying steel drums in Kentucky for a dollar apiece and hauled them to Indiana and sold them for a dollar apiece. The one finally said, "We aren't making any money." The other one said, "You're right. We ought to buy a bigger truck."

186
Kentucky Turf Layers

A couple were having a house built. The builder called them to come out to the house. He told them that they were ready to paint the rooms and asked them what colors they wanted. They went into the kitchen, where they decided on orange. The builder opened a window and shouted, "Green side up!" Next they went into the living room, which they wanted painted yellow. Upon hearing this the builder opened a window and shouted, "Green side up!" From the living room, they went down the hall into the bedroom. Their choice was blue for the bedroom. The builder once again opened a window and shouted, "Green side up!" The couple, looking more than a little amazed, asked him why no matter what color that they chose he called for green. "Oh, that's because I've got some Kentuckians working there laying sod," he replied, "and I have to keep reminding them which side goes up."

187
The Light

There's this Kentuckian and a couple . . . well, a couple Kentuckians and a couple Polacks that work in this warehouse. And one foreman comes in, and the Polacks are hangin' from . . . the warehouse . . . from their knees from the rafters, like on the And the foreman says, "Whataya doin' hangin' there by your And the Polacks said, "Well, we're lights." And the foreman

190
Kentuckian Believes He's Black

A black, a Polack, and a Kentuckian were on a bus to Chicago. On the way, they decided to save on expenses while they looked for jobs and rent a room together for a few nights. When they got to Chicago, the black and the Polack decided to live it up for a while and went to a bar. The Kentuckian wasn't going to waste any time, so he went to look for a job. He found one working in a factory. He went back to the room they had rented and found the black and the Polack drunk. He decided to go to bed and asked the other two to wake him up at 6:00 in the morning so he could go to work. They said they would, and he went to sleep.

While the Kentuckian was asleep, the black and the Polack thought they would play a joke on him and paint him black. The next morning the Kentuckian got up and went to work. The man in charge asked him what he was doing there. He said, "What do you mean? You hired me yesterday." The man in charge said, "You're wrong. We don't hire niggers here." The Kentuckian said that he wasn't a nigger, and the man told him to go look in the mirror. When the Kentuckian saw that his face was black, he said, "Damn Polack woke up the wrong guy!"

191
Marking the Place on the Boat

These two Kentuckians were out fishin' in a rented boat. And all of a sudden before they knew it, it got real dark. It was too dark for them to see to fish anymore. They were really upset because this spot was hot for fishin', and they wanted to keep on fishin' so that they could get a lot of fish from this one particular spot.

So the one Kentuckian said, "Well, I got an idea how we can come back tomorrow to the same place and get some more fish." And the other one said, "Well, what's that?" And he said, "Well, let's put an 'X' in the bottom of the boat." And the other Kentuckian said, "Well, you fool, that won't work! What if we don't get the same boat the next time?"

192

What Is Intellect?

There were these two Kentuckians, and they were diggin' a ditch, while the foreman, who was from Indiana, sat up in the shade, drinkin' a nice, cool orange. Now the Kentuckians wondered why they had to dig the ditch while he was up there drinkin' that nice, cool orange. So one of 'em said to the other one, "I think I'm gonna go up there and ask him why."

So he goes up there, and he says, "Foreman, why are we down there diggin' the ditch while you're up here sippin' a nice, cool orange?" And the guy says, "'Cause I got intellect." And the guy says, "Intellect? What's that?" Says, "You don't know what intellect is?" And the guy says, "No." He says, "Come here a minute." So he takes him over to this tree, and he holds his hand up in front of the tree. And he says, "See my hand? Hit it." And right before the guy hits his hand, he pulls it down, and the guy smashes his hand into the tree. Okay, so he says, "That's intellect."

So the other guy goes back and starts diggin' the ditch again. And his companion says, "Why is he up there?" And the guy says, "'Cause he's got intellect." And the guy says, "Intellect? What's that?" So the guy holds his hand up in front of his face and says, "See my hand? Hit it."

193

Propping Up the Barn

There were these Kentuckians trying to get a mule inside a barn. Well, they got the mule towards the barn door, and they couldn't get it in because his ears touched the top of it. So anyway they were propping the barn up trying to get the mule through it. So anyway this old Indiana guy comes up, and he goes, "What are you trying to do?" The Kentuckian looks up and says, "Well, it's like this. The mule's ears are too long, and he can't go through the doors. And the Indiana guy goes, "It would be much easier to dig a trench and let the mule through." And so he leaves. One Kentuckian says to the other Ken-

180
A Case of Diarrhea

There's one about a Kentuckian and an Indianian who are fishing. They are on opposite sides of the river. The Hoosier will fish for a while, and then he'll go back in the woods, and then he'll come back and fish for a while and then go back. And he just kept doing this all afternoon, and finally this Kentuckian just can't stand it any longer, and he goes, "What is that guy doing?" So he yells, "Hey, whatcha doing over there?" And the Hoosier goes, "What do you mean?" And he says, "You keep going back in the woods and then coming back. What are you doing?" And the Hoosier goes, "Well, I got a case of diarrhea." And the Kentuckian goes, "Wait a minute, and I'll be over to help you drink some!"

181
Talk a Little Slower

Three or four guys were sitting around telling jokes. This one started telling a Kentuckian joke. The joke started going against the grain of a Kentuckian in the group. The Kentuckian said, "Hey, wait just a minute. I'm a Kentuckian, you know." So the person telling the joke said, "Oh, I'm sorry. I'll talk a little slower."

182
Kentuckians' Brains Are Expensive

There was a man who was getting a brain transplant. The man who had the brains on display was giving his sales talk. "Now here is a brain that costs $400." "My!" said the buyer, "Whose brain was that?" "Oh, that was the brain of a great mathematician," said the salesman. "And here is a brain which costs $500. Its owner was a great scientist." "And here is a small one marked $700 down here," remarked the buyer. "Why is such a small brain $700?" "Oh, that is a Kentucky brain," said the salesman. "But why the high price on this Kentucky brain?" asked the buyer. The salesman turned to him in dismay and said, "Why, do you realize how many Kentuckians it took to make that little brain?"

183

"*My Old Kentucky Home*"

There was this guy who wanted to be a Polack more than anything else in the world. So he went to this doctor that performs operations. So they scheduled him for an operation. And the day of the operation he went to the hospital, and they had him on the operating table. And all at once the doctor had a call from outa town that he had to go to a different hospital. So he said to the guy who wanted to be this Polack that he had an able-bodied assistant that could perform the operation just as well and that if he didn't mind that, this assistant would do it. So the guy said, "Okay." So the operation went on as scheduled, and it went pretty good.

And so a couple days later the original doctor came back and was talkin' to the assistant doctor. And he said, "Well, how did the operation go?" And the assistant doctor said, "Well, okay." And he said, "You did do the operation as scheduled? You removed ten percent of his brain?" And the assistant said, "Ten percent of his brain! I took out ninety percent of his brain!" And the original doctor said, "Oh, then that explains why he was singin' 'My Old Kentucky Home'!"

184

The Kentuckian and the Chain Saw

This Kentuckian had this handsaw, and it only cut down four trees a day. Then he saw an ad in the Sears and Roebuck catalog for a chain saw guaranteed to cut down twelve trees a day. So he bought it and took it home, and it only cut down four trees a day, too. So he took it back to the guy he bought it from and told him that it didn't work right. The man took the saw over to a table and pulled the string and started the motor. The Kentuckian said, "What's that noise?"

185

Kentuckians Need a Bigger Truck

These two Kentuckians went in business and were buying steel drums in Kentucky for a dollar apiece and hauled them to Indiana and sold them for a dollar apiece. The one finally said, "We aren't making any money." The other one said, "You're right. We ought to buy a bigger truck."

186

Kentucky Turf Layers

A couple were having a house built. The builder called them to come out to the house. He told them that they were ready to paint the rooms and asked them what colors they wanted. They went into the kitchen, where they decided on orange. The builder opened a window and shouted, "Green side up!" Next they went into the living room, which they wanted painted yellow. Upon hearing this the builder opened a window and shouted, "Green side up!" From the living room, they went down the hall into the bedroom. Their choice was blue for the bedroom. The builder once again opened a window and shouted, "Green side up!" The couple, looking more than a little amazed, asked him why no matter what color that they chose he called for green. "Oh, that's because I've got some Kentuckians working out there laying sod," he replied, "and I have to keep reminding them which side goes up."

187

The Lights

There's this Kentuckian and a couple . . . well, a couple Kentuckians and a couple Polacks that work in this warehouse. And one day the foreman comes in, and the Polacks are hangin' from . . . in the warehouse . . . from their knees from the rafters, like on the ceiling. And the foreman says, "Whataya doin' hangin' there by your knees?" And the Polacks said, "Well, we're lights." And the foreman goes,

"No, you're not lights! Get down here and go to work!" And he said, "No, we're lights. We can't work. We're lights." And the foreman said, "If you're not down here in two seconds, you're gonna be fired." So, of course, the time went by, and the Polacks wouldn't come down. So the foreman said, "Get out! You're fired!" So they got down and walked out. In a little bit these two Kentuckians walked out. And the foreman said, "Where you goin', boys?" And the Kentuckian goes, "Well, we can't work without lights."

188
The Dumbest Kentuckian

Okay, there was these two executives in the office, and they both had office boys—one was a Polack and one was a Kentuckian, the office boys were. This one executive says, "Boy, I must have the dumbest office boy in the world. I just told him to take this two cents and go out and buy me a Cadillac, and he went off and tried to do it!" And this was the Kentuckian. And the other executive said, "I just told my office boy to go upstairs on the third floor and get me."

So these two boys were out, and the Polack said, "Boy, I must have the dumbest boss in the world. He told me to go up on the third floor and get him when all he had to do was get on the phone and call him himself." So this Kentuckian goes, "Well, that's nothing. My boss gave me this two cents and told me to go out and buy him a Cadillac, and he didn't even tell me what color to buy!"

189
Where the Ducks Ford

A Kentuckian was on his side of the Ohio, and an Indiana guy was on the other side. The Indiana guy wanted to get on the Kentucky side, so he asked the Kentuckian where the river was low . . . two feet or lower. The Kentuckian said, "See that rock? It's lower there." So this guy started out, and he came up fussing. The Kentuckian said, "I thought it was low 'cause three ducks have been walking on it for hours."

190

Kentuckian Believes He's Black

A black, a Polack, and a Kentuckian were on a bus to Chicago. On the way, they decided to save on expenses while they looked for jobs and rent a room together for a few nights. When they got to Chicago, the black and the Polack decided to live it up for a while and went to a bar. The Kentuckian wasn't going to waste any time, so he went to look for a job. He found one working in a factory. He went back to the room they had rented and found the black and the Polack drunk. He decided to go to bed and asked the other two to wake him up at 6:00 in the morning so he could go to work. They said they would, and he went to sleep.

While the Kentuckian was asleep, the black and the Polack thought they would play a joke on him and paint him black. The next morning the Kentuckian got up and went to work. The man in charge asked him what he was doing there. He said, "What do you mean? You hired me yesterday." The man in charge said, "You're wrong. We don't hire niggers here." The Kentuckian said that he wasn't a nigger, and the man told him to go look in the mirror. When the Kentuckian saw that his face was black, he said, "Damn Polack woke up the wrong guy!"

191

Marking the Place on the Boat

These two Kentuckians were out fishin' in a rented boat. And all of a sudden before they knew it, it got real dark. It was too dark for them to see to fish anymore. They were really upset because this spot was hot for fishin', and they wanted to keep on fishin' so that they could get a lot of fish from this one particular spot.

So the one Kentuckian said, "Well, I got an idea how we can come back tomorrow to the same place and get some more fish." And the other one said, "Well, what's that?" And he said, "Well, let's put an 'X' in the bottom of the boat." And the other Kentuckian said, "Well, you fool, that won't work! What if we don't get the same boat the next time?"

192

What Is Intellect?

There were these two Kentuckians, and they were diggin' a ditch, while the foreman, who was from Indiana, sat up in the shade, drinkin' a nice, cool orange. Now the Kentuckians wondered why they had to dig the ditch while he was up there drinkin' that nice, cool orange. So one of 'em said to the other one, "I think I'm gonna go up there and ask him why."

So he goes up there, and he says, "Foreman, why are we down there diggin' the ditch while you're up here sippin' a nice, cool orange?" And the guy says, "'Cause I got intellect." And the guy says, "Intellect? What's that?" Says, "You don't know what intellect is?" And the guy says, "No." He says, "Come here a minute." So he takes him over to this tree, and he holds his hand up in front of the tree. And he says, "See my hand? Hit it." And right before the guy hits his hand, he pulls it down, and the guy smashes his hand into the tree. Okay, so he says, "That's intellect."

So the other guy goes back and starts diggin' the ditch again. And his companion says, "Why is he up there?" And the guy says, "'Cause he's got intellect." And the guy says, "Intellect? What's that?" So the guy holds his hand up in front of his face and says, "See my hand? Hit it."

193

Propping Up the Barn

There were these Kentuckians trying to get a mule inside a barn. Well, they got the mule towards the barn door, and they couldn't get it in because his ears touched the top of it. So anyway they were propping the barn up trying to get the mule through it. So anyway this old Indiana guy comes up, and he goes, "What are you trying to do?" The Kentuckian looks up and says, "Well, it's like this. The mule's ears are too long, and he can't go through the doors. And the Indiana guy goes, "It would be much easier to dig a trench and let the mule through." And so he leaves. One Kentuckian says to the other Kentuckian, "Gosh, isn't he dumb! It's not his legs that are too long; it's his ears!"

194

Kentuckian Considers Crossing the Ohio on a Light Beam

There were two men fishing on the Ohio River. One was a Kentuckian, who was on the Kentucky side. The other was an Auroran on the Indiana side. The Kentuckian had been sitting all morning, not catching a fish, while the Auroran was pulling the fish in right and left. Every few minutes the Kentuckian saw that guy get another fish. Finally he called across the river to the Auroran, "Hey, you catch anything?" The Auroran said, "Sure, the fishing was great today." Then the Auroran asked if he was catching anything? He replied that he wasn't, so he told him to come over to the Indiana side. The Kentuckian said he couldn't swim. So the Auroran said he'd turn on his flashlight, and he could walk over on the beam. The Kentuckian said, "Ha, I'm not that dumb; I know you'll trick me. I'll get half way over, and you'll turn the light off."

195

Nail Heads on the Wrong End

A Kentuckian came up and asked for a job as a carpenter. When asked what all he could do, he replied, "Framing and outside and inside trim." The foreman told him to go nail some Celotex on the side of a building. About an hour later the foreman came by to check his work, and while watching him, saw him nail a nail or two, then throw some over his shoulder and maybe nail three or four more and throw a few more over his shoulder. The foreman came up and asked, "What the hell do you think you're doing throwing away all those good nails?" The Kentuckian replied, "The heads are on the wrong end of the nail." The foreman said, "You dumbass Kentuckian! Save those nails; they're for the other side of the house!"

196

Why He Couldn't See

There was this Hoosier and a Kentuckian applying for a job. They were waiting in the secretary's office of this firm when she told the Hoosier that the boss was ready to interview him for the job. The Hoosier went in the boss's office, and the boss said, "I have two questions for you, and if you can answer them, you can start work Monday morning." The first question the boss asked the Hoosier was, "What would happen if I poked one of your eyes out?" The Hoosier replied, "I would be half blind." The second question was, "What would happen if I poked both of your eyes out?" The Hoosier replied, "I would be totally blind." The boss said, "Very good, I'll see you bright and early Monday morning."

The Hoosier left, and on his way out stopped to talk to the Kentuckian. He told the Kentuckian that the test was really easy and that the answers were "I would be half blind" and "I would be totally blind." The Kentuckian thanked him, and the Hoosier said, "See you Monday morning."

At that time the secretary told the Kentuckian that the boss wanted to see him now. The Kentuckian went in the boss's office, and the boss told him, "I have two questions for you, and if you can answer them, you can start work Monday morning." The first question was, "What would happen if I cut one of your ears off?" The Kentuckian answered, "I would be half blind." The boss just gave him a funny look. He then asked, "What would happen if I cut both ears off?" The Kentuckian said, "I would be all the way blind." This really puzzled the boss, so he asked him how he figured he would be all the way blind if he cut off both ears. The Kentuckian said, "If you cut off both my ears, when I went to put my hat on I couldn't see."

197

Instant Replay

There was a Kentuckian and a Hoosier sittin' in a movie house, you know, and the picture was on. And it was about this Indian that was ridin' his horse around the cliff. And there's a cowboy on top of the cliff. And the Hoosier said, "I bet the cowboy jumps off the cliff and knocks the Indian off his horse." And the Kentuckian goes, "Okay, I'll betcha." So the Indian rides around the cliff, and the cowboy jumps off the rock and knocks the Indian off his horse. And the Hoosier says, "Well, I won." And the Kentuckian goes, "Yeah, I know." And the Hoosier says, "Well, I have to tell you now that I seen the film before, and I knew what was gonna happen." And the Kentuckian said, "Yeah, I saw it before, too, but I didn't think he could do it twice."

198

The Football Game

Did you hear about the Kentuckians and Polacks who were so tired of all the jokes about themselves that were going around that they decided to settle the matter once and for all? They were going to play a football game, and the loser would from then on bear the brunt of all the jokes. It was decided that the game would be held in Kentucky.

The game was a scoreless tie until the third quarter. Then a train went by and blew its whistle, and the Polacks thought the game was over and left the field. Fourteen plays later, the Kentuckians scored and won the game.

199

The Daring Kentuckian

There was this Kentuckian, and he was driving. And he got pulled over by these two big thugs. So they made him get outa the car, and they drew a circle around him. And they said, "If you step outa that circle, we're gonna beat the livin' daylights outa you." So they went over, and they picked up big sticks. And they started beatin' his car to death. And it was a brand new car. And he started laughin'. He just laughed and laughed and laughed. And the harder they hit, the more he laughed. And they finally came over and said, "What's the matter with you? Are you crazy or what?" And he said, "Well, no, but while you been beatin' that car up, I stepped outa the circle twice!"

200

The Pig Pen

There were these three poor fellows who didn't have much of a home life. One was from Ohio, another from Indiana, and the other one was from Kentucky. Well, the three of them decided to move out into the pig pen with the pigs. After the first day the Hoosier moved back home. Even home was better than the pig pen. On the second day the guy from Ohio couldn't stay another day, so he moved back home. On the third day the Kentuckian was still there. But on the fourth day the Kentuckian decided to stay, so the pigs moved out.

201

Kentuckians Need Twelve Pairs of Underwear

Heard about the Hoosier, Ohioan, and the Kentuckian who got drafted? They asked the Ohioan how many pairs of underwear he wanted, and he said, "Six—one for each day of the week and one for the weekends." They asked the Hoosier how many pairs he wanted, and he said, "Seven—one for each day of the week and one for each day of the weekend." Then they asked the Kentuckian how many pairs he wanted, and he said, "Twelve." They said, "What would you want twelve pairs for?" And the Kentuckian said, "January, February, March . . ."

202

Kentuckian Rents the Basement of an Outhouse

Once upon a time there was a traveling salesman. He stopped at a farmer's house, and he asked this farmer, said, "How come you got that television antenna on your outhouse out there?" "Well," he said, "there was a guy came along, and he wanted to rent a room, and I didn't have no room to rent. He said he just had to have a room, so I rented him the outhouse. And I guess if he wants to have a television out there, why, it's all right with me," you know. So the traveling salesman said, "Oh," he said, "I understand now," see.

And so he went on ahead, and the traveling salesman, he came back about every month or so, and he came back again, you know. He looked out there at that outhouse . . . and that was a-bothering him, you know . . . That had that television antenna on it.

And then about a month later, there was two television antennas on the outhouse, see. And so he said to the farmer, he said, "Say," he said, "Hows come that you got two television antennas on your outhouse?" "Well," he said, "there was a Kentuckian came by, and he had to rent a room," you know, "and I didn't have no room to rent him," you know, "and so he said he just had to have a room. He just had to have some place to stay," see. "So, by golly," he said, "I rented him the basement."

203

We Was Naughty Twice

This Kentuckian had been married for about a year, and his wife was pregnant. He told everybody that she was going to have twins. But when his wife finally went to the hospital she had one girl. The Kentuckian's friend said, "How come you were so sure your wife was going to have twins?" The Kentuckian whispered, "Well, we was naughty twice."

204

Kentuckians Tricked by Hoosiers

There was this Hoosier, and he went to the meeting some Kentuckians were having. Well, this Hoosier challenged a Kentuckian to fight, and the Kentuckian decided that he would, so they went off into the woods to fight. Well, the Kentuckian never did come back. In a little while the Hoosier came back and challenged five Kentuckians to fight. They never came back, either, so the Hoosier came back and got fifty Kentuckians to fight. Well, they never came back, either, so one hundred Kentuckians were going to fight this Hoosier. They were all getting ready to go fight with him when this one poor Kentuckian comes crawling back all bloody and mangled and bruised and beat up. He sees all these guys getting ready to go fight with the Hoosier, and he yells out with what energy he has left, "Don't go! Don't go! It's a trick! There's two of them!"

205

The Kentuckian Exterminators

Mayor Lindsay once declared war on the rats in New York City. So he hired nine Kentuckian exterminators. And so they all went down into the sewers, and they were gone for a month. And when they came back only six of them came back. "What happened to the other three?" said Mayor Lindsay. "They defected to the enemy, and two of the guys who came back brought back war brides," said one of the guys.

206

Only One Rabbit in These Parts

A man had lost his way somewhere in the hills of Kentucky. He went looking for a service station and spotted a little boy out in a field. The little boy was banging a bunny rabbit. The lost man couldn't figure that out, so he kept on going. Next he saw an old man on his porch playing with himself. The stranger thought this was really weird, a grown man playing with himself. Finally he got to a gas station and told the clerk about the little boy and old man he saw down the road. The attendant said, "You have to expect that around here, mister. There ain't but one rabbit in all these parts."

207

The Kentuckian's Last Words

There were three spies who got caught spying, and they were sentenced to death. One was a Frenchman, the other was a man from

Great Britain, and the other one was a Kentuckian. Well, so they took the Frenchman up, and they placed him underneath the guillotine. And they . . . the man . . . asked him, "Do you have any last words?" The Frenchman said, "Viva la France!" So they let loose the rope, blade came down, and it stopped right about an inch from his head. Well, they were all amazed, so they said, "This must be an act of God. You . . . you're obviously innocent. Go free, young man." So they let him go free.

So then they brought up the man from Great Britain and put his head underneath the guillotine. And they asked him, "Do you have anything to say?" Man said, "God save the queen!" So they let loose the rope, blade came down, and it stopped about an inch above his head. Said, "It . . . it's a miracle. He's obviously innocent. Go free, young man." So they let him go free.

So they brought the Kentuckian up. They placed his head underneath the guillotine, and they asked him, "Do you have any last words to say?" He said, "Yeah, there's a knot in that rope."

208
Remember Indiana!

Let's see . . . there were four guys in an airplane. And the pilot came back, and he told them that the airplane was gonna crash unless they got rid of some of the excess weight. So they threw everything overboard they could except the . . . you know . . . the people.

So they . . . the pilot came back again. He said, "There's still too much weight. Three of you have gotta jump off." So one of the guys stands up, and he says, "Remember Texas!" And he jumps off the airplane. The next guy, he comes up, and he says, "Remember Illinois!" And he jumps off the airplane to save everybody. Finally the guy from Indiana comes up, and he says, "Remember Indiana!" And he throws a Kentuckian overboard.

209
Take Four More with You

There was this Kentuckian at the Indianapolis airport who was buying a ticket back to Kentucky. The ticket cost $20 and the Kentuckian only had $19.95. So he said, "Hold on to this ticket for a minute, and I'll go see if I can scrape up a nickel." So he went canvassin' through the airport looking for a nickel, and nobody would give him one. Finally he went up to this businessman and says, "Please, sir, will you give me a nickel so I can get back to Kentucky?" The businessman looked at him and gave him a quarter and said, "Here you are, and take four more with you!"

210

Praise the Lord!

There was this old Kentuckian who decided that he wanted to buy a horse because all his friends had one. He asked three men if they had a horse for sale, and they all said, "No, but way up yonder on that hill you'll find a man with a horse for sale." So the Kentuckian climbed up the hill and asked the man if he had a horse for sale. The man said, "Yes, I do, but there's two things you got to know about this horse. To get him to go you have to say 'Praise the Lord!' and to get him to stop you have to say 'Amen!'" So the Kentuckian said, "I'll remember that," and paid the man his money, got on the horse, and said, "Praise the Lord," and the horse took off faster than lightnin' and headed for a cliff. The poor ol' Kentuckian couldn't think of the word to say, but right at the edge of the cliff he remembered it and said, "Amen!" He took his handkerchief out of his pocket, looked down at that deep valley, wiped his head, and said, "Praise the Lord!" And the horse went right on over the cliff.

 *Irish*

DURING THE FAMINE YEARS of the mid-nineteenth century, 1,250,000 half-starved Irish emigrated to North America. As Anna Peterson Royce points out in *Ethnic Identity* (Bloomington: Indiana University Press, 1982), "Although Americans had sent an unprecedented amount of relief to Ireland during the famine years, there was no welcome for the emaciated, indigent immigrants who seemed to be reaching their cities in hordes. In the best of times, when the Irish immigrant was a sturdy laborer unafraid of hard, dangerous physical activity, he still felt the brunt of anti-Catholic, anti-Irish sentiment. By 1847 that feeling had deepened to an active dislike. . . . The immigrants were regarded as stupid, dirty, superstitious, untrustworthy, diseased, and in despair. . . . All were resented by the American public" (pp. 115–16). Jokes about the Irish reflect this resentment, emphasizing the stupidity of the Irish.

Comic anecdotes about ignorant Irishmen were popular in nineteenth-century popular literature as well as in folklore. Stock characters in these tales were Paddy, the Irish immigrant, and Pat and Mike, two Irish numskulls, whose ignorance got them into all kinds of disagreeable predicaments. Irishman tales from Indiana incorporate familiar motifs of Irish jokes, which in the United States frequently deal with absurd misunderstandings. Thus, in the tales that follow, an Irishman thinks fireflies are mosquitoes carrying lanterns, thinks a turtle is a gourd, thinks a watch is a tick, and thinks the moon's reflection in the water is gold. Many Irish jokes are age-old numskull tales, not always told about Irishmen. For example, "Irishman Sleeps

125

on a Feather" (Tale 215) is an international folktale that goes back to at least 1512. "Dream Baloney" (Tale 217) is a version of another international folktale type, "Dream Bread," that just happens to be about Irishmen in this Hoosier version.

Today the Irish are assimilated into American culture, and jokes about the absurd ignorance of Irishmen are not easy to find in the oral tradition. Other immigrants, notably southern and eastern Europeans, who came to the United States after the Irish in the late nineteenth and early twentieth centuries, replaced the Irish as the undesirable group and therefore became the butt of the same or very similar numskull tales.

211
Irishmen Think Fireflies Are Mosquitoes Carrying Lanterns

Pat and Mike were in a place where the mosquitoes were real bad, and so they kind of got in a place where they weren't botherin' them so bad. And darkness come, and the lightning bugs started out. And old Pat says to Mike, "Well, Mike, we're out of luck; here they come with their lanterns."

212
Irishman Takes Turtle for a Gourd

Well, I'll tell you one about the . . . He was an Irishman too, you know. All them tales made up on Irish . . . And so he went . . . he put his grip on his back and run a cane through it . . . and went right down the road, you know. And he got way up toward night, and he begin to get pretty tired and sleepy, you know. And he said, "Well," he said, "I'm pert near dying for a drink of water." Says, "I'll go up there on that hill," to himself, he says, "and I'll see that lady." Says, "See if she won't give me a drink of water."

Said, "All right," and he went up there to the woman standin' there and knocked on the door, and she come to the door. He's standin' there with his grip on his back, you know. "Oh," he says, "Madam," says, "would you please give a poor old man a drink of water?" "Yeah, yeah," says, "I'll tell you the best thing you do," she says, "get you a good fresh drink of water. See that path there going right down that hill?" Says, "You get right in that path," says, "and follow that right down." Says, "That'll take you right down to the spring." Says, "There's an old-fashioned gourd hangin' there on the limb." Says, "Just take it off the limb and dip down in the spring," says, "and get you a good drink."

So he put his grip on his back, and out down toward the spring he went. And so he got pert near down there, and there's one of these old dry land terrapins in that path comin' up the hill, you know. And he says, "Land, possum, by Jesus," he says, "why," says, "that spring's gone dry!" He stood and looked there a little while. He says, "Well, that shore is the gourd." And so he just turned around and went back to the house and knocked on the door again. And she come to the door. She says, "Did you get you a drink?" "Ah, poss," he says, "no," he says, "I got pert near to the spring," says, "and I met the gourd comin' up the hill." Says, "The spring's gone dry!"

213

Irishman Takes Watch for a Tick

I'll tell you a litty-bitty short one 'bout an old Irishman. He was goin' along walkin' . . . had his grip on his back, you know, goin' along . . . goin' up the road. And so he looked down in front of him, and there laid a watch, and he picked it up. Turned it first one way and then another, and he says, "Ah" . . . the watch was runnin' yet, you know. It said, "Tick-tick-tick-tick-tick-tick." "Ah," he says, "You're a tick, huh?" He looked at it, and the old watch was still a-runnin'. Says, "Tick-tick-tick-tick-tick-tick." "Ah," he says, "I know what you are." He says, "You're one of them there great big ol' yeller ticks, hain't you?" Yeller gold watch! And says, "I'll just kill you right now." So he just slammed the watch down in the road hard as he could and just broke it all to pieces. He says, "You'll not tick me no more."

214

Moon's Reflection in Water Thought to Be Gold

Two Irishmen . . . one first by himself, then the other one was on down the road further, and said to the one going along, you know, oh, what he seen down to the river. There was a moon a-shinin' down in the water, and he walked on. He says, "Possum, by Jesus," he says, "a chunk of gold!" And he says, "Oh, now, just about how'll I get that chunk of gold?" "Well," he says, "I'll tell you," says, "I'll go up," says, "and get my buddy," says, "and get some more Irishmen up there."

And so he went ahead up on the side of the hill where they's at, and he come on, and he met his buddy up there and told him, he says, "Ah, poss," he says, "Mac," he says, "I seen a chunk of gold down there," he says, "in that river," he says. "Well, how in the world are we going to get it?" "Well," he says, "We can get them other fellas," says, "and we'll go down there to the riverside." Says, "There's a bent over tree," says, "right over that moon, that chunk of gold," says. And so he told the other'n, "Well," he says, "all right," he says. "I'll climb that tree," says, "and I'll swing out over that chunk of gold," says. "And," says, "and then the next one catch hold of my feet," says, "and go on then to the next one comes up." Says, "Let him catch ahold his feet," says, "and that-a-way we just keep goin' down till we git down to it," says.

And they got, oh, purty close to seven or eight of 'em, you know, and this here fella that seed it, why, he begin to get tired, for he's holding 'em all up, you see, and he says, "Up, Pat," he says, "possum, by Jesus, hold tight below while I spit on me hands above." So he turned loose, spit on his hands, and they all went in the river.

215

Irishman Sleeps on a Feather

Let's see, that was another Irishman goin' on an old gravel road. And so goin' along walkin' late one evenin', and he says, "Ah, poss," he says, "I'm gittin' tired and sleepy." And so he walked a little piece further, and he found a feather layin' in the road. And, "Oh," he says, "possum, by Jesus," he says, "right now," he says, "I've often heard tell of a featherbed." Says, "I'll just take this feather, pick it up," says, "and I'll walk on a little piece further till I come to a big flat rock or some place," says, "and I'll lay that feather down on that rock," says, "and I'll take me a good nap."

So, well, he walked on till he found a rock, and so he took and went and laid that feather down on that big rock and spread it out, and so he laid down awhile. First he'd lay awhile on one side, and then he'd turn over on the other side. He says, "Poss," he says, "it's not very comfortable." He says, "That feather is *not*, if that's what you call a featherbed."

And so he wallowed and wallowed on it all night, and finally next morning he got up. He couldn't hardly walk. He just wore hisself plumb out, you know, turnin' and twistin' on that big rock. So he got up. He finally made it, and he turned around and looked at it. He says, "Ah, possum, by Jesus," he says, "I've often heared talk of featherbeds," says, "but if all featherbeds," says, "is like that one," says, "I never want to sleep on another one!"

216
Irishman Has the Easier Job

There was this Irish guy who come over on the boat to the United States. He called his younger brother back in Ireland and told him that he had a job in New York City carrying hod up to the top of a 25-story building. He told his brother that he should come to the United States and get a job carrying hod because it was such easy work. All the bricklayers were doing all the work at the top.

217
Dream Baloney

Well, there were these three Irishmen, and they only had one pound of baloney between them. So one said, "Let's all go to bed, and in the morning the one who has the biggest dream gets the baloney." So when they got up in the morning, the first one said, "I dreamed I went to a banquet, and the table was spread with every kind of food imaginable." The second one said, "Well, I had a bigger dream. I dreamed that I died and went to heaven!" They then asked the third one what he had dreamed. And the third one said, "I dreamed that you went to a banquet, and that you died and went to heaven. And I figured that neither one of you was coming back, so I ate the baloney."

*Blacks*

ALL OF THE JOKES about blacks in this section, except one (Tale 227), were collected from white Hoosiers; however, as Lawrence W. Levine shows in *Black Culture and Black Consciousness* (New York: Oxford University Press, 1977), many of the same stereotypes of blacks are found in both white American and black American folklore (pp. 330–41). Common stereotypes of blacks shared by whites and blacks concern the inability of blacks to cooperate with one another, the laziness and tardiness of blacks, and the tendency of blacks to lie, steal, drink too much, spend money foolishly, and buy big cars. A dominant theme in jokes about blacks concerns their sexual prowess (See Tales 220, 221, 223). As Alan Dundes points out in *Mother Wit from the Laughing Barrel* (Englewood Cliffs, N.J.: Prentice-Hall, 1973), "The theme of genital superiority appears to be a widespread one and it seems to be shared by both Negroes and whites. In fact, it is not clear whether the notion was originally part of the white stereotype of the Negro which was eventually borrowed by the Negro or whether the notion started in Negro culture. Evidence from other cultures suggests that it is quite common for a 'dominant' group to attribute greater sexual capacity and drive to members of an oppressed minority, e.g., during World War II, some Germans claimed that Jews possessed super sexual appetites" (p. 642). In "Blacks and Jews in American Folklore " (*Western Folklore*, 33 [October 1974]: 301–25),

Nathan Hurvitz examines this stereotype and others attributed to both blacks and Jews in American and West European folklore. For a brief treatment of white stereotypes in jokes told by two black informants, see Paulette Cross, "Jokes and Black Consciousness: A Collection with Interviews" (in *Mother Wit from the Laughing Barrel*, pp. 649–69).

218
Dividing Souls

There was these two boys who'd been out nuttin' and were gonna divide out the nuts. So they went in a graveyard, but on their way in, by the opening, they dropped two nuts. When they go it, they started dividing them—"You take this one, and I'll take that one. You take this one, and I'll take that one."—until they got 'em all divided up. These two colored boys were standing outside the graveyard and heard them talking. "The Lord and the devil is dividin' up the bodies," one said. Then the two boys inside said, "Now let's go out there and get the other two." Them two colored boys thought they meant them and got scared and ran off!

219
The Voice from the Grave

They got two colored guys to bury him . . . you know, to carry the casket—pallbearers. And this old boy thought he'd have some fun, you know. He could throw his voice, and he slipped around, you know, and kinda hid. And these guys had this casket lowerin' it down in the grave, you know. And this old boy said, "Let me down e-e-easy, boys." And them guys stopped, you know, and looked at one another. Their eyes got great big. You know how they shine up anyway, them colored. And they started lowerin' the casket down a little more. And he said, "Let me down e-e-easy, boys." They say they dropped that casket and took off hard as they could go!

220

Cold, Deep Water

Niggers have the biggest dicks in the world. And they wanted to have a contest, but, you know, they didn't want to have everyone watch them. So these two, they were going in some secluded place. They were going across the Golden Gate Bridge. Nigger saw the water, and it made him want to piss. So he walked up to the side of the bridge, pulled his thing out, and commenced to pissin'. The other nigger saw the other nigger pissin', so it made him want to piss. So he whips his thing out and goes at it. The first nigger says, "Goddamn, the water's cold!" The other one says, "Yeah, and it's deep, too."

221

The Heart Transplant

Did you hear about the white man who had a heart transplant? The donor was a Negro. After the operation the white man was sent home with apparently no side effects. But six months later the man came back for a checkup, and the doctor asked the man how he felt and if there were any side effects. The man said that there were some side effects, but that they were all good. The doctor asked what were the side effects. And his patient said, "Well, my dick has grown two inches, and I've been getting welfare checks every month."

222

Boo!

Liza and Rastus were walking through the woods on the same path when the path diverged, so Rastus told Liza to go on one path and he would go on the other. Well, Liza got to the place where the path came back together first, and she was standing there waiting on him and didn't see him come up. Rastus came up and said, "Boo!" And Liza said, "Rastus, you nearly scared the pants off me." And Rastus said, "Boo! Boo!"

223

The Black Astronaut

The NAACP wrote to congress and said that all of the astronauts were white and that there had to be some colored ones. So congress told them if they found any that were smart enough they would send them into space. Well, they looked and looked and finally found a Negro who was smart enough. So they trained him, and finally he was sent into space.

When he got up there he turned around, and there was a monkey sitting there. He was, well, you know, kind of surprised, so he called ground control and asked them what the monkey was for. So they said that when the red light came on the monkey would do his stuff, and when the blue light came on he should do what he had been trained for.

So the red light came on, and the monkey really went to town. He pushed buttons and did all kinda technical stuff like that. The Negro was really impressed, but the blue light never came on. Just as he was getting ready to call ground control again, the blue light came on, and out popped a lever with a note on it. And he took it and read it. It said, "Now feed the monkey."

224

Smartin' Pills

There was this Negro standing on a corner with some dried up rabbit turds. And this other jig came up and asked him what they were, and he said, "Why, these are old smartin' pills." So the other nigger said, "Why not give me some?" And the other one said, "Hell, I'll sell you some!" The guy sold him some. And he said, "My gosh, these taste like shit!" The other guy said, "See, you're smarter already."

225

Play Fair!

Back in the days of the Roman Empire some black guy went to Rome and wanted to become a citizen. They told him they'd give him a few simple tests, and if he passed he would be a citizen of Rome. First, they took him over to the Coliseum where thousands of people were watching him. For his first test he had to fight ten of the toughest gladiators. To the Romans' surprise, he easily defeated them.

For the next test they dug a big hole and made him lay on his stomach while they covered him and filled the hole with rock and piled the rocks high above the ground. The crowd was just beginning to smile when the rocks quivered and the black man jumped up to the top of the heap in his torn clothing.

They said, "If you can just pass one more test, we will make you a citizen." So they buried him up to his neck in the center of the Coliseum and turned a wild, ferocious and hungry lion loose. The lion charged him, and he ducked to the left. The lion charged again, and he ducked to the right. The lion charged again, and this time he stretched his neck and grabbed the lion's balls in his teeth. The crowd yelled, "Play fair, nigger!"

226

The Black Bartender and the Italian

This Italian walked into a bar and sat down. He noticed there was a Negro bartender, and yelled "Hey, nigger, give me a beer." The bartender said, "Okay, but don't call me nigger." The Italian agreed to this, but after he finished his first beer, he said again, "Hey, nigger, give me another beer." "Listen," said the bartender, "I thought I told you not to call me nigger." But he handed him another beer after the Italian agreed not to repeat his mistake.

But a little while later, the Italian again yelled, "Hey, nigger, give me a beer." By now the bartender was getting pretty pissed, and he said, "Listen, buddy, how would you like it if we traded places for a while, so you could see how it feels to be called names." The Italian thought a minute; then he said, "Okay." So they traded places. The Negro sits down at the bar and says, "Hey, wop, how about a beer?" The Italian looked at him for a minute, then said, "Not on your life; we don't serve niggers here!"

227

Black Man, Jew, and White Man

A Jew, a black, and a white were fighting in a war, and they were killed and went to heaven. God said it was too crowded in heaven, and if they gave him $100, he would send them back. The white man gave him $100, and God sent him back. Then the general came by and asked the white man where had he been, and he told him what happened. Then the general said, "Well, where is that Jew and Negro I saw with you?" He said, "The last time I saw that Jew he had God down to $75.95; and the last time I saw the Negro he was running around looking for a cosigner."

228

Something Spectacular

This black man went up to heaven and met St. Peter, and he asked him, he says, "Well, before you can come in here you'll have to tell me something spectacular that you've done during your lifetime." He said, "Oh, I did something very spectacular." "What was that?" He says, "Well, I'm a black man. I married a white girl on the steps of the courthouse in Selma, Alabama." He says, "Well, when did you do that?" He says, "Ten minutes ago."

229

Are You Catholic?

There was two little boys sittin' on a corner—one white and one black. A priest walked by, and the white boy said, "Hello, Father." "Hello, son," said the priest and walks on by. The black boy says, "Is that your father?" And the white boy says, "No, that's my heavenly father." The white boy left. A little while later the priest walked past again, and the black boy said, "Hello, Father." And the Priest says, "Hello, son. Are you Catholic?" And the black boy says, "Hell, no, being black is bad enough!"

230

The Piano Player at the Revival Meeting

There was a revival meeting held by a Negro Baptist church in which everybody who was anybody attended. The preacher delivered his opening remarks about the goodness of God and then opened his hymn book. "Brothers, turn to hymn 32." The piano player looked at the preacher. "But Brother Preacher, I don't know that song," he said. The preacher turned to the congregation a second time. "Brothers, turn to hymn number 13." Once again the piano player turned to the preacher. "But Brother Preacher, I don't know that song." The preacher turned to the congregation again. "Brothers, turn to hymn number 54." And again the piano player turned to the preacher. "But Brother Preacher, I don't know that song." From the back of the hall came a yell: "Throw the mother fucker out!"

The preacher was appalled. He was absolutely shocked. "Now, brothers, we can't allow that kind of talk in the house of our Lord! I want the person who called Brother Piano Player a mother fucker to stand and confess his sin before God and this congregation!" Nobody stirred. Once again the preacher spoke: "Then I want the person sitting next to the person who called Brother Piano Player a mother fucker to stand." Nobody stirred, and in desperation the preacher said, "I want the person sitting next to the person sitting next to the person who called Brother Piano Player a mother fucker to stand." But nobody moved.

Presently a man in the back of the hall stood, "Brother Preacher, now I'm not the mother fucker who called Brother Piano Player a mother fucker, but what I want to know is, who's the mother fucker that called him a piano player?"

231

A Choice of Costumes

A black couple was invited to a costume party. The fella couldn't go out and get his own costume, so he asked his wife to go out and get him one. So she went out and got him a Superman costume. When he got home he asked to see the costume. And he said, "I can't wear that thing; it's a white man's costume!" So the next day she took it back and got a Captain Marvel costume and got the same response, that he couldn't go to the costume party in a white man's costume.

So she went shopping the next day, and she brought a white scarf, two new baseballs, and a two-by-four. When he came home from work that evening, he asked his wife about the costume, and she handed him the white scarf, two baseballs and the two-by-four. He said, "What am I supposed to do with these?" She said, "Well, you can tie the scarf around your middle and go as an Oreo cookie, or you can put the two baseballs on your chest and go as a domino, of if you don't like that you can stick the two-by-four up your rear and go as a fudgesicle."

 *Poles*

In spite of the efforts of some Polish-Americans to have Polack jokes declared illegal, jokes about Poles have remained popular in the American oral tradition since the 1960s. Many of these jokes did not originate as jokes about Poles but are familiar forms of numskull tales that were told earlier about other regional and ethnic groups in Europe and Canada as well as in the United States. Most of these tales are still told about other groups. As William M. Clements has pointed out in the introduction (p. 3) to his useful index, *The Types of the Polack Joke* (Bibliographic and Special Series no. 3 of *Folklore Forum*, 1969), the Polack "is known by such aliases as Kentuckian (Brier, Hillbilly) in Indiana and Ohio, Buckeye or Hoosier in Kentucky, Cajun in Louisiana, Aggie in Texas, Okie in California, Newfie in Canada, and Negro everywhere. Polack jokes may also be told about Irishmen, Little Morons, Jews, Italians, Puerto Ricans, and Texans (is no one sacred?)."

While *Polack* often is simply one name for a numskull stereotype found throughout western culture, other groups, such as blacks and Jews, do not share all the stereotypic features or the cluster of slurs attributed to Poles in Polack jokes. As Alan Dundes has noted in "A Study of Ethnic Slurs" (*Journal of American Folklore*, 84 [1971]: 200–02), the dominant traits of Poles in Polack jokes are that they are poor, dirty, stupid, inept, vulgar, boorish, and tasteless; and the "stereotypic features of poverty, dirtiness, stupidity, ineptness, and vulgarity are not to be found in the stereotype of the Jew." From 1880 to 1920 a considerable number of Poles settled in Indiana, especially in the northern counties, where Polish jokes are especially popular.

232
The Three Babies

There were three babies born in this hospital: One to a Jewish woman, one to a Polish woman, and one to a German woman. Well, after a nurse bathed the three children, it was discovered that they didn't know who each child belonged to. So after careful consideration a doctor came up with this conclusion. He brought in a picture of Hitler. The German baby saluted, the Jewish baby shit in his pants, and the Polish baby ate it.

233
The Polish Astronaut

There were these three astronauts trying to figure out where to go. One was an Italian, one was a Negro, and the third was a Polack. The Negro said, "Let's go to the moon." "Oh, no," said the Italian, "Venus is the planet of love. We should go there."

The Polack said, "I don't care where you guys are going. Me and my friends are going to go to the sun." His friends were amazed. "But you can't go to the sun. It's too hot. You'll die from the heat." The Polack smiled and said, "Oh, no, we won't. We're going to wait and go when it gets dark."

234
The Battlefield

The Polish army and the Russian army were fighting a war, and the Russians came up with a way to get the Poles to come up out of their trenches. The Russians would yell out, "Hey, Kawalski," and a Pole would stand up and say, "What?" And then "bang," they would shoot him. Then the Russians would move down the trench and do it again. After a while one of the Polish generals decided to try the same thing on the Russians. He figured someone in the Russian Army must be named Khrushev, so he yelled out, "Hey, Khrushev," and a voice from the Russian lines called, "Yeah, Kawalski, what do you want?" And when the Polish general stood up and said, "Nothing," they shot him.

235
The Polack at the Indy 500

There was this race driver who was a Polack, and he won the 500, but he made five pit stops when all the other drivers only made two. The reporter wanted to know why, so he asked some of the pit crew. And they didn't know, so he decided to ask the driver himself. The driver said he made two stops for gas and three stops to ask directions.

236
The Polack Goes Ice Fishing

There was this Polack who wanted to go ice fishing, you see. So he asked his neighbor if he could borrow his saw. He used the saw for three days, trying to saw a hole in the ice to go fishing. Finally his neighbor asked for the saw back. And the Polack said, "But I haven't even got my boat in the water yet!"

237
The Polish Trackers

One time two Polacks went hunting. They were walking along and came upon a set of tracks. One of them said, "Well, what do you know! These here are bear tracks." "No, they aren't. Those are deer tracks; any fool can see that," said the other. They argued about it for some time and finally decided to follow the tracks until they came upon what was making them. All at once the tracks led into a cave. "See, I told you that those were bear tracks. Everyone knows that deer don't live in caves," said the first one. Then the other Polack said, "I still say they aren't; they're too close together." About that time they heard a loud whistle, and a train ran over them.

238

Game

This Polack and Greek went hunting. Half a day went by, and they didn't see any game. So they stopped for lunch, and the Greek said to the Polack, "If we don't see any game within the next two hours, we'll go home." They both agreed. A couple hours went by, and they don't see any game, but they came upon this clearing and saw a nude girl. The girl waves to them, and they go over to the nude girl. The Greek goes up to the girl and says, "Are you game?" And she says, "Yes." And the Polack shot her.

239

The Lost Polack

Three Polacks went hunting. It was a big place, so they decided that if one of them should become lost, he should shoot into the air three times, and the others would come looking for him. Sure enough, one got lost. He shot into the air three times, waited, and nothing happened. Nobody showed up. He shot into the air again. He waited. Nobody showed up again. He decided he had better start walkin'. He hadn't walked very far when he ran into one of the other guys. "Hows come you didn't come after me when I was lost?" he asked. "Did you shoot in the air three times?" "Yeah, I shot in the air three times, and no one came. Then I shot in the air three times again, and no one came. That only left me one arrow, so I started walkin'."

240

The Polack's New Car

This Polack bought a new car and had driven it for about a week or so. One day he locked the keys in the car and rolled up the windows. So he called the dealer and asked him if he could do anything. The dealer said he probably could, but it would be the next morning before he could get there. Anyway, the dealer asked him if he would be needing the car before then. The Polack says, "No, but couldn't you come anyway? It's getting cloudy and looks as if it might rain, and I left the top down."

241

The Flagpole Measurement

One Polack was holding a pole up in the air, and the other was climbing up it with a tape measure when the job foreman came along and said, "What the hell's going on here?" The first Pole said, "We're measuring the pole; you said you wanted to know how tall it was." He said, "Why in the hell don't you lay it down and measure it?" The first Polack said, "You wanted to know how tall it was, not how long it was."

242

The Pizza

Did you hear about the Polack that went to the Pizza Barn? He didn't know what he wanted. He didn't know whether he wanted sausage or what kind. So he finally decided what he wanted to order. So he said to the guy, "Well, I want a large sausage pizza." So when he came to get it, the guy said, "Well, how many pieces do you want it cut into? Do you want it cut into eight or ten?" And the Polack stands there, and he scratches his head, and he says, "God, eight or ten? Well, you better cut it into eight. I don't think I can eat ten."

243
The Polish Window Washer

Did you hear about the Polack whose wife was always nagging him to wash the basement windows? She kept after him for weeks until he finally said he would do it. After three hours he came back in the house, and he was covered with mud. His wife asked if he was done yet. The Polack answered, "Hell, no, I'm not done yet! I just finished digging the hole for the ladder!"

244
Telling Their Horses Apart

There were two Polacks. Each owned a horse, and they couldn't tell them apart. First they tried cutting the mane off of one horse, but in a short while it grew back, and they had the same problem all over again. Next they tried cutting the tail off of one horse, but just like the mane it also grew back. Then they decided to measure them and see if they could tell them apart by their height. One Polack measured them, and looking up very disappointed, he said, "Well, this won't work either. The black one is just as tall as the white one."

245
Two Assholes on a Camel

Did you hear the one about the two Polacks that worked in a factory, and they kept hearing everyone talking about how much money they saved with a car pool? Well, the two Polacks decided that if these guys could save that much money and live 35 or 40 miles away, just think how much they could save living only two blocks away. So they decided to buy a car. They put together all their money and went downtown to a used car lot. When they got there they told the guy they needed a used car. He said, "Well, I've got a '59 Edsel that I'll sell for $395." The Polacks only had $150 between them, and the guy's junkers started at $300, so they started to leave.

They were just about to leave when the guy yelled, "Wait a minute! I think I've got something here that you might like. It's a trained camel that somebody left in trade. It stops at stop signs and red lights and even signals turns. Take him around the block, and if you like him, I'll let you have him for $150." So the Polacks got on the camel and took off. About two hours later they came walking back. The used car dealer came running out and yelled, "Where in the hell is my camel?" "Well," they said, "we were riding along, and we had to stop at a red light. Then some guys pulled up in a car and started yelling, 'Look at the two assholes on that camel!' So we got off to look, and the light changed and the camel went on without us."

246
Polish Coalminers

A guy walks into a bar, and he was taking a piss. He comes out of the rest room, and his face was as white as a sheet. The bartender says, "What's wrong?" The guy said, "There's three black guys in there taking a piss, and the one in the middle has a white dick." The bartender says, "You have to be kidding." And the guy says, "No, I'm serious. The guy in the middle has a white dick." A few minutes later three black guys come walking out of the bathroom, and the bartender asked the guy, "Are you talking about those three?" And he said, "The one in the middle has a white dick!" The bartender says, "Hell, those guys aren't black. They're Polish coalminers, and the one in the middle got married last week."

247
The Polack and the Frog

This Polack had a problem. He had this frog on his head, and he couldn't figure out how to get rid of it. Finally he went to the doctor, and when he went into the examining room, the doctor asked him what his problem was. "Can't you see, man?" shouted the Polack. "I've got a frog on my head!" "You think you got problems," the frog piped up. "Hell, I've got a damn Polack on my ass!"

248
The Polack Finds a Pig

There was this Polack, and he found a pig. And he didn't know what to do with it, so he asked his friend. And his friend told him, "Why don't you take it to the zoo?" The Polack said, "Okay," and left with the pig. The next day his friend saw him driving down the street in his car, and the pig was in the front seat beside him. The friend flagged him down and said, "I thought I told you to take that pig to the zoo!" The Polack said, "Yes, I took him to the zoo yesterday, and today I'm taking him to the ballgame."

249
The Polish Virgin

This Polack got married and took his bride off for their honeymoon. Well, they were only gone about an hour when all of a sudden the Polack comes running home to his mom and starts crying. Well, of course, his mom asked him what his problem was, and he told her that his new wife was a virgin. So his mom goes, "I don't blame you, son. If she's not good enough for others, then she's not good enough for you!"

250
Rape by a Polack

A woman was in a police station explaining how she was raped. She told the police officer that the man who raped her was a Polack. The officer asked her how she could be sure that the man that raped her was a Polack. She said, "Well, I had to show him how."

251
The Nude Polack on the Street Corner

A woman was arrested in town for not having any clothes on. When the policeman asked her why, she told this story: "Well, officer, I was at a Polish party. We were dancing and singing and drinking and dancing and drinking. Then the lights went out, and a man came over the P.A. and said that all the men were supposed to take off their clothes. So they started unzipping. The lights came on again. And we started drinking and dancing again. Pretty soon the lights went out again, and a voice came over the P.A. and said for all the women to take off their clothes. The lights came on again, and we started dancing and drinking. The lights went out again, and the voice said for everyone to go to town. Well, officer, I was the first one out of that party!"

252
Stretching a Dime

Did I ever tell you about the value of a dime? One day a Polack and a Jew were bragging about how far they could stretch a dime. Each one agreed to try it and meet a few days later to see who got the most out of a dime. The Jew bought a cigar. He smoked one-third, saved the ashes; smoked one-third, saved the ashes; smoked the rest, saved the ashes. On the fourth day he gave the ashes to his wife to use as fertilizer on her roses. He told the Polack, "You can't beat that for stretching a dime."

The Polack said, "I have you beat. I bought a Polish sausage for a dime. The first day I ate half. The second day I ate half. The third day I used the skin for a rubber. The fourth day I took a shit in the skin and sewed it back up. The fifth day I took it back to the butcher and said it smelled like shit. He said it smelled like shit, too, and gave me my dime back." Now there's a lesson in economics you won't learn in college!

253
Everything is Big in Texas

This Polack was truckin' through Texas, and he goes into this bar and says, "You Texans think everything is so goddamn big down here. Well, I don't think everything's so big. Bartender, give me a beer." So the bartender brings him a beer in a glass about the size of a bucket, and this Polack starts gettin' pretty drunk, so he says, "Bartender, where's the bathroom?" The bartender says, "First door on your left." Well, this Polack, he goes through the first door on his right and falls in the swimming pool, and when he comes up he starts yellin', "Don't flush it! Don't flush it!"

Jews

JOKES ABOUT JEWS are fairly common in Indiana and repeat the main traits of the Jewish stereotype in American folklore that Alan Dundes delineates in "A Study of Ethnic Slurs: The Jew and Polack in the United States" (*Journal of American Folklore*, 84 [April–June 1971]: 193–99): concern with mercantile trade and money, desire for professionalism and status, and pride in Jewish heritage and fear of losing ethnic identity. As Dundes shows, "the principal mercenary and status-seeking elements of the Jewish stereotype are not to be found to any great extent" in jokes about Poles and other ethnic minorities. Thus, Dundes suggests that Jewish stereotypes "may have some basis in ethnographic fact. If Jews are at all materialistic, if Jews do stress family solidarity, if Jews are ambitious in terms of the careers of their children, then these slurs serve to reinforce the group's value system," for most of these jokes are told and appreciated by Jews as well as by gentiles (p. 202).

On the other hand, it has been argued that ethnic humor is dysfunctional since it has the potential for promoting conflict between groups. While the jokes that Dundes discusses and the ones that follow may be rather bland and harmless, other traditional material might be vicious and hostile. As Nathan Hurvitz has stressed in "Blacks and Jews in American Folklore" (*Western Folklore*, 33 [October 1974]: 324–25), tolerating "the bland and amusing may foster a permissive atmosphere for the expression of the vicious and hostile" and "create cleavages between groups that must work together." Still, as Dundes counters, "the slurs are used by the folk whether the folklorist studies them or not . . . and an objective analysis of the stereotypes contained therein could do no harm and might possibly do a great deal of good in fighting bigotry and prejudice" (p. 203). Since jokes provide outlets for aggressions engendered by the conflicts and frustrations of living with others, Dundes probably is right.

254
Virgin Wool

A Jewish woman goes into a store to buy a dress. She asks the saleslady the price of a particular dress. The saleslady tells her that the dress costs $150. Then the Jewish woman, being tight with her money, says, "Another store down the street has the same dress for $50. What's the difference?" Then the saleslady says, "But, madam, our dress is made of virgin wool." "So," says the Jewish lady, "who cares what the sheep do at night?"

255
Doing It the Jewish Way

A man goes to the door of a cathouse and asks the madam if any of the girls know how to do it the Jewish way. The madam thinks he is joking and slams the door in his face. This happens to him about six times, until finally a girl overhears him asking the madam and says, "Wait a minute; I've never tried it the Jewish way. I'll do it for nothing." The man says, "See, you're catching on already!"

256
The Crafty Rabbi

Three members of the clergy go up to the old philanthropist, and each of them asks him for a million dollars for each of their respective churches. The old fellow says, "Yeah, under one condition; when I die you must replace the money in my casket." A few years later at the funeral service for the old fellow, the Catholic priest walks up, tears in his eyes, and places a million dollars in the casket. He's followed by the Methodist minister who tearfully places a million dollars in the old codger's casket. The Jewish rabbi walks up, smile on his face, places a three million dollar check in the casket and takes the change.

257
Who's Minding the Store?

There was this old Jewish man, and he was dying. He and his family lived on top of a grocery store, which they owned. As he laid on his bed, he said, "Is my oldest son, Isaac, here?" "Yes, Poppa, I'm here." "Is my oldest daughter, Ruth, here?" "Yes, Poppa, I'm here." "Is my second oldest son, Joseph, here?" "Yes, Poppa, I'm here." "Is my second oldest daughter, Sara, here?" "Yes, Poppa, I'm here." "Is my youngest son, Abraham, here?" "Yes, Poppa, I'm here." "Is my youngest, Ester, here?" "Yes, Poppa, I'm here." "Is my beloved wife of 40 years here?" "Yes, dear, I'm here." "Then who the hell is minding the store?"

258
The Jew's Wishes

Did you ever hear the story about the two Jews that lived in Palestine? Of course, these two Jews are very devoted to their religion, and they are very much devoted to one another. One of them is named Jacob, and the other is named Isaac. So one day the angel came over and was talking to Jacob. He said, "Jake, you know your prayers have been heard very much, and the Lord sent me over here to see what you would like to have." Jake started asking for money by the million, but the angel said, "Wait a minute. Whatever we grant or give you, Isaac gets double." So he says, "All right, I'll tell you what I would like to have. I'd like to have a castle with fifty rooms, the finest that was ever made." The angel said, "Granted, but there are two castles for Isaac."

Next couple or three days he comes back again and says, "All right, you've got the castle. What do you want to have in that castle?" He says, "I'd like to have fifty of the most beautiful women ever created." He says, "Well, that's fine, but Ike gets a hundred." So that was granted. Two or three days later, the angel comes back and said, "Now, Jake, now you've got the castle and the women. What would you like to have now? He says, "I'd like for you to remove one of my nuts."

259
Bargaining with the Devil

There once was a Negro, a Jew and a Polack who were all in a car accident and died. They went to hell, and it was so crowded that the devil said if they paid him $5.00 apiece they could all return to the living. The Polack pulled out $5.00 and left. He met someone who knew him, and the guy said, "I thought you died and went to hell. Where are the other two guys?" He explained the $5.00 deal with the devil and said, "The Negro was telling the devil he'd pay him on Saturday night, and Jew was trying to talk him into letting him go for $4.95.

260
The Boss's Relation

A Baptist minister died and went to heaven. He met St. Peter at the gate, and Peter says to him, "You've been a minister and a good man. You sacrificed and worked hard, so I'm going to reward you." So Peter gives him a Ford Falcon. Next a Catholic priest enters, and Peter says to him, "You've sacrificed all of your life. You didn't marry and were a good man, so I'm going to reward you." So he gives him a Cadillac. Next a Methodist minister comes in, and he was right behind the priest and heard Peter give the priest a Cadillac. Peter says, "You've sacrificed and lived a good life, so I'm going to reward you." So he gives him a Chevy Nova. The Methodist says, "Well, the priest got a Cadillac. Why do I only get a Chevy Nova." And Peter answered, "Well, the priest gave up more. He didn't marry, and he sacrificed more than you." So the Methodist minister was satisfied, and he was walking down the street when he saw a Jewish rabbi go by in a Lincoln Continental. He hurried back to Peter and asked why the rabbi had the Lincoln and he only got a Chevy Nova. Peter says, "He's related to the boss."

261

One of Our Boys Made It

There was this Catholic and Jew sitting at a bar. They were talking about their families. The Catholic said, "My boy just graduated from high school, and I'm really proud of him. He's going to a seminary to become a priest." The Jew then said, "Big deal, buddy, I could really care less if your son's going to become a priest or not." The Catholic then says, "Just think of it; if he's a good priest, he can go on to become a bishop!" The Jew says, "So your son's a bishop; I could care less." The Catholic says, "If he's a good bishop, he can go on and become a cardinal maybe!" The Jews replies, "I don't even know what a cardinal is and could care a lot less." The Catholic says, "Then if he's really good, he can go on and become a pope someday." The Jew says, "The Pope has never done anything for me." The Catholic says, "Well, who do you want him to be, Jesus Christ?" "Why not?" asked the Jew. "One of our boys made it!"

262

Walking on Water

Well, there were three men in a boat: a Catholic priest, a Protestant minister, and a Jewish rabbi. And the Catholic and the Protestant decided to get out of the boat and walk across the lake. Well, the rabbi wanted to prove he could do this, too, so he stepped out of the boat, and he sank in the water. And the Catholic said to the Protestant, "Joe sure didn't know where the stumps were, did he?"

263

Better than Pork

There is a priest and a rabbi riding together on a train. The priest says to the rabbi, "You aren't allowed to taste pork, are you?" The rabbi answers, "No." The priest says, "Well, between you and me, have you ever tasted it?" The rabbi answers, "Well, between you and me, yes, I've tasted pork." The train moves on and the rabbi asks the priest, "You believe in celibacy don't you?" The priest answers, "Yes." The rabbi asks, "Well, between you and me, have you ever had sex with a woman?" The priest answers, "Well, between you and me, I have had some sex." The rabbi answers, "It sure is a hell of a lot better than pork, isn't it?"

264

Three for Ten

There was a rabbi and a priest, and the rabbi asked the priest if he wanted to go golfing. The priest said, "Yeah, I sure would like to go golfing except that I've got to hear confessions today. And I've also got to write a sermon for tomorrow, so I won't have time." The rabbi thought a minute, and he said, "Well, why don't I listen to the confessions and you write the sermon, and then we'll still have enough time to go golfing." So the priest said, "Well, okay, but you'll have to listen to me to find out how it's done."

So they both went into the confessional booth, and the first man comes in. He says, "Father, bless me, for I have committed adultery three times this week." The father says, "That will be ten dollars, please." So the man pays it, and he leaves. Second man comes in. He says, "Father, I went to the house of ill fame three times this week." Father says, "That will be ten dollars, please." And the second man leaves.

So the rabbi says, "Yeah, I get the hang of this. You go write your sermon. I can take over. I'll do just fine." So the third man comes in. He says, "Father, I committed adultery this week one time. So the rabbi says, "Well, go away. It's three for ten this week."

265
The Rabbi Attends Mass

This rabbi knew this preacher or minister who was Catholic. And he wanted to find out how they did things, so the minister said, "Well, come on down Sunday." So I guess the rabbi did, 'cause then he was talking to his assistant or somebody who asked him what happened. And the rabbi said, "Well, they were gamblin'." "Gamblin'?" "Yeah, this guy in a white robe stood up in front and said, "Betcha I can beatcha at a game of dominoes." And the people said, "Betcha can't!" And then he passed around a plate and took up the bets!"

266
Jewish Christmas

A Methodist, a Catholic and a Jew were all asked how they celebrate Christmas. The Methodist said he and his family sang carols and gathered around the Christmas tree to exchange presents. The Catholic said he and his family lit candles and sang. The Jew looked at them, thought a minute, then replied that he and his family gathered around the cash register and sang "What a Friend We Have in Jesus."

267
The Jew Who Converted to Catholicism

There was this Jew that moved into the Catholic neighborhood, and every Friday he would go out on the barbeque grill and grill steaks. Well, at that time all the Catholics in this neighborhood couldn't eat meat on Friday, so after several Fridays the Catholics appointed a delegation to go down and talk to this Jew and try to smooth things over and talk him out of broiling steaks on Friday. So they went down there, and they found out he was Jewish, and they figured they couldn't do anything about it except talk him into becoming Catholic. So they told him all the good points of Catholicism, and really talked it up, and finally he agreed to take catechism to become a Catholic.

So finally the big day arrived where he was going to be baptized a

Catholic. All the Catholics in the neighborhood are there, and the bishop comes in and goes through his little ritual, and he says, "You were born a Jew; you were raised a Jew; you are now a Catholic."

Well, the next Friday rolls around, and the ex-Jew, now Catholic, comes home from work, puts on his sports clothes, goes out to the grill and flops a couple of big steaks on, and starts broiling them. Well, the aroma starts drifting all over the Catholic neighborhood, and all of a sudden, a delegation of Catholics appear from nowhere, and they say, "You can't broil meat! You can't eat meat on Friday! You're a Catholic now!" Well, the Jew looks at the Catholics, looks back at the steaks, and then looks back at the Catholics, and looks at the steaks, and he says, "You were born a steak; you were raised a steak; you are now a fish."

268

The Last Wish

Three men lay dying in a hospital ward. Their doctor, making rounds, went up to the first and asked him his last wish. The patient was a Catholic. "My last wish," he murmured, "is to see a priest and make confession." The doctor assured him he would arrange it and moved on. The second patient was a Protestant. When asked his last wish, he replied, "My last wish is to see my family and say good-bye." The third patient was, of course, a Jew. "And what is your last wish?" the doctor asked. "My last wish," came the feeble, hoarse reply, "is to see another doctor."

Catholics

RELIGIOUS JOKES are very popular in the contemporary oral tradition. As Barre Toelken points out in *The Dynamics of Folklore* (Boston: Houghton Mifflin, 1979), "If we were to list the most common jokes told in our culture, I believe we could relate most of them to anxieties, threats, and concerns felt by different groups at different, noticeable periods of time in our history. Probably the bulk of American jokes concern sex, politics, religion, and ethnicity—just the very subjects that cause us continual malaise in conversation, the topics our mothers told us never to discuss in public" (p. 270). Religious jokes are by no means a modern invention, though. In medieval satire, hypocritical and lecherous parish priests, monks, and friars were stock characters. Today priests and nuns who fail to uphold their vows of poverty, obedience, and chastity are the butt of similar jokes. Clerical incontinence especially was a popular theme in medieval fabliaux, and it remains a dominant motif in the tales presented below.

269

The Nervous Priest's First Mass

There was this new priest, and it was his first time to give Mass, so he was a little nervous, you know. He began swinging his rosary, and

156

pretty soon he began seeing people going like this [The informant reels her head slowly and closes her eyes halfway]. "Well," he figures, "I've got them hypnotized. I'll try something." So he says, "Everyone put five dollars in the collection basket." And they did. He said, "Well, I've got something going here, so I'll ask for ten dollars next week."

So next week he started swinging his rosary again, and the people started going like this [The informant reels her head slowly and closes her eyes halfway]. And he asked for ten dollars. Sure enough, everyone put in ten dollars, so he says, "I'm going to make some money here. Next week I'm going to ask for twenty dollars." So next week he started swinging his rosary, and it broke. He said, "Shit!" And it took them three months to clean out the church.

270

Everyone in the Parish Will Die

During a sermon the priest said, "Everyone in this parish will die." A man sitting in the front pew just laughed out loud. The priest repeated, "Everyone in this parish will die." Again the man laughed. Finally the priest asked him what was so funny. The man replied, "I'm not from this parish."

271

The Priest's Three Conditions

This Catholic priest had a permanent erection. And he went to mass every Sunday, and it showed in his pants. And he tried to hide it under an overcoat, but it seemed he was wearing an overcoat even in the summer trying to hide it. And another priest talked to him about his problem and told him he should do something about it. So this other priest told him to go to a doctor. The doctor told him he was perfectly normal and there wasn't anything he could do medically. "I won't charge you for an office call," the doctor said, "but the only thing I can suggest would be intercourse." But the priest said he couldn't do that.

So he started back to church every Sunday with the bulge in his pants. So the bishop found out about it, and the bishop called him in and told him he would have to do something about it. He said he had tried, but the only thing that the doctor had suggested was intercourse but he couldn't do that. The bishop told him he would give him a one time reprieve for doing it, but the priest didn't want to do this. So he asked the bishop if it was an order, and the bishop said it was so he could get this cleared up. If it was an order he would go along with it only on three conditions. The bishop said, "Okay, what are the conditions?" "One, she would have to be blind. I wouldn't want a woman to see a priest making love to her." The bishop said, "That's a pretty good thought. What's two?" "She would have to be completely sterile. I couldn't stand the thought of me making a woman pregnant." "I see you thought this out real good. That's a real good idea. What's three?" The priest said, "She has to have big tits; I'm crazy about big tits!"

272

Sure Is Dark in Here

One day a little boy walked into his mother's bedroom and saw his mother in bed with another man. The mother jumped up and said, "Son, go back outside and play." Well, at that time she heard her husband drive home. So she told the man to go stay in the closet and take her son with him. So the man and the little boy went and hid in the closet. The little boy started playing with some toys but then said, "Boy, sure is dark in here." The man was real nervous and gave the boy some money and told him to keep quiet and told him not to tell anyone who gave him the money. Well, later on the little boy said, "Boy, sure is dark in here." The man gave him some more money and told him to be quiet. This kept on until finally the husband left, and then the other man left.

The next day the little boy was out on the sidewalk counting his money when his father walked up and asked him where he got the money. The little boy told him that he promised not to tell. The father kept asking, and the little boy said that he couldn't tell. Finally, the father said that the little boy had to go to confession. So the father took the boy to the church, and the little boy went in the confessional booth. As the boy sat down, he said, "Boy, sure is dark in here." At that time the priest said, "Oh, no, I thought I got rid of you in the closet!"

273

The Pope's Reward

One day God decided to reward the priests and nuns according to how pure and sin-free their lives had been. So he sent down his chief angel to listen to the life stories of these people and give each of them a car on the basis of how virtuous they'd been. One nun confessed that she'd once had a love affair with a priest. "That's not too good for you, Sister," the angel remarked, "but since you have been good other than that one little slip, we'll give you a Chevy." Next, he talked to a priest, who admitted he'd had several affairs, one with the mother superior. The angel thought a minute, then said, "Well, that's a bit more serious. I think we can only give you a VW." This continued for several days. One day a priest driving a Buick saw another priest on a bicycle. "Man, you really must have had a swinging time," the Buick owner remarked, laughing. "Swinging time, hell," the other remarked, "you should see the Pope on his roller skates!"

274

The Priest and the Profane Mechanic

This car mechanic was fixing a priest's car, and he mashed his finger with a car wrench. He yells, "Goddamn it, son of a bitch!" And the priest says, "No, my son, you mustn't say that. Say 'Lord help me'." Then the tire fell off the car, and the mechanic yells, "Goddamn it, son of a bitch!" And the priest says, "My son, don't talk like that. Ask forgiveness and say, 'Jesus bless me!'" Then the car falls on him, and he says, "O Lord, please help me. Don't let me die, O Jesus." All of a sudden, the car goes back up, and his body heals, and he's okay. And the priest says, "Son of a bitch!"

275
Missed Again

One day this nun and priest decided to go out and play golf together. This priest had a terrible habit of cursing whenever he goofed up. They went to the first hole, and as the priest swung at the ball, he missed it. Then he got really mad and yelled, "Shit!" The nun said, "Father, you're going to have to quit that cussing if you want me to play with you." They kept on playing, and pretty soon the priest missed again. This time he yelled, "I missed again, goddamn it!" The nun looked at him and said that God was going to punish him one of these days for his terrible language. Well, the next time the priest hit the ball, it went in the water. He yelled, "Goddamn, I missed that son of a bitching hole again!" Just then a bolt of lightning came down from the sky and struck the nun dead, right there on the green. A voice from the sky then said, "Goddamn, I missed again!"

276
What's a Quickie?

This priest is walking down the alley, and a prostitute walks up to him and says, "Hey, Father, just "$2.50 a quickie." Priest says, "Oh, no, no, my child." He walks down a little farther, and a second prostitute asks him, "Father, want a quickie? Just $2.50." Father says, "Oh, no, no, my child." Gets to the end of the alley and sees a prostitute leaning on a lamp post. The prostitute says, "$2.50 a quickie, honey." Father says, "Oh, no, no, my child." Father gets back to the parish house and is walking down the hall when he passes a nun. He asks, "Sister, what's a quickie?" Nun says, "$2.50, Father; same as downtown!"

277
The Creator of Life

There was a nun and a priest going across a desert on a camel. Finally, the camel died, and the nun and priest were left on foot. The priest then looked at the nun and said, "Sister, I've never seen a nude nun before." The nun then looked at the priest and said, "Priest, I've never seen a nude priest before." So they both took off their clothes, and the nun looked at the priest and asked, "What's that between your legs?" So the priest says, "That's the creator of life." At that, the nun said, "Well, hell, stick it in that camel, and let's get the hell out of here!"

278
The Key to the Golden Gate

You heard the one 'bout the nuns that took turns each day washin' the Pope's back? See, they washed the Pope's back, you know, and so this one nun goes in, and it was her turn to wash his back. He told her, "Okay," he says, "whatever you do, don't look over my shoulder." So she's settin' there washin' his back, and she looks over his shoulder. Says, "My God!" She says, "What is that, sir? What is that there?" And he says, "That's the key to the Golden Gate. If you'll lay down, I'll unlock your Golden Gate."

So things went on, you know, and she went out, and this old nun comes up to her, and she says, "How'd it go? How'd it go?" And she says, "I looked over his shoulder." She says, "You what? You looked over his shoulder?" And she says, "Yeah, I looked over his shoulder." Says, "What'd he tell you?" Says, "Oh, he told me it was the key to the Golden Gate, and he laid me down and unlocked my Golden Gate." She says, "Well, that lying son of a bitch told me it was Peter Pan's horn, and I've been blowin' it for fifteen years!"

279
What the Nuns Found in the Priest's Room

Three nuns were cleaning the priest's room, and the first nun says to the other two, "Do you know what I found under Father Michael's pillow? A vile, dirty, filthy pornographic magazine." "Oh, no, not that!" cried the other two nuns. "Yes, but don't worry. I took care of that right away; I burned the awful thing." "Oh, good," the others said. The second nun said, "Do you know what I found in Father Michael's right-hand drawer? One of those awful, dirty, disgusting, disgraceful, lewd, sinful condoms." "Oh, no, not that! Oh, that's awful," the other nuns said. They were really upset. "Oh, don't worry; I took care of that. I cut the end off of that disgusting, horrible thing." The third nun passed out.

280

The Nuns' Penance

There was this nun. She went to the Pope, and she goes, "Father, I've just seen a part of the man's body that really I never should have seen at all." So the Pope goes, "Well, just go into the back room of the church there and wash your eyes with holy water, and you will be saved." So she goes back in there and starts washing her eyes out. So another nun comes in. She says, "Father, I've just touched a part of the man's body that . . . I've really sinned. I shouldn't have ever done it, but I've touched it, and I really don't know what to do." And he goes, "Sister, just go into the back room and wash your hands in holy water, and you will be saved." So, you know, the one nun's back there; she's washin' her eyes out. And the next nun, she's back there washin' her hands with holy water. And, boy, there they are just a-scrubbin' away. The one's just scrubbin' away, and the other's flippin' that holy water right in her eyes! 'Bout that time they hear, "Gangway, girls! I've gotta gargle!"

281

Mother Superior's Laxative

A nun went into a bar and said to the bartender, "I want to buy a bottle of scotch." The bartender says, "Why would you want to buy liquor, Sister?" The nun answered that the mother superior used it for a laxative. After he got off work, the bartender was driving, and he saw the nun wrapped around the lamp post, really stinking drunk. He said, "But I thought the liquor was for Mother Superior." She said, "It is. When she finds out that I drank that scotch, she'll shit."

282
Mother Superior's Guidance

There was this Catholic mother superior at a Catholic girls' school. And one day she called three of her little pupils together to ask them about their future careers. The first little girl said, "Oh, Mother Superior, I want to be a nurse so I can help mankind." The mother superior was very pleased at this answer. The second little girl replied that she wanted to be a teacher, so she could educate the people of the world. This answer also pleased the mother superior. "Oh, I'm so proud of you girls."

Then she turned to the third student. "And what do you want to be, dear?" The little girl answered, "Oh, Mother, I want to be a prostitute, because then I'll be able to help mankind, too." The mother superior was so horrified that she fainted. After she was revived, she again asked the little girl, to make sure she had heard her right. And the little girl again said she wanted to be a prostitute. "Oh, thank God," the mother superior sighed, "I thought you said you wanted to be a Protestant!"

283
The Nun Teaches Spelling

There was this nun, and she had a spelling class. She asked each of the kids to spell a word. The first little girl stands up and says, "My name is Mary Smith, and I'm going to spell cat. Cat—C-A-T." The next little girl gets up and says, "My name is Linda Jones, and I'm going to spell dog. Dog—D-O-G." The nun says, "That's fine, Linda. Next." This little boy gets up and says, "My name is Jesus Christ Allen, and I'm going to spell pig. Pig—P-I-G." The nun says then, "That's fine, Jesus, but when the priest comes in, just tell him your name is J. C. 'cause that's shorter and won't take so much time."

The next day, Father John comes in, and the first little girl stands up and says, "My name is Mary Smith, and I'm going to spell cat. Cat—C-A-T." Father John says, "That's fine, Mary." The next little girl stands up and says, "My name is Linda Jones, and I'm going to spell dog. Dog—D-O-G." Father John says, "That's really excellent,

Linda." The little boy stands up then and says, "My name is J. C. Allen, and I'm going to spell aluminum." The nun says, "Jesus Christ, you can't spell that." And the priest says, "Well, goddamn, Sister, let him try!"

284

The Nun and the Little Boy

A little boy was going down the street crossing himself. A nun walked by and saw him making the sign of the cross and thought, "What a nice little boy." She said to him, "Does your mother send you to church all of the time?" "No, she just sent me to the store, and I'm trying to remember what she wanted—a head of lettuce, two jugs of milk and a package of wieners."

285

More Powerful than Holy Water

A small boy was sitting on a curb, shaking a bottle of turpentine, watching it foam. The pastor of his church happened to come by and asked him what he was doing. The boy held up the bottle of turpentine and replied, "This is the most powerful liquid in the whole world." The preacher said, "No, son, holy water is the most powerful liquid in the world. You can sprinkle a drop of it on a pregnant woman's belly, and she will pass a baby boy." The boy just looked up at the preacher and said, "That's nothing. You put a drop of this on a cat's ass, and it will pass a motorcycle."

 *Preachers*

In *No Laughing Matter* (Bloomington: Indiana University Press, 1968), G. Legman maintains that "the very few jokes still to be encountered accusing the ministry of immorality, indicate by their small numbers . . . the very great decay into which religion has fallen in the last century. In the centuries when the gentry and the clergy were at the height of their power, it was the gentry and the clergy about whom the sexual accusations of the folktale were made to center" (vol. I, p. 417). In *Black Culture and Black Consciousness* (New York: Oxford University Press, 1977), Lawrence W. Levine agrees with Legman about the decline of religion, but he reaches a different conclusion about the popularity of religious jokes in the modern oral tradition. Levine says, "The decline of the sacred world view was reflected throughout the twentieth century in the proliferation of jokes at the expense of religion" (p. 326). Admittedly, Levine is speaking only of black American culture, but what he says about religious jokes applies to white American culture, too. Both blacks and whites sense "the hypocrisy and dishonesty of the 'respectable' world around them" and project these qualities onto the figure of the preacher, "whose lofty pretensions were constantly pictured as being undermined by his compulsive lust for chicken, liquor, money, and women" (p. 326).

286

There Are No Lutherans There

Two Lutheran ministers were at a ballgame, and these two guys were sitting behind them, and these two guys didn't like Lutherans and were trying to get rid of the two ministers. The first guy said, "I think I'm going to Arkansas 'cause there's only 500 Lutherans there." And the ministers just sat there and didn't turn around or say anything. After a while, the second guy says, "I'm going to Africa 'cause there's only 20 of those goddamn Lutherans there." Still, the ministers didn't turn around or say anything. So during the whole ballgame the two guys kept insulting Lutherans and everything. Finally, one of the ministers turned around and said, "Why don't you go to hell; there are no Lutherans there!"

287

The Preacher Who Didn't Know His Ass

There is a community in the Andes Mountains. And there is no cars, so their only means of power and transportation is their asses. Well, everyone in the town has an ass. There are small asses, round asses, and fat asses. But the preacher's wife has the prettiest ass in the whole town. Also everyone in the town has to keep track of their own asses. Well, one day the preacher is delivering his message at church, and everyone has brought his ass. All of the sudden the church catches on fire, and the preacher screams for everyone to get their asses and get out of the building. Everyone is scrambling around, and they can't find their asses. Finally everyone gets hold of their own ass and gets out of the building. The preacher jumps out the window of the church and lands in a well. And this just goes to show you the preacher don't know his ass from a hole in the ground.

288

The First Sermon

This young minister, he was going to give his first sermon. He was real scared. There was an older minister there, too. The young one was real scared and asked the other one, "What shall I do?" He said to put this bottle of whiskey in your side pocket, and whenever you get nervous, just turn around and take a little swig.

So he started giving the sermon the next Sunday, and pretty soon he started getting nervous, so he turned around and took a little swig. He talked a little longer before he started getting nervous again. Then he turned around and took another swig. After a while, he was real nervous, so he just turned around and chugged the whole bottle. Then he turned around and started giving the sermon again.

He thought he was doing real good, but all the people started leaving, and the only one left was the old minister who was just laughing and laughing. The young minister said he couldn't understand what he did wrong. The old minister said, "Well, there's four main things wrong." First, David slew Goliath, not beat the shit out of him. You don't call Jesus Christ, J. C. Jesus rode to town on an ass, not looking for some. And it's a taffy pull at St. Peter's, not a peter pull at St. Taffy's.

289

Preacher's Sermon Saves Man

After discovering that he had lost his hat, a man decided the simplest way to replace it was to go to church and steal one from the entry. Once inside, he heard a sermon on the Ten Commandments. At the end of the service he said to the minister, "I want you to know that you saved me from crime. I came in here with sin in my heart. I was going to steal a hat. But after hearing your sermon, I changed my mind." "What did I say to change your mind?" asked the minister. "When you got to the part about 'Thou shalt not commit adultery,' I remembered where I left my hat."

290

The Preacher's Lesson

Once there was a man who fell asleep in church during the sermon every Sunday. The minister noticed this and thought he would teach this man a lesson by asking a question. So he said to him, "Mr. Brown, who is our Father in heaven?" Mr. Brown's wife took her hat pin and stuck him. Mr. Brown felt this and yelled, "God!" But he soon fell asleep again. The minister again decided to ask a question. He said, "Mr. Brown, who is our Savior?" Mrs. Brown again stuck him with her hat pin. He cried, "Jesus Christ!" The same thing happened again. The minister said, "Mr. Brown, what did Eve say after she had her thirteenth child?" Mrs. Brown stuck him with her hat pin, and he yelled, "If you stick me with that thing again I'll break it off!"

291

The Preacher Acts It Out

One day a girl came in the house and said, "Goddamn!" Her mother said, "Darling, you are not supposed to say that. I am going to tell your father." When her father got home, she said, "Goddamn!" Her father says, "Dear, you are not supposed to say that. I am going to tell the minister on you." They go to the minister, and the minister says, "Now, honey, why are you upset?" She stumbles. Then he says, "Let's act it out." She said, "I went out with my boyfriend in his convertible car." The minister says, "Let's get my convertible, and let's go out." "He was driving down the highway, and he turned off the main road." So the minister did the same. "We got out of the car and went over to the bushes." The minister and the girl did the same. "He started kissing me." So the minister kissed her. "He pulled down my panties." And the minister did the same. "Then we got back in the car." And the minister said, "Goddamn!"

292

The Preacher and the Little Boy

One day there was this preacher sitting on his front porch. A little boy walked by, and the preacher said, "Son, what's that you got in your jar?" "A horsefly," said the little boy. "What are you gonna do with it?" said the preacher. "Trade it for a horse," said the little boy. Later that day the little boy comes by with a horse. The next day the little boy walks by, and the preacher asked him what he had in his jar this time. "Cream. I'm going to trade for butter." Later that day the little boy came back by with some butter. The next day the little boy walked by the preacher again. The preacher asked him what he had in his jar this time, and the little boy said, "A cockroach." The preacher then said, "Wait a minute, son. Let me get my hat, and I'll go with you!"

293

Three Preachers Confess Their Sins

There were once three preachers who got together and confessed their sins to each other. The first preacher said, "Well, my sin is women. I just have a weakness for women, and I find it very hard to overcome." The second preacher said, "Well, you know, I have a little taste for liquors . . . alcoholic, and I just really enjoy taking a little nip now and then." The two preachers turned to the third preacher who was very quiet and said, "What is your sin since we are all confessing to each other?" The third man looked at the other two and said, "Well, you know, my sin is gossip, and I just can't wait to get out of here and tell someone."

294

Lining a Hymn

In the old days when hymn books were scarce the preacher would read two lines of a hymn, and the chorister would lead in the singing—the singers of the congregation falling in, one after the other, until by the time the end of the two lines were reached, most of them would be singing. It was this custom that gave rise to an incident that has been credited to many a congregation.

One night the preacher arose and said, "I cannot see to read the hymn. I left my specs behind." The chorister, quick to act, put the words to a long metered tune, and the congregation trailed in. As the last note sounded, the preacher was quite irritated and said, "I did not mean that for a hymn; I only said my eyes were dim." But to no avail. The words sounded good to the singers, and they went right ahead singing the second couplet: "I did not mean that for a hymn,/I only said my eyes were dim."

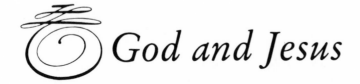# God and Jesus

PEOPLE WHO TELL religious jokes are not necessarily agnostics and atheists. In fact, those who appreciate religious jokes may be deeply religious. As G. Legman says in *No Laughing Matter* (Bloomington: Indiana University Press, 1975), "People who tell anti-clerical jokes . . . or who express themselves sacrilegiously concerning God and the clergy are not necessarily irreligious people, nor do their jests and mockeries, however broad, necessarily express any serious anti-religious feelings. More often, and profoundly, it is the reverse: the underlying emotion is actually that of a deep religiosity, for which the jokes and mockery serve as a way of letting off steam" (vol. II, p. 760). Thus, jokes about God or Jesus may be told by religious people to relieve them of the pressure of a too ideal model.

Some of the jokes about Jesus in this section are varieties of the modern sick joke. In the 1970s, a whole cycle of sick Jesus jokes developed, mostly in the form of short riddle jokes. (See the headnote to the section on Doctors, Nurses, and Patients for reference to other kinds of sick riddle jokes.) Some people find sick jokes especially offensive, but as Alan Dundes points out in his discussion of one sick joke cycle, "The Dead Baby Joke Cycle" (*Western Folklore,* 38 [July 1979]: 155), "Folklore is always a reflection of the age in which it flourishes and so whether we like it or not, the dead baby joke cycle is a reflection of American culture in the 1960s and 1970s. If we do not

171

like the image, we should not blame the mirror. If anything is sick, it is the society which produces sick humor."

295

God's Gift to Man

Adam is in the garden, and God has given him twenty years of normal sex life, and he's just not satisfied with these twenty years because he's using them up, and like the only person around is Eve, and so he's gotta get his kicks in. So he goes up to this monkey, and he says, "Monkey, how many years of sex life do you have?" And the monkey says, "Twenty, like you, but I only need ten." Adam goes, "Well, I wonder if I could have the other ten." The monkey goes, "Well, go back to God and ask Him." So he goes back to God, and God says, "Sure, Adam, you can have them."

So the next person he goes to is a tiger, and he says, "How many years of sex life do you have?" And the tiger says, "Twenty, but I only need ten." So he goes back to God, and God says, "Sure, you can have the other ten."

So the last one he goes to is the donkey, and he says, "Are you like all these others who have twenty years of sex life but only need ten?" And the donkey says, "Yeah." So he goes back to God, and he says, "Can I have the donkey's other ten years of sex life?" And God says, "Sure, Adam." And ever since then man has had twenty years of normal sex life, ten years of monkeying around, ten years to act like he's got a tiger in his tank, and the last ten years to act like an ass.

296

God Needs a Vacation

One day God was up in heaven talking to his main angel, Gabriel. He said, "Gabriel, I'd like to take a vacation this year, but I don't know where to go. Can you think of anywhere?" Gabriel thought a minute and said, "How about Venus?" God said, "No, it's too cold there this time of year." Then Gabriel said, "How about Jupiter?" God said,

"No, I went there last year." Finally Gabriel said, "I've got just the place for you to go, earth." God looked at Gabriel a minute and said, "How dumb can you be, Gabriel? You know I can't go there. I went down there about a million years ago. I knocked up some Jewish broad, and they're still talking about it."

297

God Helps Them Who Help Themselves

A man was kneeling in church, and he was praying to God. He says, "O God, give us world peace, freedom from starvation; stop the hatred and mistrust; let everyone love one another; keep the world population down; clear the smog from the cities, and stop the war." A puff of smoke appears, and a big voice booms out, "Do it yourself, you lazy bum!"

298

Why Me, God?

There was a man, and his wife died. Then his children burned to death when his house burned down. Then he got hit by a car and got his leg cut off. He went to church and fell on his knees and started crying. "O God, what did I do wrong? My wife died, then my children; my house burned, and then I got my leg cut off. O Lord, why me, why me?" And the voice of God thunders out, "'Cause you piss me off, that's why!"

299

God Thinks He's Bobby Knight

There was a basketball player from Indy who died and went to heaven. When he got to heaven he told St. Peter that it was all right that he died as long as they played basketball in heaven. St. Peter said they did, but instead of numbers on the jerseys they used letters. The man from Indy didn't understand, so St. Peter said he would just show him. When they got to the court he explained that the man with the "C" on his jersey was a center, the players with "G" were guards, and since the man from Indy was a forward he would have an "F" on his shirt. The player from Indy said he understood everything except who the man was with "BK" on his shirt. St. Peter just laughed and replied, "That's just God; he thinks he's Bobby Knight."

300

Oral Roberts Goes to Heaven

Oral Roberts died, so he was on his way up to heaven. And he got to the main gate, and there was Saint Peter. And Saint Peter says, "Hey, man, what's your name?" And he goes, "Well, I'm Oral Roberts." And Saint Peter goes, "Oral Roberts! Hey, man, we've heard of you up here. You know, you're pretty famous around here. I'll take you in to see Jesus here. You know, he might wanta talk to you."

So he took old Oral over to Jesus, and Jesus said, "Who's this man?" And Saint Peter said, "Well, that's Oral Roberts!" And Jesus said, "Man, I've heard of him; he's pretty well known around here. I'll tell you what; we'll take him in to see my dad here—God, you know."

So they took him in to see God, and here's Saint Peter and Jesus and Oral Roberts, you know. They come in here to see God. "Who is this man?" Jesus spoke up and said, "Well, Father, this is Oral Roberts." And God said, "Oral Roberts! I've heard of you. There's something you can do for me." And Oral Roberts says, "Well, I'll be glad to help wherever I can. What is it?" And God said, "I've got this pain here in my back."

301

Them Plaguey Indians

An old woman who lived near the frontier during our disturbance with Great Britain had possessed a marvelous propensity for learning the news and frequently used to make inquiries of the soldiers. On one occasion she called to a passing soldier whom she had frequently saluted before: "What's the news?"

"Why," said he, "the Indians have fixed a crowbar under Lake Erie, and are going to turn it over and drown the world." "Oh, massy, massy! What shall I do?" she cried, and ran away to tell the neighbors of the danger and inquire of her minister how such a calamity might be averted. "Why," says he, "you need not be alarmed; we have our Maker's promise that He will not again destroy the world by water."

"I know that," returned the old lady hastily, "but He's nothing to do with it; it's them plaguey Indians!"

302

How Jesus Was Named

You know how on Christmas cards with the three wise men on them, one wise man is taller than the others. Well, on Christmas Eve when they came to see the infant in the stable, the tallest wise man hit his head on the stable doorway. "Jesus Christ!" he shouted. Joseph turned to Mary and said, "Jot that down, Mary. I like that name better than Clyde."

303

He Who Is without Sin

Jesus was in Jerusalem. He saw a crowd of women throwing rocks at another woman, who was a harlot. They were stoning the shit out of her. It kinda bothered him, so he pushed through the crowd of women and stood in front of the harlot. He began quoting scriptures to them about "He who is without sin, cast the first stone," and one of the women from the back threw a stone and hit the harlot. He pushed his way back to the lady and said, "Mother, sometimes you really piss me off!"

304

I Love a Parade

The Romans had just won an important battle, and Caesar wanted to show his appreciation. They lined the Appian Way with Christians. The Roman legions, with trumpets blaring, marched down the street, and a general sees this man on a cross mumbling something. The general stopped the procession and rode his horse up to the cross. He can't understand what the man is saying, so he asks for a ladder and climbs closer to the man and asks him again what he said. The man mumbles again. The general gets even closer, asks him again, and hears the man on the cross humming, "I love a parade."

305

Jesus on the Cross

Jesus was up on the cross when he saw Peter in the crowd. He then called out and said, "Peter, come here." Peter fought his way through the crowd and said, "Yes, Lord?" However, the guards saw Peter, quickly grabbed him, cut off an arm, and threw him back into the crowd. Jesus called again, "Peter, come here." Peter once again fought his way through the crowd and was caught by the guards. This time the guards cut off his other arm and threw him back into the crowd. Jesus cried again, "Peter!" Peter again fought through the crowd with blood running from where his arms had been and said, "Yes, Lord?" Once again the guards grabbed him, cut off a leg, and threw him into the crowd. Jesus cried again, "Peter, where are you?" Peter hopped on his only leg through the mass of people and once again was caught by the guards, and his last leg was cut off. Then the guards threw him back into the crowd, and Jesus called again, "Peter, come quickly!" Peter clawed at the ground with his chin to drag his bloody stump of a body up the hill to the cross, and this time he made it to the cross because the guards were sorry for him. Peter looked up to Jesus and said, "Yes, Lord, what is it?" And Jesus said, "Peter, I can see your house from up here."

306

Pull out the Nails

It was the day of the crucifixion. J. C. was on the cross, and there was a little kid there who really felt sorry for Jesus. The little kid pushed his way up through the crowd to the cross and asked, "Jesus, is there anything I can do for you?" Christ looked down at him and said, "Yes." The kid said, "What is it?" Jesus said, "Do you see the nails in my hands?" The kid said, "Yes." Jesus said, "Pull out the nails." The kid said, "Okay." He went and got a ladder, climbed up on the right side, and pulled the nail out of his right hand. The kid asked again, "Is there anything else I can do?" Jesus replied, "Pull out the nail in the left hand." The kid did it and said, "Now is there anything else I can do?" Jesus replied, "Get the FEET!" [Informant plants feet and, with arms extended from each side, falls forward.]

307

The Second Coming

Jesus Christ thought he would come back and see how he would be received a second time, so he went first to the priest's home, and disguised himself as a dirty old beggar, and knocked at the door. The priest answered the door and let Jesus in. Jesus said, "I'm Jesus Christ, and I would like some food and a place to stay." So the priest fell on his knees and kissed Jesus' feet and gave him food and a place to rest. He received him with great hospitality. The next day, Jesus went to the Protestant minister's home and said, "I'm Jesus Christ, and I would like some food and a bed." So the minister fell on his knees and cried and hugged Jesus and gave him food and a place to rest. The next day, Jesus went to the synagogue and knocked on the door. The rabbi answered, and Jesus said, "I'm Jesus Christ, and I would like some food and a bed." The rabbi turned around and yelled, "Hey, Mack, get the cross! The troublemaker's back!"

Salesmen and Other Travelers

OLD BRITISH BALLADS like "The Broomfield Hill" (Child 43), "The Knight and the Shepherd's Daughter" (Child 110), and "The Baffled Knight" (Child 112) deal with the seduction, or the attempted seduction, of a shepherdess by a wandering knight. In more recent treatments of this popular theme in folk literature, the feudal setting disappears, and the characters are modernized. The knight becomes a soldier or sailor, and the shepherdess becomes an innocent country girl. For instance, one American ballad, "The Fair Maid by the Seashore"—apparently from a British broadside and certainly a close analogue, if not merely a modernization, of "The Broomfield Hill"— is about the attempted seduction of a maiden by a sea captain. Jokes about traveling salesmen and farmer's daughters are contemporary descendants of the old pastourelles dealing with the seduction of a shepherdess by a roving knight.

The traveling salesman, then, is but one name for an Outsider viewed as a potential interloper, a threat to conjugal rights. As Barre Toelken points out in *The Dynamics of Folkore* (Boston: Houghton Mifflin, 1979), the traveling salesman joke is not really about salesmen. Toelken suggests that the traveling salesman in contemporary jokes is "perhaps the symbol of that marital threat felt by many men, also experienced to some extent in movie characters like Shane. . . . These homeless wanderers move into other people's towns, sometimes

178

solving the local problem, often threatening the men and entrancing the women. It is important to note that the traveling salesman is outrageously funny only insofar as he remains in the joke; if he arrives on our front doorstep, the joke is over" (pp. 270–71).

308

The Traveling Salesman Gets Lost

A traveling salesman got lost one day out in the country. After a while he saw a boy mowing along a fence row, so he stopped and said, "Where's the nearest town?" The boy answered, "I don't know." The salesman then asked, "Where's the nearest bus station?" The boy answered, "I don't know." Frustrated, the salesman asked, "Where's the nearest phone?" The boy answered, "I don't know." The salesman then got mad and said, "You sure don't know much, do you?" The boy answered, "I may not know much, but I sure as hell ain't lost!"

309

The Salesman and the Little Boy

There was this little boy who went to the door because someone was at the door. It was a salesman that asked if his mother was there. The little boy said no, and the salesman asked where she was. The little kid said she was down at the whorehouse. The salesman asked, "Is she a prostitute?" And the little boy answered, "No, a substitute." The salesman stood there a long time, and then he goes, "Well, I'll be a son of a bitch." The little boy said, "Well, I am too, but I don't go around telling people."

310

The Thirsty Traveler

Once there was a man traveling along a deserted road, and he was hungry and very, very thirsty. He finally came upon an old rundown farmhouse. He knocked at the door, but no one answered. So he walked to the back, and there was a bedraggled, dirty old woman with horrible rotten teeth and her young grandson. The man asked for a drink of water, and they pointed to the water pail on the back porch. He went onto the porch and felt kinda sick thinking he would be drinking after that filthy old woman, so he turned the dipper upside down and drank through the handle. The little boy, who had followed him, said, "That's funny. Grandma drinks out of our dipper that way, too."

311

Out for Blood

There was a bean salesman driving down the highway one day when he noticed this big barn that had one side facing the highway that would be just perfect for a billboard. So he stopped, and he asked the farmer if he would accept fifty dollars a month for him to advertise on the side of this barn. And the farmer thought, "Well, that sounds pretty good; I might as well let him do it." So he said, "Okay," and the salesman went away.

And a couple of days later a Kotex salesman drove down the road, and he noticed the same barn. And he stopped and talked to the same farmer, and he offered him a hundred dollars a month to put a sign on the side of the barn. And the farmer thought about it, and then he said, "Well, listen, the only thing I don't understand is a bean sales- man came down the road the other day, and he only offered me fifty dollars and you offer me a hundred. Why is that?" And the Kotex salesman said, "Well, those bean people are just fartin' around, but we're out for blood."

312

Keeping Score

One night this traveling salesman was having trouble out in the country with his car, so he went up to this farmhouse and asked the farmer if he could spend the night and then fix his car in the morning.

The old farmer told him he could stay there, but he would have to sleep with his daughter. So he said he didn't mind. He went into the bedroom, and there was the most gorgeous girl he had ever seen. So a little later, the girl just wanted him so badly that the salesman just had to oblige her. But the daughter said, "You had better go in and see if my pop is asleep." So he went in, and the old farmer was laying there in the nude, so he pulled a hair out of the old farmer's ass. The old farmer didn't move a muscle, so he went back in and screwed the daughter. They got the urge about six times that night, but each time the salesman had to check to see if the farmer was asleep. Each time he pulled a hair out of the farmer's ass, and the farmer didn't move. So early in the morning, they got the urge again. So again the salesman went in and pulled a hair out of the farmer's ass. So the farmer rolled over and said, "I don't care if you screw my daughter, but I wish you'd quit using my ass for a scoreboard."

313

It's Just the Cat

There's these three traveling salesmen. Two of them are ex-football players from Indiana, and the other is a dumb Kentuckian. They're all riding in the same car to this business conference, and so happens they get lost. They come upon this old farmer's house, and it's getting kind of late, so they decide to stop and see if they could put them up for the night. They stop and ask, and the farmer says they can stay in the barn loft, just as long as they don't mess around with his daughter. They all agree and go to the barn for some sleep.

A few minutes later one of the men looks out the window and notices the farmer's daughter undressing by the window, so he takes this long board and puts it to her window and climbs across and screws her. He starts back across the board, gets halfway, and the farmer comes running out of the house with his shotgun and yells, "Who's up there?" And the ex-football player says, "Meow, meow." And the farmer says, "Oh, damn, it's just the cat," and goes back into the house.

He gets back, and the other football player goes across and screws the daughter. He starts running back across and gets halfway across, and the farmer comes running out with his shotgun and says, "Who's up there?" And the ex-football player replies with a meow, and the farmer says, "Oh, shit, it's just that damn cat," and returns back to the house.

So the Kentuckian sees that both of them went and had a good time, so he decided to go. He got across and screwed the farmer's daughter. So he starts running back across, and once again, the farmer runs out with his shotgun and yells, "Who's up there?" And the Kentuckian says, "It's just the cat!"

314

The Naive Traveling Salesman

There was this traveling salesman, see, and his car broke down, so he had to look for a place to stay for the night. Well, he came to this farmhouse, and he asked the farmer if he would give him a place to sleep for the night. The farmer said sure, but the salesman would have to sleep with his daughter. The salesman said okay, and so they all went to bed. The farmer cautioned the salesman to avoid screwing his daughter.

The salesman and the young, beautiful daughter were in bed, and the girl scooted over next to him and began to fondle him. The salesman got up and went around the bed to lay on the other side. Once again, the daughter scooted over next to him and began to play with him. The salesman got up, went around the end of the bed, and laid down on the other side. This time the daughter scooted over, played with the salesman and asked, "Don't you know what I want?" The salesman said, "Hell, yes, you want the whole goddamn bed!"

315

The Traveling Salesmen's Punishment

There was these three traveling salesmen, and they had car trouble out by this farmer's house. They wanted to get it repaired, so they went up to the farmer's house and asked if they could use his phone. The farmer didn't have a phone, but offered to take them into town in the morning. So they asked if they could stay there, and the farmer said, "All right, but I don't want you bothering my daughter because that's the only room you can sleep in." So the old farmer went to bed, and sure enough the salesmen all screwed his daughter.

So the next morning the daughter told the farmer what had happened, and he got steaming mad. So he took the first guy out in the barn and said, "I want you to go pick ten of your favorite fruits or vegetables and bring them back here." So he went out and picked ten apples. The farmer then took 'em and stuffed 'em up the salesman's ass for punishment for screwing his daughter. The farmer then took the second salesman out to the barn and told him the same thing. The second salesman went out and picked ten oranges, and the farmer stuck them up his ass.

So the farmer then took the third salesman out to the barn and told him the same thing. The farmer then went to the house, and on his way back to the barn he saw the first two salesmen just laughing to beat hell. So he went over to them and said, "I thought your punishment was painful, so what are you laughing about?" The salesmen turned and said, "That damn poor George is out pickin' watermelons!"

316
The Broken Eggs

There was this traveling salesman. His car had broke down. And it was real bad outside and the middle of the night, so he went to this farmer's house. He told him his car had broke down and he needed a place to sleep. So the farmer said, "All right, you can sleep here, but the only place you can sleep is with my daughter. And I don't want you to screw her, or I'll kill you. To make sure, I'll put these eggs in bed between you, and if they're broken in the morning, I'll kill you." So the salesman got in bed, and the farmer placed the eggs between them. When the farmer left, the daughter started to tease him. And finally he couldn't take it anymore, so he rolled over and stuck it to her. They went on about it, and when they got done the daughter said, "What are we going to do? He'll kill you in the morning when he sees these eggs are broken." So the traveling salesman, he's pretty slick, so he picks up all the pieces and glued them back together, just perfect, so you couldn't tell the difference.

So the old farmer came in the next morning. They weren't broken at all, so he took them in and began preparing breakfast. Well, he opened this one egg, cracked it open, and there was nothing in it. So he took the other egg and cracked it open, and there was nothing in it. So he went and he grabbed his shotgun. Before you know it, he ran outside. He went to the hen house, and he said, "All right, which one of you goddamned roosters has been using rubbers?"

317

Hoosier Hospitality

This takes place in southern Indiana, and it goes like this. There's this traveling salesman passing through this part of Indiana, and his car broke down. He needed some kind of transportation, so he kept trying the car but finally gave up on it. So he walks up to this old farmhouse and tells the mister of the house that he needs a place to stay for the night or the next day until help could come. Well, the daughter of the house says, "Sir, you may stay here if you like." The man said, "That's mighty nice of you." She said, "Just call it Hoosier hospitality." So she fixed him a great big supper that night. He said, "That sure was a great supper. I don't know how I'll be able to thank you." The daughter said, " Don't think nothing of it, sir. This is just Hoosier hospitality."

So that night they were getting ready for bed, and he said, "You want me to sleep out in the barn?" The daughter said, "Oh, no, sir. You can sleep in this bed. It has nice clean sheets on it." He said, "That's awfully nice of you." She said, "Think nothing of it. It's just Hoosier hospitality." That night she brought him some blankets because he was a little chilly. He said, "Thank you." She said, "It's just Hoosier hospitality."

That night passed, and the next morning she fixed him a huge breakfast. He said, "This is great. How am I ever going to thank you?" She said, "Think nothing of it. This is Hoosier hospitality."

One thing led to another, and his hormones was working pretty good. They just started fuckin' right on the floor. He was just a-ramming it into her, and the daddy walks in. He said, "Goddamn it, girl, you been talking about Hoosier hospitality all day. Arch your back and get his balls off this cold linoleum floor!"

318

Sleeping with the Farmer and His Wife

A traveling salesman was stranded in a midwestern snowstorm and asked to spend the night at a farmer's house. The farmer said, "Yes, but we have only one bed, and you'll have to sleep with my wife and me." To the salesman's surprise, he was told to sleep beside the wife, and the farmer took the foot of the bed. After a while, when he felt sure the farmer was asleep, the salesman began to feel around two great round globes and asked what they were. "Those are my milk factories," she replied. Then he put his finger on the top of her stomach and found a tiny round cavity. He asked what it was, and she replied, "That's the knot from my mother's apron string." He moved his hand a little farther down and said, "And what is this?" Just then the farmer spoke up, "That's my foot, and it's staying right there!"

319

Sleeping with the Farmer's Wife

A traveling salesman came in the farmer's house and asked to spend the night. The farmer was busy cranking the hand phone and said, "Sure, just go on upstairs and sleep with my wife." So he did. The next morning the salesman found the farmer still cranking the hand telephone and trying to get it to work. He told the farmer, "Thanks for letting me sleep with your wife, but she sure does have a cold butt." The farmer said, "I'm not surprised. She's been dead three days, and I'm still trying to get the coroner."

320

He Who Laughs Last

There were these two guys driving a car down a country road real late at night, and their car broke down. And they couldn't get it started, and they tried and tried and couldn't get it started. So there was a farmhouse nearby, so the two men talked it over and decided that they should go and ask whoever lived in the farmhouse if they could use the phone. They went up to the door and knocked on the door, and this real old lady answered the door. She must have been 60 years old. They asked her if they could use the phone, and she said of course they could use the phone. So they called this guy to come out and get their car started, but he couldn't come because it was too late at night. The one man said to the other he could probably fix the car if it were daylight and he could see because he didn't think there was very much wrong with it, so they decided to ask the lady if they could stay there for the night. The lady said they could stay there, but they would have to sleep downstairs because she slept upstairs. And they said that would be okay with them. So in the morning they got up, fixed their car, and went on their way.

About nine months later this one guy gets a letter in the mail, so he immediately calls his friend and says, "Do you remember the night we were stranded on the road and stayed all night in that old country farmhouse?" The friend said yeah, he remembered that night. And the other man said, "You didn't happen to wander around during the night did you?" His friend said, "Seems to me that I can remember wandering around in the middle of the night." And the other man said, "You didn't happen to wander upstairs did you?" The friend says, "I do remember wandering upstairs. I did go upstairs." The other man said, "You didn't happen to wander in the old lady's bedroom did you?" "I do remember something about going in the lady's bedroom." "You didn't happen to use my name by any chance?" His friend says, "Yeah, I think I do remember using your name." So his friend said, "I sure do want to thank you. That old lady just died and left me her farm and $200,000."

Doctors, Nurses, and Patients

Physicians have been the subject of satirical folk humor since the Middle Ages and continue to be popular figures in contemporary jokelore. A very general motif in some of the tales in this section is "Repartee concerning doctors and patients"; however, most of the jokes presented below are forms of contemporary sick humor, and some follow the good news/bad news format. As Alan Dundes notes in "The Dead Baby Joke Cycle" (*Western Folklore*, 38 [July 1979]: 149), the good news/bad news opposition is a common format in contemporary sick humor, and most good news/bad news jokes "have to do with medical malpractice, unnecessary surgery, and the like. It is certainly appropriate for sick humor to treat illness and hospital care." Dundes provides examples of seven sick jokes involving conversations with doctors, including versions of jokes in this section.

Much sick humor in the oral tradition today takes the form of short riddle jokes, which are faddish and sometimes topical. The Helen Keller joke discussed in the Introduction is an example of a riddle joke from a cycle popular a few years ago. Other cycles of sick jokes in recent years have dealt with Jesus and the Kennedy family. Simon J. Bronner discusses a current cycle of sick jokes in "'What's Grosser Than Gross?': New Sick Joke Cycles" (*Midwestern Journal of Language and Folklore*, 11 [Spring 1985]: 39–49). According to Bronner, "For those who tell or listen to the [sick] jokes, the extreme in-

187

congruity between an expectation of what is acceptable and appropriate and the actual response contributes to the perception of gross humor" (p. 43).

321
One Thing at a Time

This woman went to her doctor and told him, "Doctor, I have this problem. It's more of a bother than anything, but I do a lot of entertaining," she says, "and, well, I pass gas a lot. It doesn't smell or make any noise, but it's bothersome anyways. Oops, there goes one!" Well, the doctor just kind of looked at her for a moment, and then gave her some pills and told her to come back in two weeks. So two weeks later the old girl comes back, only she was pretty mad this time because now not only did she still pass gas a lot, but they were real loud ones at that, she claimed, Well, the doctor just kind of smiled and said, "Good, now that we've got your hearing cleared up, we can work on your nose!"

322
The Doctor and the Constipated Woman

This woman went to the doctor because she could not go to the john. He examined her, and there wasn't anything wrong with her. So he told her to go to the pharmacy and pick up these suppositories. So she went and picked them up, and about a week later she came back to the doctor and wanted some more. It had been a month's supply she had gotten, and the doc, he couldn't figure out why she had used so many. He said, "What the hell you been doing, eating those things?" She said, "Hell, yes! What do you think I was doing with them, stuffing them up my ass?"

323
April Fool

There was this guy waiting for his wife to have a baby, see, and he was real nervous sitting around in the waiting room smoking cigarettes and walking the floor. Then this woman came out and said, "Mr. Parker, your wife has had her baby. If you'll step to the window, the nurse will show you your baby." So he goes over to the window, see, and this nurse brings out a little bundle, brings it to the window, and then grabs it by the feet and starts swinging it around the room and bashing its head on the walls and throwing it up on the ceiling and letting it fall on the floor. And the man is just standing there clawing at the window. Then the nurse comes out and says to him, "Ha, ha, April Fool! Dead on arrival!"

324
Bad News and Good News

This doctor comes into this room where this guy is a patient there, you know, in a hospital. And he says, "Well, I have good news for you, and I have bad news for you." And the patient goes, "What's the bad news?" And he goes, "Well, we're gonna have to remove both of your legs." And he says, "What's the good news?" And he goes, "Well, the guy down the hall wants to buy your house slippers."

325
Good News and Bad News

There is this man, and his wife was going to have a baby. He's at the hospital, and he's going back and forth for an hour. The doctor comes out and says, "Well, I have good news and bad news. The good news is that you have a baby boy." The guy says, "My God, that's good!" He's really happy. The doctor says, "Well, here's the bad news." He says, "He has one leg and four buck teeth." The guy says, "My God, what am I gonna do?" The doctor says, "Well, you could take him home and use him for a rake."

326
What Could Be Worse?

This man brought his pregnant wife to the hospital. He went into the waiting room, and his wife went into the delivery room. About an hour later, the doctor came into the waiting room and said, "Sir, I'm sorry, but your baby is going to be deformed. It won't have any legs." Half an hour later, the doctor came back into the waiting room and told the man, "Your baby won't have arms either." The man was terribly upset, but he told himself it didn't matter and that he would love the baby anyway.

Then the doctor came in again. And this time the doctor said that the baby would not have a trunk. "Your baby is only going to have a head," he said. The father cried out but still said he would love the child. Ten minutes later the doctor burst into the waiting room again. He said, "Sir, I'm so very sorry, but your baby is only an eye!" The poor father was heartbroken. "What could be worse?" shrieked the father. The doctor replied, "It's blind!"

Schoolteachers

THE SCHOOLMARM is a popular figure in American jokelore. She is both the symbol of female dominance and the model of moral authority. A dominant figure in the classroom, the female teacher is envisioned by schoolboys as also a dominant figure in the bedroom. In schoolboy fantasy, as reflected in these jokes, the schoolmarm is the subject of sexual desire and conquest, almost always by a stock character, Little Johnny. More precocious than his schoolmates, Johnny possesses sexual knowledge far beyond what is normal for his age. Johnny sometimes speaks profanely in inappropriate contexts, but the humor in most of the jokes is based on punning or other wordplay, such as trick names. Most often learned and recited in adolescence, these jokes about schoolteachers serve important psychological functions for young males. They reduce their fear about sex since Johnny always gets the best of a woman considered sexually dominant. The jokes also reduce adolescent male hostilities toward the oppressive moral authority of adults since an authority figure, the schoolmarm, is presented as not so very moral.

327

You Were Thinkin'

There was this little boy, and he was in first grade, and his name was Johnny. And in the first grade lots of times the teacher will have guessing games, you know, and she puts something behind her back, you know, and she describes it, and they have to figure out what it is and guess. Well, one day Johnny's teacher decided to do that, so she goes, "Okay, class, I have something behind my back, and it's long and green. What is it?" And Johnny goes, "Oh, teacher, I know! I know, teacher! I know!" And she goes, "Okay, Johnny, what is it?" And he goes, "A pickle!" And she goes, "No, Johnny, it's a cucumber. But you were almost right. You were thinkin'!"

So she goes, "Okay, class, now I have something else behind my back, and it's round and orange. What is it?" And Johnny goes, "Oh, I know, teacher! I know! I know!" And she goes, "Well, what is it, Johnny?" And he goes, "It's an orange!" And she goes, "No, Johnny, it's not an orange. It's a tangerine, but you were thinkin', Johnny. You were almost right."

And Johnny goes, "Okay, teacher, now I've got something for you." So Johnny sticks his hand in his pocket, and he goes, "I have something in my hand. It's long and narrow and has a pink tip. What is it?" And the teacher goes, "Johnny! You mustn't say things like that in school!" You know, and he goes, "Okay, teacher, it was only my pencil. But you were thinkin'!"

328
The Spelling Bee

The teacher was having a spelling bee. And she had this one little boy who always made something nasty out of everything she said, so she was a little bit leery about having this kid in the bee. But, anyway, it came time for him to spell, so she said, "Okay, Harold, your word is *cat*." He said, "C-A-T, cat, and he's a mean son of a bitch." She said, "Harold, I don't want to hear another word like that out of you. Just don't want to hear it!" So she went around the room again, and it came Harold's turn to spell again, and she said, "Harold, your word is *lion*." He said, "Lion, L-I-O-N, and he's a big son of a bitch!" She said, "I told you I didn't want to hear another word like that, and if I do again you're going to the principal's office." So it went around again and came back to Harold, and she looked at the word and thought, "Oh, my God, I can't give this word to him, but she did anyway. And she said, "Okay, Harold, your word is *pussy.*" He said, "Pussy, P-U-S-S-Y." She waited a moment, and nothing happened, and she said, "That's very, very good, Harold!" And he said, "You bet your sweet ass it is, sister!"

329
How 'Bout That?

Little Johnny was in school, and he had this real bad habit of saying "How 'bout that?" Every time the teacher would ask some question or he would make some statement, he would always say, "How 'bout that?" So the teacher said one day, "Johnny, you're just going to have to stand in the hall till you can learn to quit saying 'How 'bout that?'" So she took him out in the hall and stuck his nose against the wall and said he had to stand there for an hour.

So when the hour was up, the teacher went out, and she said, "Well, Johnny, are you about ready to quit this bad habit of saying 'How 'bout that'?" Johnny said yes he was, and he said, "You know, teacher, while I was standing out here I made up a poem." Teacher said, "Oh? Let's hear it." He said, "As I was standing in the hall,/ I saw a cockroach run up the wall." She said, "Johnny, that's just real cute. But I'll tell you what," she said, "when you go back into the room, I'm gonna ask you to say this in front of the students. But do me a favor, please. Leave the cock part out. Just say the roach ran up the wall." So they went back into the room, and she took Johnny up in front and told the class he was going to recite a poem he had just made up. So Johnny said, "As I was standing in the hall,/ I saw a roach run up the wall . . . with the cock out. How 'bout that?"

330
Sticking It Out till Noon

This is the story of the little boy who went to school after having received a circumcision late in life. He was sitting there in class one day, and he was squirming all over his seat. And the teacher said, "Johnny, what is wrong with you?" And the little boy proceeds, you know, to tell the teacher what had happened, and she said, "Well, I'll tell you what, Johnny. Why don't you go to the superintendent's office and see if he can help you in some way so that maybe you can return to class and be okay and a little more comfortable."

So he went out, and shortly thereafter he came back in. And the fly of his britches was open, and his little ol' pedinkus was just sailin' on, hangin' on out there. And the teacher said, "Johnny, why did you return to class in this way, in this manner?" And he said, "Well, the superintendent said if I could stick it out till noon I could go home."

331

The Foxy Teacher

There was a third grade class with a very foxy teacher. Johnny was a very advanced student, and he kept watching the teacher all day. At the end of the day the teacher was erasing the board and dropped the eraser. Johnny said, "Teacher, you're wearing panty hose." The teacher expelled Johnny for two days. When Johnny came back, he again started watching the teacher. She dropped the chalk and bent over to pick it up. Johnny said, "Teacher, you're not wearing a girdle." Johnny was expelled for two weeks. The next time Johnny was in class he did pretty good until the end of the day. The teacher was sweeping up and bent way over. Johnny got up and started to walk out of class. The teacher said, "Where in the hell do you think you're going?" Johnny said, "After what I just saw my school days are over."

332

The Teacher Assigns an Essay

This teacher instructed her class to write an essay including four subjects: religion, royalty, sex, and mystery. "It'll take quite some time to write an essay of this nature and smoothly incorporate all subjects, so please begin."

About fifteen minutes later, a boy raised his hand and announced that he was finished. The teacher said, "I don't see how you can be finished with an essay of that nature in that short of time." "Well, I have," said the boy. "If you think you have, please read it." The boy read, " 'My God,' said the queen, 'I'm pregnant. I wonder whose it is?' "

333

Not Even a Coffee Break

A new teacher had just come to teach at a local school, and she was calling the roll one day when she came to the name Peter Period. Well, the teacher thought there must be a mistake, so she skipped over the name and went through the rest of the roll. Later on, she went to the principal's office, and she asked, "I don't know quite how to ask this, but is there a Peter Period in this school?" "Hell, no," exclaimed the principal, "we don't even have time for a coffee break!"

334

Why Schoolmarms Make Good Prostitutes

This guy ran a whorehouse, and on the first floor he had the house-keepers, on the second floor he had the models, and on the third floor he had the schoolteachers. And it seemed like the third floor was getting all the business. And he couldn't figure out why the school-teachers were gettin' all the business. So he went to the first floor, and he listened to the housekeepers, and they said, "Come in. Hang up your clothes! Don't mess up the bed!" So then he went up to the second floor, and he listened to the models, and they said, "Don't mess my lipstick up! Don't mess my hair!" So then he went up to the third floor where the schoolteachers were. And he listened in, and they said, "If you don't do it right the first time, you'll have to do it again."

 *Farmers*

Until World War I, the population of Indiana was largely rural, and the economy was mainly agricultural. Even in 1920 when the urban population slightly outnumbered the rural, most Hoosier towns were surrounded by farms and dominated by rural influences. Some counties, especially in southern Indiana, still are largely rural and sparsely populated. As a character type, however, the farmer is not a prominent figure in Hoosier jokelore. One might expect tales of dull witted farmers in this section, but the only numskulls in the tales that follow are a novice farmer and a naive farmer's son, not experienced farmers. A dominant theme, though, in the tales below is the farmer as clever deceiver and wit (Tales 337, 338). The marginal economy of farming is reflected in the tale about the farmer who probably will not turn a profit for the third straight year (Tale 335) and the two tales about farmers anxious to marry off their daughters, apparently to ease their financial burdens (Tales 339, 340).

335

Hard Luck

There was this farmer who always took his produce into the city to sell it. This farmer was going from door to door and came up to this one and knocked. A woman dressed in a sheer negligé answered. He introduced himself and said that he was selling produce. This year it was peaches. The woman took the farmer's hand and put it on her breast and asked him, "Are they firm and round like these?" The farmer, looking down at the ground, said, "Yes." Then she took his hand and put it between her legs and asked, "Are they fuzzy and soft like this?" The farmer said, "Yes." Then, much to the surprise of the woman, the farmer broke down and started crying. The woman, all upset, asked if she had done something to upset him. The farmer said, "Oh, ma'am, it's just that two years ago I lost my corn crop with the flood, and last year the bugs got all of my beans, and now this year I'm going to get screwed out of my peaches!"

336

The Would-Be Farmer

This man wanted to become a farmer, so he went down to the store and said, "Sir, I want to become a farmer, so I'll need a rooster." And the man replied, "We call those cocks." The farmer said, "Okay, give me one of those. I guess now I'll need a hen." The man replied, "We call those pullets." The farmer said, "Okay, give me one of those." Then he said, "Well, I'm gonna need a mule, too." The man replied, "We call those asses. I have one here, but he's pretty stubborn. He'll sit down a lot, but if you scratch him, he'll usually get back up." The farmer said, "I'll take him anyway."

So he starts walking down the road with his rooster under one arm, the hen under the other, and the mule behind him. All of a sudden the mule decided to sit down. The farmer said, "What am I going to do?" About that time a lady came walking by, and he asked her, "Miss, could you hold my cock and pullet while I scratch my ass?"

337

The Farmer's Prize Mule

There was an old farmer who had a mule with sweezy. That's like rheumatism. Every time you'd touch his right shoulder, he'd hold his head straight out and point his tail. Well, one day, two hunters came to the farmer and asked if they could run their prize dogs and look for quail. The farmer said sure, and he believed he'd go along. Well, they hunted and hunted, but the dogs didn't find anything. The farmer said, "I bet my prize mule can find some." He took the mule to a good thicket and when the hunters weren't looking touched the sore shoulder. The mule raised his head and stuck out his tail, and up flew a bunch of birds. The hunters were excited and asked the farmer to try it again. The same thing happened.

One hunter said, "I have to have that mule. What's she worth?" The farmer wouldn't sell at first but finally took $175. The hunter said he just had to try out the mule before they left and asked the farmer where the best place was. The farmer pointed to a thicket across a creek, and the hunter got on the mule and started across. Halfway across he found it was deeper than he thought and raised his legs to keep dry. His shoe touched the mule's shoulder, and it stopped dead and lifted its tail and head. The old farmer seeing what happened said, "I forgot to tell you. He points fish as good as birds."

338

The Farmer Visits the Doctor

This farmer says to the other farmer he wasn't feeling good. And the other farmer says, "Well, you'd better get to town and get examined." So he came into town and was examined, and three or four days later he saw his fellow farmer. The farmer said, "Well, Bill, did you get examined?" "Yep." "What did they find?" Said, "They found ten dollars, and they let me keep two."

339

The Farmer Tests His Daughter's Suitors

The farmer wanted to marry off his daughter, so he put an ad in the paper. A man came answering the ad. The farmer said the man had to prove himself worthy. The guy says, "Okay, what do you want me to do?" The farmer says, "Well, you see the old cow in the pasture?" The guy says, "Yes." The farmer says, "Well, you have to screw the old cow for an hour. If you can do that, you're worthy of my daughter." The guy says, "Cool." He goes out there in the pasture, and he jumps on the old cow and is really going to town. About fifteen minutes later the guy is exhausted. I mean he just goes pouf. The old farmer digs a hole and buries him.

Another guy comes and answers the ad. The farmer tells him he has to prove himself worthy by screwing the cow for an hour. "If you do, then you are worthy to marry my daughter." The second guy is out there, and he's been at it for about a half hour, and he drops dead from exhaustion. The old farmer buries him.

A third guy comes and says, "I want to marry your daughter." So the farmer says, "You have to prove yourself worthy. You have to screw the old cow for an hour. If you can do that, then you can marry my daughter." The guy says, "Fine." And he goes out there, and he's just going to town, see? And about forty-five minutes has passed, and the farmer remembers he has to go to town. So he goes to town and gets some grain and some food and has a couple beers. Before he knows it, four hours has passed. He looks at his watch and says, "Oh, my God, the poor guy's dead! I'll just go out and bury him, too." So he gets in his truck and screams back to his farm. The guy is still going to town, having a good old time. The farmer runs out there and yells, "Stop! Stop! Stop! All right, you can marry my daughter." The guy says, "The hell with your daughter. How much do you want for the cow?"

340

Just a Little Bit

You see, there was this here farmer, a Farmer Jones. Well, his son had just come home from either fightin' or college. Well, something like that. Anyway, he'd been gone for a while. His dad, Farmer Jones, set him to workin' in the fields, plowin' with a horse and a plow. Well, he was plowin' furrows. Farmer Jones' land ran along Farmer Brown's land. And Farmer Brown saw the boy plowin' and decided he would be a good match for one of his daughters. So he timed his plowin' so he'd meet the boy when he came down to his land.

So one day he timed it just right. And he said, "Son, how would you like to get married? You're young and strong and a hard worker. You'd be a good match for one of my daughters. Now, my oldest girl is perfect for you. You're about twenty-two. Well, she's a little older, about twenty-eight, but a real pretty girl. Only one thing wrong with her though. She's a little bit cross-eyed, not much, just a little bit." The boy said, "No, I don't think I'd care much for her." The farmer said, "Well, you're in luck. I've got another daughter who's prettier than the first, and she's just your age, twenty-two. And is she ever a good cook. Only one thing wrong with her though. She's just a little bit bowlegged, not much, just a little bit." The young man said, "No, I don't think so." The farmer said, "I'll tell you what. My youngest daughter is the best of the bunch. She's only eighteen. See that bungalow over there? If you'll marry her, I'll give you that, plus you can join up with me and farm this land. There's only one thing wrong with her. She's a little bit pregnant, not much, just a little bit."

341
The Farmer's Son

There was this ol' farmer. And he was going to town, so he told his boy to watch the sow 'cause it was going to have pigs today. When the ol' man came home, the sow was turned around eatin' one of her pigs. His boy said, "Dad, don't worry. It'll come back out again. That makes nine times she's ate it." That sow had eat up all nine of its litter!

342
The Preacher and the Farmer's Wife

Back in the old days a farmer used to spend all day in the field working. Well, there was this farmer who always expected his wife to have the meal on the table when he got in from the field. One afternoon he was coming up to the house and saw his wife outside chasing a chicken. He said, "What are you doing out here chasing a chicken? And why haven't you got supper fixed for me?" His wife said that she didn't have a chance to because the preacher came. The old farmer yelled, "Fuck the preacher! I want my supper!" His wife simply replied, "I already did that, and now he wants a chicken."

Politicians

OVER FIFTY YEARS AGO in *The Science of Folklore* (1930; reprint, New York: Norton, 1964), Alexander H. Krappe observed that "the good stories about the practices of American lawyers and politicians would fill a handsome volume and afford no less choice reading than the mediaeval tales with their constant attacks on the women and the clergy" (p. 54). Jokes about politicians continue to be very popular in the oral tradition, reflecting the age-old tendency of the folk to mock certain trades and professions. In contemporary political humor, which most often is topical, no political party or figure is safe. The folk tell jokes about Republicans and Democrats, about Richard Nixon and John F. Kennedy, about George Wallace and Jesse Jackson. Politicians as a class are distrusted in contemporary jokelore.

One of the jokes below (Tale 343) is a familiar story in the American oral tradition and the title tale in Vance Randolph's collection of bawdy folktales, *Pissing in the Snow and Other Ozark Folktales* (Urbana: University of Illinois Press, 1976). The joke does not always concern a politician, but the Hoosier version conforms to other forms of the tale in the contemporary oral tradition. As Frank A. Hoffmann points out in his annotation of Randolph's version (p. 6), "In recent years, the story has had renewed currency, adapted to the structure of the 'there's some good news, and there's some bad news' joke. In this form it is used as a put-down on a well-known political figure who is informed of the act as a means of getting rid of an unwanted colleague (the good news), and then of the fact that the handwriting is his wife's (the bad news)."

343
Pissing in the Snow

President Nixon was walking around the White House grounds one day, and he noticed that somebody had pissed on the snow and had written out the words "Tricky Dicky." He didn't know what to think of this, so he called his Secret Service men and asked them to check into who had done it and make sure no unauthorized people had gotten onto the grounds. The next morning the Secret Service reported back to him. The agent said, "Mr. President, we've got some good news and some bad news for you. First, the good news. The person who did it was part of your staff, Henry Kissinger, and no unauthorized people were on the grounds. The bad news is that it was in your wife's handwriting."

344
Pat Nixon's Problem

Pat Nixon went to the doctor for a physical. Five doctors examined her, and all five of them came up with the same diagnosis: crabs. The doctors just didn't know how they could ever get up enough guts to tell their patient . . . the President's wife, of all people . . . what was the matter with her. Finally, the anesthesiologist popped up and said, "It's all right, fellas; when she wakes up, I'll just tell her that her watergate's been bugged."

345
The Governor of Indiana Gets a Bargain

The Governor of Indiana went around the state looking for a call girl. He found three in a bar: a redhead, a blonde, and a brunette. To the redhead, he said, "How much will it cost me to go to bed with you?" The redhead replied, "Two dollars." He asked the same question to the blonde, and she said, "One dollar." When he asked the brunette the same question, she replied, "Mister, if you can raise my skirt as high as taxes, get my panties as low as wages, get that thing of yours as hard as the times, and screw me like you do the public, it won't cost you a damn cent!"

346

George Wallace Gets a Checkup

George Wallace went to the doctor's office one day for a checkup. A few days later he went back to get the results. "George," the doctor said, "I've got some good news and some bad news." "Well, give me the good news first," Wallace said. The doctor said, "The good news is that it's terminal." "It's terminal?" Wallace exclaimed. "That's the good news? What's the bad news?" the doctor replied, "It's sickle-cell."

 *Golfers*

Jokes about golf and golfers are plentiful in the contemporary oral tradition. There are humorous tales about novice golfers, women golfers, and golf widows. There are jokes about clerics and religious figures on the golf course, numskulls on the golf course, and frustrations on the golf course. As "The Golf Lesson" (Tale 352) shows, there is even a shaggy dog story, a rare one approaching obscenity, about golf. An especially popular theme in golf jokes is the callous golfer who thinks only of his game. One joke, for instance, that I recently collected is about a golfer who lived next to the golf course. One day while playing the hole near his house, he hit a ball into his own yard, and the ball bounced on his carport. A friend playing with him talked him into playing the ball off the carport to avoid a penalty. Just as the golfer hit the ball, his wife opened the back door, and the ball hit her right between the eyes and killed her. A few years later, after the golfer remarried, the same thing happened on the hole by his house: he hit the ball on his own yard, and it bounced on the carport. His friend again tried to convince him to play the ball off the carport, but the golfer argued, "Are you kidding? The last time I tried that I took a seven on that hole!" The many golf jokes in the oral tradition suggest that golfers constitute a modern folk group, and their jokes offer some relief from pressures experienced on the golf course.

205

347

The Sentimental Golfer

There were these two men playing golf, and they were like on the ninth hole at Rea Park, right by the road, when a funeral procession goes by. One of the men stops where he is and takes off his hat and stands with his head bowed until the procession gets by. The other man watched him and then said, "I didn't know you were so sentimental about funeral processions." The first man says, "Ordinarily I'm not, but I was married to her for twenty-five years."

348

A Rough Day on the Golf Course

There were these two old men who played golf every Saturday, and their names were Dick and Harry. Well, one Saturday Dick came home real tired, more than he usually was when he played golf, and his wife asked him what the problem was. He said, "Boy, it was really a rough game today. Harry had a heart attack and died on the fourth tee, and all the rest of the time it was hit the ball and drag Harry, hit the ball and drag Harry."

349

Change for a Five

There were these two guys who were out playing golf, and this one had to go to the bathroom real bad. And so he went behind this bush, and he had to do number two. And he went to the bathroom. And all of a sudden he started thinking that he didn't have any toilet paper or anything. So he went up to this one guy, and he said, "Hey, buddy, do you have any toilet paper or a handkerchief or Kleenex or anything?" And he said, "No, sorry, buddy, I'm afraid I can't help you there." So he went up and he asked this other guy, and he said, "Hey, do you have a handkerchief or anything? I just don't know what I'm going to do if I don't find one." And this guy said, "No, I'm afraid I can't help you." And so that kept going on for about four or five more times. And so finally he went up to this lady, and he said, "Lady, do you have change for a five?"

350

The Preacher Who Played Golf on Sunday

There was this preacher that liked to sneak out early on Sunday morning and play nine holes of golf so he could think about what he was going to talk about in church. And the angels said to God, "He's not supposed to do that. Why don't you punish him?" God said, "I'm going to. I'm going to. Just wait a minute." The preacher made par on the first hole, and on the second hole he made a good drive and a good second shot and sunk the putt for a birdie. The angels said, "God, I thought you were going to punish him." God said, "Just wait a minute; I'm going to." The third hole was a 180-yard, par three hole. The preacher teed up the ball and hit it and got a hole-in-one. The angels got real upset and said, "I thought you were going to punish him." God said, "I just did. Who's he going to be able to tell?"

351

Jesus and Moses at Golf

One day Jesus and Moses decide to go golfing. They arrive at the course and are ready to tee off. Moses steps up, and he uses a nine iron. He hits the ball, and it lands on the green. Jesus steps up and says that he can do better than that. He says that he'll use the ten iron because Arnold Palmer uses the ten iron. Well, Jesus steps up and hits the ball, and it lands in a body of water. Moses says that he'll give Jesus another try and that he'll go get the ball. So Moses goes over and parts the water and brings the ball back to Jesus. Well, Jesus insists on using the ten iron again because Arnold Palmer uses the ten iron. Well, he hits the ball, and again it goes in the water. Jesus says that he'll go get the ball this time. Well, he goes out and walks across the water to get the ball and another golfer sees him. The other golfer walks up to Jesus and says, "Who do you think you are anyway, Jesus Christ?" Jesus replies, "No, Arnold Palmer."

352

The Golf Lesson

A man was teaching a woman the proper swing on the golf course when the zipper on the back of her pants got fastened to the zipper on the front of his. They tried for hours to get unfastened. Finally, when they realized that dark was setting in, they decided to walk back to the clubhouse fastened together and then get help in getting unfastened. As they were passing a utility building on their way back to the clubhouse, a dog stepped out and threw a pan of water on them.

Sources and Notes

Unless otherwise noted, texts are from the Indiana State University Folklore Archives. The following short-title listings and abbreviations are used throughout the notes:

Baughman: Ernest W. Baughman, *Type and Motif-Index of the Folktales of England and North America,* Indiana University Folklore Series, no. 20 (The Hague: Mouton, 1966).

Brunvand: Jan Harold Brunvand, "A Classification for Shaggy Dog Stories," *Journal of American Folklore,* 76 (January–March 1963): 42–68.

Buehler: Richard Edward Buehler, "An Annotated Collection of Contemporary Obscene Humor from the Bloomington Campus of Indiana University," (M.A. thesis, Indiana University, 1964).

Clements: William M. Clements, *The Types of the Polack Joke,* Folklore Forum Bibliographic and Special Series, no. 3, 1969; and "The Polack Joke in 1970: An Addendum," *Folklore Forum,* 4 (January–March 1971): 19–29.

Cray: Ed Cray, "The Rabbi Trickster," *Journal of American Folklore,* 77 (October–December 1964): 331–45.

Dance: Daryl Cumber Dance, *Shuckin' and Jivin': Folklore from Contemporary Black Americans* (Bloomington: Indiana University Press, 1978).

Hoffmann: Frank Hoffmann, *An Analytical Survey of Anglo-American Traditional Erotica* (Bowling Green, Ohio: Bowling Green University Popular Press, 1973).

Legman I: Gershon Legman, *No Laughing Matter: An Analysis of Sexual Humor* (Bloomington: Indiana University Press, 1968), vol. I.

Legman II: Gershon Legman, *No Laughing Matter: An Analysis of Sexual Humor* (Bloomington: Indiana University Press, 1975), vol. II.

Motif: Stith Thompson, *Motif-Index of Folk-Literature,* 6 vols. (Bloomington: Indiana University Press, 1966).

Orso: Ethelyn G. Orso, *Modern Greek Humor: A Collection of Jokes and Ribald Tales* (Bloomington: Indiana University Press, 1979).

Randolph: Vance Randolph, *Pissing in the Snow and Other Ozark Folktales* (Urbana: University of Illinois Press, 1976).

Ranke: Kurt Ranke, ed., *European Anecdotes and Jests,* trans. Timothy Buck (Copenhagen: Rosenkilde and Bagger, 1972).

Type: Antti Aarne and Stith Thompson, *The Types of the Folktale*, Folklore
Fellows Communication, no. 184 (Helsinki: Suomalainen Tiedeakatemia,
1961).

WPA: Works Progress Administration, Indiana Files of the Federal Writers'
Project, Cunningham Memorial Library, Indiana State University, Terre
Haute, Indiana. Thirty-four humorous tales from the WPA collection
were printed in a mimeographed booklet, *Hoosier Tall Stories* (Federal
Writers' Project in Indiana, 1937), and have been reprinted here since the
booklet is now rare.

1. Collected in Chesterton, December 1968, from a 45-year-old male
steel mill foreman. Baughman X584.1, "Bear chases man back to camp." For
another version from Indiana, see Buehler, pp. 165–66.
2. This tale, collected in the 1930s, is from the WPA files. Type 1920D,
"The Liar Reduces the Size of his Lie." Baughman X904.1(a), "Liar tells of
barn he has seen which was three hundred feet long (his brother steps on his
toes to remind him of lying)." Baughman notes another version from Texas.
3. Collected in Farmersburg, May 1971, from a 57-year-old male retired
grocer. Type 1920B, "The one says, 'I Have not Time to Lie' and yet lies."
Motif X905.4, "The liar: 'I have no time to lie today'; lies nevertheless." The
following tale is a version.
4. This tale, collected in the 1930s, is from the WPA files. Type 1920B,
"The one says, 'I Have not Time to Lie' and yet lies." Motif X905.4, "The
liar: 'I have no time to lie today'; lies nevertheless." The preceding tale is a
version.
5. Collected in the 1930s, this tale is from the WPA files. The several
motifs in Baughman are: X907.1(d), "The fast woodchopper"; X986(f), "Man
cuts trees so fast that ax has to be cooled in lake or river while chopper cuts
with spare ax"; X1651.2.1*(c), "River boats float on Wabash River fogs";
X1796.4*(aaa), "River gets too hot to cool man's axes"; X1796 X1796.4 (aab),
"Men scald hogs below spot where man cools axes in river."
6. Collected in Farmersburg, April 1971, from an 18-year-old male high
school student. Baughman X909.1(a), "Liar lies so much he has to have
someone else call his pigs." Baughman notes only a version from Texas.
7. Collected in Jasper, December 1970, from an 80-year-old male retired
farmer. Baughman X921, "Lie: remarkably tall person."
8. Collected in Elnora, November 1982, from a 73-year-old male retired
farmer. Baughman X981*, "Lie: skillful marksman." Motif X1100, "Lie: the
remarkable hunter."
9. This tale, collected in the 1930s, is from the WPA files. Baughman
X981*(dc), "Duellists [sic] aim at each other's left eye. The bullets meet in
mid-air, fall to the ground, fused into mass of hot lead."
10. Collected in Farmersburg, May 1971, from a 57-year-old male retired
grocer. The informant heard this tale from Rufe, himself, who was his
neighbor in the 1930s. Type 1894, "The Man Shoots a Ramrod Full of
Ducks." Motif X1111, "Hunter shoots ram-rod full of ducks." Cf. Type
1890D (Baughman), "Ramrod Shot." The following tale is a version.
11. Collected in the 1930s, this tale is from the WPA files. Type 1894,

"The Man Shoots a Ramrod Full of Ducks." Motif X1111, "Hunter shoots ram-rod full of ducks." Cf. Type 1890D (Baughman), "Ramrod Shot." The preceding tale is a version.

12. Collected in Farmersburg, April 1971, from an 82-year-old male retired miner. The informant, an active bearer of tradition, especially local folk history, learned this tale and other stories about Rufe directly from Rufe at a barbershop in Farmersburg between 1920 and 1940. Baughman X981*, "Lie: skillful marksman." Baughman X1121.1*, "Lie: great gun shoots bullet a great distance."

13. Collected in Farmersburg, April 1971, from an 18-year-old male high school student. Baughman X906, "Would not lie for a trifle." Baughman X1122.2(a), "Person shoots twenty ducks in a line with one shot."

14. This tale, collected in the 1930s, is from the WPA files. Type 1890E, "Gun Barrel Bent." Baughman X1122.3.2*, "Hunter bends gun in curve, bullet chases deer (fox) around mountain several times before catching up with, killing deer."

15. Collected in Farmersburg, April 1971, from an 82-year-old male retired miner. Motif X1124, "Lie: the hunter catches or kills game by ingenious or unorthodox method." Cf. Baughman X1123*, "Lie: poor marksmanship."

16. Collected in Chesterton, December 1968, from a 45-year-old male steel mill foreman. Type 1891B*, "Rabbits (hares) Caught by making them Sneeze." Aarne and Thompson report versions only from Finland. Baughman X1124(h), "Hunter puts pepper on flat rock and a shining object on top of the pepper. Rabbits investigate, sneeze, hit heads on rock, die." Baughman reports this motif only from Alberta.

17. Collected in Mitchell, December 1970, from a 52-year-old male chemical engineer. Type 1890, "The Lucky Shot." Motif X1124.3, "Accidental discharge of gun kills much game." As Baughman notes (p. 54), in American and English forms of this tale, the gun generally is not discharged accidentally but is used luckily. The following tale is a version.

18. Collected in the 1930s, this tale is from the WPA files. Type 1890, "The Lucky Shot." Motif X1124.3, "Accidental discharge of gun kills much game." See note 17, as the preceding tale is a version.

19. This tale, collected in the 1930s, is from the WPA files. Baughman X1133.2, "Man escapes bear by running for a long time, from summer to winter." Baughman X1124.6*, "Man stops shocking wheat to chase a deer. Just as he is about to grab it, he slips on the ice. (It is now winter.)"

20. Collected in the 1930s, this tale is from the WPA files. Type 1890A, "Shot Splits Tree Limb." Motif X1124.3.1, "Gunshot splits limb and catches feet of birds."

21. Collected in Greensburg, May 1969, from a 47-year-old male construction worker. Type 1920H*, "Will Blow Out Lantern." Baughman X1154(c), "Man catches lantern while fishing; the lantern is lighted."

22. This tale, collected in the 1930s, is from the WPA files. Baughman X1154(d), "Woman on bridge sneezes, loses false teeth in water. An elderly, skinny fish appropriates them, grows fat with their aid."

23. Collected in Farmersburg, April 1971, from an 82-year-old male retired miner. Motif X1156, "Lie: other unusual methods of catching fish." Baughman X981*, "Lie: skillful marksman."

24. Collected in Mitchell, August 1968, from a 53-year-old male laborer. Type 1889M, "Snakebite Causes Object to Swell." Baughman X1321.3.1, "Lie: hoop snake." Baughman X1321.3.1.1*, "Venom of hoop snake causes wood to swell after snake bites it." Baughman X1205.1(g), "Small wooden object struck by snake swells so that man cuts great quantity of lumber from it." The hoop snake (Cf. Motif B765.1, "Snake takes tail in mouth and rolls like wheel.") also appears in legends. See Ronald L. Baker, *Hoosier Folk Legends* (Bloomington: Indiana University Press, 1982), p. 123. The following three tales are versions.

25. Collected in the 1930s, this tale is from the WPA files. Type 1889M, "Snakebite Causes Object to Swell." Baughman X1205.1(a), "Snake strikes wagon tongue, causing it to swell with various results." Baughman X1205.1(g), "Small wooden object struck by snake swells so that man cuts great quantity of lumber from it." See note 24.

26. Collected in Martinsville, November 1981, from a 51-year-old male car salesman. Type 1889M, "Snakebite Causes Object to Swell." Baughman X1205.1(g), "Small wooden object struck by snake swells so that man cuts great quantity lumber from it." See note 24.

27. Collected in September 1971 from a 20-year-old student from Princeton. Type 1889M, "Snakebite Causes Object to Swell." Baughman X1205.1(g), "Small wooden object struck by snake swells so that man cuts great quantity of lumber from it." See note 24.

28. Collected in Ladoga, March 1982, from a 50-year-old female nurse. Type 1912, "Crippled Cat Uses Wooden Leg to Kill Mice." Baughman X1211.2, "Crippled cat uses wooden leg to kill mice."

29. Collected in Terre Haute, November 1967, from a 55-year-old male farmer. Baughman X1212(a), "Wildcats fight; . . . fur drifts down for two days."

30. Collected in the 1930s, this tale is from the WPA files. Baughman X1213(a), "Panther jumps into kettle of boiling syrup instead of on man sleeping beside fire. Man finds quantities of hair in the syrup."

31. Collected in Frankton, October 1981, from a 77-year-old male farmer-sportsman. Motif X1215.8, "Lie: intelligent dog."

32. Collected in Elnora, November 1982, from a 73-year-old male retired farmer. Baughman X1215.8(a), "Intelligent hunting dog."

33. Collected in Cayuga, May 1972, from a 37-year-old male. Baughman X1215.8(aa), "Master shows dog a skin stretching-board; the dog brings in a raccoon just the size of the board."

34. Collected in Elnora, November 1982, from a 73-year-old male retired farmer. Baughman X1215.8(ac), "Hunting dog chases birds into hole, releases them one at a time for master to shoot."

35. Collected in Elnora, November 1982, from a 73-year-old male retired farmer. Type 1889N, "The Long Hunt." Baughman X1215.9(ab), "Hunter loses his bird dog while hunting; a year later he discovers the skeleton of the dog still pointing skeleton covey."

36. Collected in Waynetown, January 1972, from a 93-year-old male retiree. Baughman X1215.10, "Lie: dog with remarkable scent."

37. Collected in April 1970 from a 21-year-old male student from Shoals. Type 1889L, "Lie: the Split Dog." Baughman X1215.11(b), "Hunting dog runs into sharp object . . . splits self down the middle. His master claps him back together in a hurry, gets right legs up, left legs down."

38. Collected in Whiting, April 1968, from a 52-year-old male chemist. Baughman X1218*(aa), "Fox eludes dogs by running into shed where pelts are stored, hanging upside down on wall."

39. Collected in Chesterton, December 1968, from a 45-year-old male steel mill foreman. Baughman X1218*(ab), "Foxes spell one another when chased by dogs." The following tale is a version.

40. Collected in the 1930s, this tale is from the WPA files. Baughman X1218*(ab), "Foxes spell one another when chased by dogs." The preceding tale is a version.

41. This tale, collected in the 1930s, is from the WPA files. Baughman X1221(ac), "Bear is so large that man cannot carry him out of woods. He drives him twenty miles closer to home . . . before shooting him."

42. Collected in Farmersburg, April 1971, from an 18-year-old male high school student. The informant is an active bearer of tradition, mainly jokes. He heard about Rufe from another high school student, who heard tales about Rufe at a barbershop in Hymera. Baughman X1223.1*(a), "Squirrels steal corn and store it in hollow tree." Baughman X1223*(ab), "Squirrels are used to climbing certain tree. The owner cuts it down. The squirrels run fifty feet up in the air before they discover the tree is gone." Baughman X1741.1(b), "Squirrels run up into air for fifty feet before they realize their favorite tree has been cut down."

43. Collected in Chesterton, December 1968, from a 45-year-old male steel mill foreman. Baughman X1233(gb), "Razorback hog runs through hollow log under fence to get out of pasture."

44. Collected in Greensburg, May 1969, from a 47-year-old male construction worker. Baughman X1235.2(a), "Cow falls into sinkhole, drowns in her own milk, but churns one hundred pounds of butter in the process."

45. Collected in the 1930s, this tale is from the WPA files. Baughman X1237.1(c), "General Grant plowing canal plows through stump which closes on his coattails." Baughman X1237.1.1, "Man plows through stump which catches the back of his pants in cleft."

46. Collected in Frankton, October 1981, from a 77-year-old male farmer-sportsman. The informant's tales about coon hunting are well known in Madison County. Baughman X1241.1(fa), "Horse crosses swollen stream on narrow stringer or beam of bridge."

47. Collected in Greensburg, May 1969, from a 47-year-old male construction worker. Motif X1242, "Lies about mules." Baughman X1741.7*(d), "Man and horse jump off canyon rim; near the bottom the man calls out *whoa* and the horse stops three feet from floor of canyon."

48. Collected in Terre Haute, November 1967, from a 74-year-old male retired oil well pumper. Baughman X1286.2, "Lies about ferocious mosquitoes."

49. This tale, collected in the 1930s, is from the WPA files. Baughman X1301.5*(b), "Big fish gets away as man tries to land it. He gets enough meat on the gig to last for two weeks." This tale shares a bottomless lake motif (Motif F713.2, "Bottomless lakes") with legends. See Ronald L. Baker, *Hoosier Folk Legends* (Bloomington: Indiana University Press, 1982), pp. 116–71.

50. Collected in the 1930s, this tale is from the WPA files. Baughman X1303.2(a), "Large fish swallows string of fish tied to flatboat, rocking the boat in the attempt to free them."

51. Collected in April 1970 from a 19-year-old female student from Palmyra. Baughman X1306.3*, "Tragic end of tame fish. Tame fish falls into water, usually while crossing footbridge, drowns." This text is suspiciously close to a variant from Kentucky in Leonard W. Roberts, *South from Hellfer-Sartin* (Berea, Kentucky: The Council of Southern Mountains, 1964), p. 154. The following text is a version.

52. This tale, collected in the 1930s, is from the WPA files. Baughman X1306.3*, "Tragic end of tame fish. Tame fish falls into water, usually while crossing footbridge, drowns." The preceding tale is a version.

53. Collected in Cayuga, May 1972, from a 65-year-old male retired laborer. Motif X1321.1.2, "Lie: great snake is thought to be a log." Baughman X1321.1.2.2*, "Men sitting on log stick or cut it with knife or ax. The snake moves, sometimes carrying men some distance before they realize their plight."

54. This tale, collected in the 1930s, is from the WPA files. Baughman X1321.4.4.2*(a), "Grateful snake catches fish for fisherman after the fisherman gives it a drink."

55. Collected in Beech Grove, July 1971, from a 76-year-old housewife. Baughman X1342, "Lies about frogs." Cf. Baughman X1306.1*(a), "Tame fish churns butter."

56. Collected in the 1930s, this tale is from the WPA files. Baughman X1402.1*(ca), "Man plants seeds; the seeds come up immediately, and vine chases man across field." Baughman X1431.1(d), "Three turnips fill a half bushel."

57. Collected in Marshall, March 1974, from an 81-year-old male retired farmer. Baughman X1455.1(i), "Remarkable stalk of corn yields shelled corn." Baughman X1402.3.4*, "Lie: length of great cornstalk."

58. Collected in Valparaiso, March 1974, from a 50-year-old male steel mill supervisor. Baughman X1533*, "Rich land grows crop or fruit from inanimate object." Baughman X1460*, "Lie: crops produced from inanimate objects." Baughman X1462*(a), "Man sticks a stake into ground to serve as landmark while planting corn. It grows four ears of corn."

59. Collected in Cayuga, May 1972, from a 65-year-old male retired farmer. Baughman X1611.1.7*(cc), "Wind blows rooster into a jug."

60. Collected in Greenfield, March 1983, from a middle-aged male. Exact age and occupation withheld. Motifs X1620, "Lies about cold weather"; X1286, "Remarkable mosquitoes"; X1623, "Lies about freezing"; X1623.3, "Lie: flame freezes: startling results."

61. Collected in September 1971 from a 20-year-old male student from Princeton. Baughman X1651(a), "Man walks on thick fog."

62. This tale, collected in the 1930s, is from the WPA files. Baughman X1651.1, "Man, shingling building during thick fog, shingles several feet of fog when he gets beyond the roof line."

63. Collected in Valparaiso, March 1974, from a 50-year-old male steel mill supervisor. Baughman X1651.3.1*(a), "Fish swims out of water into thick fog."

64. Collected in the 1930s, this tale is from the WPA files. Type 1920P (Baughman), "Bad Weather." Baughman X1652*(a), "Large hailstones. Hailstone bounces off silo, kills calf."

65. This tale, collected in the 1930s, is from the WPA files. Baughman

X1654.3.1*(a), "In hard rain, the rain goes into bunghole of barrel faster than it can run out both ends."

66. Collected in the 1930s, this tale is from the WPA files. Baughman X1733.3*(c), "Basket of dirt and rock falls on man in well, knocks him in rock to knees." Cf. Baughman X1733.1, "Man lifts heavy load, sinks into solid rock."

67. Collected in Bedford, August 1969, from an 82-year-old male retired railroader and farmer. Type 1917, "The Stretching and Shrinking Harness." Baughman X1785.1, "The stretching and shrinking harness." The following tale is a version.

68. This tale, collected in the 1930s, is from the WPA files. Type 1917, "The Stretching and Shrinking Harness." Baughman X1785.1, "The stretching and shrinking harness." The preceding tale is a version.

69. Collected in Farmersburg, April 1971, from an 18-year-old male high school student. Baughman X1796.3.1*(a), "Horses or mules pull buckboard so fast that showers fill the back end of the wagon or buckboard, while front stays dry."

70. Collected in Washington, April 1974, from a 22-year-old female student. Type 366, "The Man from the Gallows." Motif Z13.1, "Taleteller frightens listener: yells 'Boo' at exciting point." Cf. texts 8 and 11 from Spencer in John M. Vlach, "One Black Eye and Other Horrors: A Case for the Humorous Anti-Legend," *Indiana Folklore*, IV:2 (1971): 105, 108.

71. Collected in December 1971 from a 19-year-old housewife and part-time student from Anderson. Type 2204, "The Dog's Cigar." Baughman Z13.4*(b), "Woman in streetcar or railroad car, throws out of window the cigar or pipe of soldier."

72. Collected in Terre Haute, November 1969, from a 19-year-old female student. Baughman Z13.4*, "Sells. The joke is on the listener." A version from Spencer appears in John M. Vlach, "One Black Eye and Other Horrors: A Case for the Humorous Anti-Legend," *Indiana Folklore*, IV:2 (1971): 101–102.

73. Collected in Evansville, May 1968, from a 22-year-old female student. Baughman Z13.4*(j), "Man is chased by coffin." Brunvand C620, "The Walking Coffin." This tale also contains legend motifs: Motif H1410, "Fear test: staying in frightful place." Motif F1041.7, "Hair turns gray from terror." See William M. Clements, "The Walking Coffin," *Indiana Folklore*, II:2 (1969): 3–10.

74. Collected in Terre Haute, November 1969, from a 19-year-old female student. Baughman Z13.4*(k), "Man takes shelter in haunted house, is disturbed by rapping noise in room above." Brunvand C665, "The Rapping Paper."

75. Collected in Washington, April 1974, from a 22-year-old female student. Type 2200, "Catch-tales." Baughman Z13.4*(i), "Escaped inmate from insane asylum chases man. . . . touches victim . . . says 'Tag!'" Brunvand D100, "The Encounter with a Horrible Monster." For a version from Spencer, see John M. Vlach, "One Black Eye and Other Horrors: A Case for the Humorous Anti-Legend," *Indiana Folklore*, IV:2 (1971): 103–104.

76. Collected in Indianapolis, May 1970, from a 20-year-old female student. The informant said, "This is another one of those stories I often tell my friends. Details change to suit the place I happen to be and the people I tell.

I've been telling this for many years." Type 2200, "Catch-tales." Brunvand D200, "Pulling the Leg."

77. Collected in Indianapolis, April 1981, from a 20-year-old female student, who learned the tale in high school. Type 2200, "Catch-tales." Motif J1511.14, "Things on highway belong to the public." Brunvand D210, "Feeding Baloney."

78. Collected in Columbus, January 1974, from a 50-year-old male quality control inspector. Type 2200, "Catch-tales." Brunvand D220, "The Dog that Drank Gasoline."

79. Collected in Terre Haute, May 1970, from a 20-year-old female student from Indianapolis. The informant said, "This is a story I have told many times, but details have changed each time according to where I happened to be. It must be told as a true story to get the proper effect." Type 2200, "Catch-tales." Brunvand D240, "The Two Bumps."

80. Collected in Terre Haute, January 1968, from a 19-year-old female student. Baughman Z13.4*(a), "The 'kleshmaker,' 'cushmaker,' etc." Brunvand D500, "The Kush-Maker." See Alan Dundes, "The Kushmaker," in *Folklore on Two Continents,* ed. Nikolai Burlakoff et al. (Bloomington: Trickster Press, 1980), pp. 210–22; and William Hugh Jansen, "The Klesh-Maker," *Hoosier Folklore,* 7 (1948): 47–50. Jansen found an analogue attributed to Davy Crockett.

81. Collected in Terre Haute, May 1969, from a 21-year-old female student. The informant learned the tale in 1961 at a slumber party when she was in junior high school. Baughman Z13.4*(1), "Person receives a mysterious document in a foreign language. Each time he presents it to someone for translation, he is rebuffed with horror, often violently." Brunvand D501.1, "The Purple Passion." See Legman I, pp. 504–16, for variants and discussion of this tale.

82. Collected in Aurora, May 1970, from a 20-year-old female student, who heard the tale in 1965. Brunvand C50, "The Boy who Wanted Eternal Youth."

83. Collected in Terre Haute, March 1970, from a 22-year-old male student. Brunvand C55, "The Foo Bird."

84. Collected in October 1979 from a 22-year-old male student from Evansville. Brunvand C425, "The Midget Knight and his Mount."

85. Collected in April 1969 from a 19-year-old female student from Winamac. Brunvand C455, "The Gossiping Snakes."

86. Collected in Chesterton, December 1968, from a 16-year-old male high school student. There are five other versions of this tale in the ISU Folklore Archives. Cf. Brunvand, pp. 59–65, "Stories with Punning Punch Lines."

87. Collected in Chesterton, December 1968, from a 45-year-old male steel mill foreman. Cf. Brunvand, pp. 59–65, "Stories with Punning Punch Lines."

88. Collected in Terre Haute, December 1968, from a 19-year-old female student. Brunvand C625, "The Hardy Sailor."

89. Collected in Columbus, December 1969, from a 29-year-old male student, who learned the tale in 1965. Brunvand C635, "The Guilty Moth."

90. Collected in Rosedale, May 1969, from a 19-year-old female student. Brunvand C1025, "The Missile Shot."

91. Collected in Rosedale, May 1969, from a 19-year-old female student. Brunvand C1625, "Don't Fly Off the Handle." Cf. Legman II, p. 895.

92. Collected in Leavenworth, August 1968, from a 72-year-old male retired schoolteacher. Brunvand C1650, "Don't Lose Your Head." Legman II, p. 483.

93. Collected in Highland, January 1968, from a 50-year-old male high school coach, who learned the tale in 1963. Type 1215, "The Miller, his Son, and the Ass: Trying to Please Everyone." Motif J1041.2, "Miller, his son, and the ass." Brunvand C1675, "You Can't Please Everyone." A modern version from Greece is in Orso, pp. 78–79.

94. Collected in Burney, April 1974, from a 13-year-old male student. Hoffmann X716.3.1, "Mr. Rabbit is here with the—fertilizer." This popular tale is found in several collections of humorous folktales, including Buehler, pp. 140–43; Dance, pp. 259–60; Legman II, p. 683; and Randolph, pp. 32–33.

95. Collected in Princeton, December 1969, from a 25-year-old housewife. Legman I, p. 194. Another variant (Legman II, p. 166) has a homosexual element. The punch line goes: "Wham, bam! Oh, pardon me, Sam."

96. Collected in Terre Haute, November 1972, from a 20-year-old male furnace repairman. For versions, see Legman I, p. 196; Legman II, p. 634; and Orso, p. 196.

97. Collected in November 1972 from a 21-year-old male student from Seymour. Cf. Hoffmann X712.3.1, "Injury to testicles," and Motif H1024, "Tasks contrary to the nature of animals."

98. Collected in Terre Haute, July 1970, from a 51-year-old male railroader. Hoffmann X734.3, "Intercourse between male and animal." Legman II, p. 753, reports a version collected in Los Angeles in 1968 "and encountered much earlier in French."

99. Collected in July 1969 from a 22-year-old male student from Hammond. Hoffmann X734.3, "Intercourse between male and animal." Two versions of this tale appear in Legman I, p. 210.

100. Collected in Terre Haute, March 1982, from a 28-year-old male policeman. Hoffmann X749.4.1, "Man with huge member." Orso, p. 160, gives a version from Greece.

101. Collected in Linton, December 1969, from a 16-year-old male high school student. Hoffmann X714, "Humor concerning castrations." Cf. Hoffmann X714.3, "Castration of pet animals."

102. Collected in Terre Huate, May 1971, from a 28-year-old male student. Dance, pp. 257–58, gives a version from Virginia, and Orso, p. 196, gives a version from Greece.

103. Collected in Terre Haute, March 1982, from a 22-year-old female nurse. See Legman I, p. 197, for an American version and Legman II, p. 252, for a British version.

104. Collected in April 1969 from a 22-year-old female student from Richmond. Hoffmann X734.5.3, "Sparrow has intercourse with elephant; wonders if he is hurting her." Legman I, p. 196; Orso, p. 197.

105. Collected in Scottsburg, December 1970, from a 45-year-old female advertising manager. Two versions of this joke are in Neil V. Rosenberg, "An Annotated Collection of Parrot Jokes," (M.A. thesis, Indiana University, 1964), pp. 44–46. Also see Legman I, p. 203. Cf. Type 1422, "Parrot Unable to Tell Husband Details of Wife's Infidelity."

106. Collected in Logansport, August 1969, from a 52-year-old male railroad conductor. According to the informant, "There has been and still is a kind of professional jealousy between the engineer's crew and the train's crew, each claiming they are more important than the other. . . . Anything waved violently on or about the railroad tracks means *stop*." For the origin of "highball," see B. A. Botkin and Alvin F. Harlow, *A Treasury of Railroad Folklore* (New York: Bonanza Books, 1953), p. 292.

107. Collected in Trinity Springs, October 1972, from a 35-year-old male welder. Baughman J1495.1, "Man runs from actual or from supposed ghost."

108. Collected in Terre Haute, May 1969, from a 22-year-old male student. Legman II, p. 981, reports a New York version collected in 1940; and Orso, p. 202, prints a version from Greece. For additional references, see Neil V. Rosenberg, "An Annotated Collection of Parrot Jokes," (M.A. thesis, Indiana University, 1964), pp. 38–39.

109. Collected in Brooklyn, April 1978, from a 30-year-old male service station attendant. Five versions of this tale appear in Neil V. Rosenberg, "An Annotated Collection of Parrot Jokes," (M.A. thesis, Indiana University, 1964), pp. 26–31. Legman I, p. 202, reports a version collected in 1945 in Washington, D.C.

110. Collected in North Vernon, July 1969, from a 20-year-old male factory worker. Type 901, "Taming of the Shrew." Motif T251.2.3, "Wife becomes obedient on seeing husband slay a recalcitrant horse." See Jan Harold Brunvand, *"The Taming of the Shrew:* A Comparative Study of Oral and Literary Versions," (Ph.D. diss., Indiana University, 1961).

111. Collected in Dugger, September 1968, from a 43-year-old male coal miner. This tale has been reported as a legend ("true story") as well as a joke. William Hugh Jansen classifies it as one of three subtypes of a modern legend. See his essay, "The Surpriser Surprised: A Modern Legend," in *Readings in American Folklore*, ed. Jan Harold Brunvand (New York: Norton, 1979), pp. 64–90. This "flatulent form" of the tale appeared in Carson McCullers's novel, *The Heart Is a Lonely Hunter*, which was originally published in 1940. Legman II, pp. 860–61, reports a version.

112. This tale, collected in the 1930s, is from the WPA files. Cf. Motif J1545, "Wife outwits her husband."

113. Collected in Fort Wayne, July 1965, from a 29-year-old male Boy Scout executive. Two versions of this tale are in Legman I, p. 269.

114. Collected in Carthage, March 1983, from a 24-year-old male pool supervisor. Motifs J1540, "Retorts between husband and wife," and T283, "Wife withholds intercourse from husband to enforce demand."

115. Collected in Evansville, March 1970, from an 18-year-old male apprentice butcher. Cf. Motifs X800, "Humor based on drunkenness"; J1766, "One person mistaken for another"; J1485, "Mistaken identity." Versions of this tale appear in Legman I, p. 668, and Legman II, p. 201.

116. Collected in Scottsburg, January 1971, from a 40-year-old female photographer. Dance says this is a popular tale in the Richmond, Virginia, area (p. 337) and prints two versions (pp. 19–20). Another version is in Legman II, p. 919.

117. Collected in Terre Haute, July 1970, from a 49-year-old male truck driver. For a version, see Legman II, p. 585. According to Legman, "This type of pronunciational or homonym-humor is of the *Joe Miller* era of the 18th century, living on mostly in admitted puns."

118. Collected in November 1972 from a 20-year-old female student from Indianapolis. See Legman II, p. 593, for a similar tale about "an aphrodisiac which turns out badly."

119. Collected in Jasper, January 1969, from a 52-year-old male factory worker. Cf. Motif J1540, "Retorts between husband and wife."

120. Collected in Brazil, June 1971, from a 75-year-old male retired farmer. Motif J1805.1, "Similar sounding words mistaken for each other."

121. Collected in Terre Haute, January 1968, from a 21-year-old female student. This is a humorous treatment of Motif D1225, "Magic Whistle," applied to the Indian rope trick.

122. Collected in Scottsburg, November 1970, from a 21-year-old female secretary. See Legman II, p. 592, for an analogue.

123. Collected in December 1971 from a 22-year-old female student from Lawrence. In some versions of this joke the wife claims she is going to a raffle, and the husband says, "I didn't want to get your raffle ticket wet." Motifs J1532, "Adulteress's absurdity rebuked," and J1540, "Retorts between husband and wife."

124. Collected in Terre Haute, May 1969, from a 20-year-old female student. Type 1425B*, "Why Seventh has Red Hair."

125. Collected in April 1970 from an 18-year-old female student from Bloomfield. Cf. Motifs Q411.0.1.1, "Adulterer killed," and J865, "Consolation by thinking of some good aspect of a situation."

126. Collected in Terre Haute, January 1970, from a 44-year-old male traffic manager. A version of this tale can be found in Phyllis Potter, "St. Peter Jokes," *Southwest Folklore*, 3 (Spring 1979): 44–45. Cf. Type 1419K*, "Lover Hidden in Chest, etc."; and Motifs K1555.0.2, "Chest containing paramour unwittingly taken away by husband," and A661.0.1.2, "Saint Peter as porter of heaven."

127. Collected in Washington, April 1974, from a 25-year-old male farmer. Motif J1321, "The unrepentent drunkard." Cf. Motif J343.1, "Drunkard refuses cure of fever if it is to take away his thirst."

128. Collected in Unionville, April 1974, from a 39-year-old male carpenter. Motif X800, "Humor based on drunkenness."

129. Collected in Westport, April 1974, from a 21-year-old female factory worker. Motif X800, "Humor based on drunkenness." Cf. Motif J1805.1, "Similar sounding words mistaken for each other."

130. Collected in Staunton, March 1968, from a 28-year-old male state highway worker. For a version, see Legman II, p. 942. Cf. Type 1832B*, "What Kind of Dung."

131. Collected in Terre Haute, November 1972, from a 20-year-old housewife. Motif X800, "Humor based on drunkenness." Cf. Motif J1805.1, "Similar sounding words mistaken for each other."

132. Collected in Terre Haute, July 1970, from a middle-aged male railroader. Exact age withheld. Motif X137, "Humor of ugliness." Cf. Motifs X800, "Humor based on drunkenness," and J1765, "Person thought to be animal."

133. Collected in Terre Haute, April 1973, from a middle-aged female factory worker. Exact age withheld. For a variant, see Legman II, p. 719.

134. Collected in Dubois, November 1979, from a 22-year-old male student. Dance, pp. 62–63, gives a version from Virginia. Vance Randolph also reports a version from the Ozarks in *Hot Springs and Hell* (Hatboro, Pa.: Folklore Associates, 1965), p. 41.

135. Collected in Indianapolis, December 1972, from a 23-year-old male city government intern. Buehler (pp. 36–37, 64, 106–07) reports three versions of this tale. Cf. Legman I, p. 63.

136. Collected in Jasper, January 1969, from a 55-year-old male farmer. Baughman X828*, "Drunk person falls in open grave with humorous results." Vance Randolph has a version of this tale in *Hot Springs and Hell* (Hatboro, Pa.: Folklore Associates, 1965), p. 125. This motif also appears in the following tale. Cf. tale and note 149.

137. Collected in Mitchell, December 1967, from a 46-year-old male optometrist. Baughman X828*, "Drunk person falls in open grave with humorous results." This motif also appears in the preceding tale. Cf. tale and note 149.

138. This tale, collected in the 1930s, is from the WPA files. Type 1561, "The Lazy Boy Eats Breakfast, Dinner, and Supper One after the Other without working." Motif W111.2.6, "The boy eats breakfast, dinner, and supper one immediately after the other; then lies down to sleep."

139. Collected in the 1930s, this tale is from the WPA files. Type 1951, "Is Wood Split?" According to Baughman (p. 62), "In common American form, the lazy man asks if the corn is shelled." Baughman W111.5.10.1, "Lazy man is being taken to poorhouse or out of town to cemetery to be buried alive. The group take pity on him."

140. Collected in Terre Haute, April 1972, from a 36-year-old female service representative. Motif J1115.1, "Clever gambler." For versions see Orso, p. 53; Legman I, pp. 107–08; Legman II, pp. 543–44.

141. Collected in Columbus, October 1969, from a 27-year-old male factory worker. Cf. Motif K523.1, "Escape by shamming madness."

142. Collected in the 1930s, this tale is from the WPA files. Baughman J1155.1.1*(b), "Hunter (or fisherman) meets stranger, tells him about all the animals, birds, or fish he has caught that day." The following two tales are versions.

143. Collected in Farmersburg, May 1971, from a 57-year-old male retired grocer. Baughman J1155.1.1*(b), "Hunter (or fisherman) meets stranger, tells him about all the animals, birds, or fish he has caught that day." The preceding tale and following tale are versions.

144. Collected in Farmersburg, April 1971, from an 18-year-old male high school student. Baughman J1155.1.1*(b), "Hunter (or fisherman) meets stranger, tells him about all the animals, birds, or fish he has caught that day." The preceding two tales are versions.

145. Collected in Farmersburg, April 1971, from an 82-year-old male retired miner. Baughman K1699*(jb), "Game warden trying to catch fish dynamiter is tricked into lighting the fuse." Cf. Motif J1180, "Clever means of avoiding legal punishment."

146. This tale, collected in the 1930s, is from the WPA files. Baughman J1369.6*, "Candidate at political meeting explains that he is a country boy, that he had grown up between two rows of corn."

147. Collected in the 1930s, this tale is from the WPA files. Baughman J1499.13*(d), "American is contemptuous of sizes of things in England."

148. Collected in Frankton, October 1981, from a 77-year-old male farmer-sportsman. Baughman K134.5(a), "Owner tells victim, 'There is nothing wrong with this horse except that he don't look so good.'"

149. Collected in Linton, February 1968, from a 31-year-old male salesperson. Motif J1782.6, "Person in white thought to be ghost." Cf. tales and notes 136, 137.

150. Collected in September 1968 from a 19-year-old male student from Jasper. Baughman J1499.13*(g), "Man is amazed at high prices in hotel." Legman I, p. 245, reports a similar tale about Abraham Lincoln.

151. Collected in Terre Haute, April 1973, from a middle-aged female factory worker. Exact age withheld. Motif J1761, "Animal or person mistaken for something else." Versions appear in Orso, p. 213, and Legman I, pp. 213–14. Cf. Hoffmann J1772.18.2, "Man's member taken for gosling's neck," which appears in tale 186.

152. Collected in December 1971 from a 23-year-old male student from Indianapolis. Motif J1772.9, "Excrement thought to be meat and therefore eaten." Clements E6.9, "The Pile of Excrement." For a version from Greece, see Orso, pp. 129–30.

153. Collected in Vincennes, December 1970, from a 70-year-old male retired bus driver. Motif J1772, "One object thought to be another." A version of this tale is in Legman I, pp. 213–14. Cf. Legman II, p. 635.

154. Collected in Hope, February 1974, from a 13-year-old male student. Hoffmann J1772.19, "Buttocks mistaken for face." See Legman II, p. 822, for a version.

155. Collected in Dale, February 1970, from a 20-year-old male student. Hoffmann J1842, "Useless surgical operation from misunderstanding." Cf. Type 1687, "The Forgotten Word." Legman II, p. 538, reports a version of this joke.

156. Collected in Brazil, December 1971, from a 28-year-old male postal clerk. Hoffmann X733.1.1, "Man mounts Indian squaw, who continually shouts 'Wahoo' as he has her. Later is told that 'Wahoo' means 'wrong hole.'" For versions, see Legman II, p. 165; Orso, p. 166; Randolph, pp. 118–19.

157. Collected in Mitchell, December 1970, from a 79-year-old male retired stone mill worker. Motif J1811.1, "Owl's hoot misunderstood by lost simpleton."

158. Collected in Scottsburg, January 1970, from a 40-year-old female photographer. Cf. Motif J2460.1, "Disastrous following of misunderstood instructions." Legman II, p. 463, gives a version in which the doctor shouts to a nurse with scissors chasing a male patient, "Nurse! Nurse! I said 'Slip off his spectacles!'"

159. Collected in Indianapolis, November 1971, from a middle-aged male. Exact age and occupation withheld. Cf. Motif J2460.1, "Disastrous following of misunderstood instructions." Cf. Baughman Z510*, "The fatal fraternity initiation." For a version dealing with a fraternity initiation, see Ronald L. Baker, "The Folklore of Students," in *The Handbook of American Folklore*, ed. Richard M. Dorson (Bloomington: Indiana University Press, 1983), p. 110.

160. Collected in Greensburg, April 1969, from a 47-year-old male construction worker. Motif J1905, "Absurd ignorance about milking animals." Cf. Motif J1903.2, "Numskull puts the milk back."

161. Collected in Terre Haute, November 1972, from a 51-year-old male grain elevator operator. For a version of this tale from Maine, see Richard M. Dorson, "Just B'ars," *Appalachia*, NS 8 (December 1942): 178–79. A literary treatment can be found in Rowland E. Robinson, *Uncle Lisha's Shop and A Danvis Pioneer* (Rutland, Vt.: Charles E. Tuttle Co., 1937), pp. 128–36.

162. Collected in Elnora, November 1967, from a 20-year-old female student. Hoffmann J2046.1, "Bus driver forgets his announcement, utters absurd twisted versions." Legman II, p. 809. Cf. Type 1204, "Fool Keeps Repeating his Instructions."

163. Collected in Sullivan, October 1968, from a 70-year-old male retired construction worker. Motif J2071, "Three foolish wishes." This is an international tale, with recent versions reported from Denmark and Hungary as well as from the United States. See Ranke, pp. 11, 134; Richard M. Dorson, *American Negro Folktales* (Greenwich, Conn.: Fawcett, 1967), pp. 343–44; and Legman II, p. 619. Cf. tale 258.

164. Collected in Mitchell, December 1970, from a 79-year-old male retired stone mill worker. Type 1562, "Think Thrice before You Speak." Motif J2516.1, "Think thrice before you speak."

165. Collected in Terre Haute, November 1969, from a 20-year-old female student. Motif J2260, "Absurd scientific theories." Brunvand F125, "The Flea-Jumping Experiment." Clements E6.8, "The Experiment."

166. Collected in Scottsburg, January 1971, from a 40-year-old female photographer. This tale is reported in Buehler, pp. 140–41, and Legman I, p. 149.

167. Collected in May 1969 from a 21-year-old male student from Hammond. Clements F2.30.6, "Farther, Farther.":

168. Collected in Elnora, March 1972, from a 23-year-old male welder. Hoffmann X732.1, "Male ignorant of sexual intercourse." Motifs J1745, "Absurd ignorance of sex," and J1805, "Other misunderstandings of words."

169. Collected in Jasper, January 1969, from a 21-year-old housewife. Hoffmann X732.1, "Male ignorant of sexual intercourse." Motifs J1745, "Absurd ignorance of sex," and J1742, "The countryman in the great world." Cf. Motifs J1803, "Learned words misunderstood by uneducated," and J2400, "Foolish imitation."

170. Collected in Jasper, January 1969, from a 52-year-old male factory worker. Hoffmann X732.1, "Male ignorant of sexual intercourse." Motifs J1805.1, "Similar sounding words mistaken for each other," J1745, "Absurd ignorance of sex," and J2450, "Literal fool."

171. Collected in West Terre Haute, October 1971, from a 32-year-old male auto mechanic. Hoffmann X733.1, "Unwitting anal intercourse." Orso, pp. 181–82, reports a version from Greece. An analogue, but without buggery, from Greece is in Ranke, pp. 50–51.

172. Collected in April 1969 from a 22-year-old female student from Princeton. Cf. Orso, p. 36, and Legman I, p. 93. This probably is a tale of sexual preference, homosexuality, rather than one of sexual ignorance. Legman II, p. 78, reports a similar tale about a girl who describes her wedding night to her mother: "Well, he laid me on the bed and undressed me completely. Then he undressed too. Then he put on all *my* clothes, and I haven't seen the son-of-a-bitch since!"

173. Collected in June 1971 from a 22-year-old male student from Logansport. Hoffmann X761, "Call him Houdini." Versions can be found in Dance, pp. 118–19, and Legman I, p. 434.

174. Collected in March 1969 from a 20-year-old female student from Indianapolis. A version from Greece appears in Orso, p. 37.

175. Collected in Mooresville, December 1968, from a 55-year-old female retired schoolteacher. Hoffman J1772.18.2, "Man's member taken for a gosling's neck." Versions appear in Buehler, pp. 117–18; Dance, p. 294; Legman I, pp. 99–100. Another version, collected from an 8-year-old female, is in Rosemary Zumwalt, "Plain and Fancy: A Content Analysis of Children's Jokes Dealing with Adult Sexuality," *Western Folklore*, 35 (October 1976): 264.

176. Collected in West Terre Haute, November 1979, from a 22-year-old female secretary. For a version of this tale, see Legman I, p. 58.

177. Collected in St. Mary-of-the-Woods, October 1968, from a 19-year-old female student. Motif J1745, "Absurd ignorance of sex."

178. Collected in May 1970 from a 21-year-old male student from Shelbyville. Clements D1.11, "The Brown Line."

179. Collected in Bowling Green, January 1969, from a 21-year-old male student. Cf. Clements D1.0, "Excrement," ff. Legman II, p. 964, reports a version of this tale about a Texan.

180. Collected in November 1972 from a 20-year-old female student from Indianapolis. Clements F2.36, "The Case of Diarrhea."

181. Collected in Bloomington, April 1973, from a 25-year-old female student. Cf. Clements E1.0, "Inherent Stupidity," ff.

182. Collected in Jasonville, April 1969, from a 37-year-old male minister. Clements E1.5, "Polish Brains."

183. Collected in Evansville, October 1973, from an 18-year-old male student and part-time stock clerk. Baughman X691.3*, "Characteristic: few brains or lack of brains or substitute brains." Cf. Clements E1.6, "The Operation."

184. Collected in Evansville, April 1970, from a 25-year-old male electrician. Clements E3.3, "The Polish Lumberjack."

185. Collected in Evansville, April 1970, from a 54-year-old housewife. Cf. Clements E3.0, "Polacks at Work," ff.

186. Collected in Terre Haute, April 1973, from a 20-year-old male student. Clements E3.4, "Polish Turf Layers."

187. Collected in Evansville, October 1973, from an 18-year-old male student and part-time stock clerk. Clements E3.6, "The Light."

188. Collected in Indianapolis, November 1973, from a 17-year-old male student. Clements E3.8, "Test of the Dumbest Polack."

189. Collected in Evansville, April 1970, from a 54-year-old housewife. Motif J1919.2, "Where the ducks ford."

190. Collected in Evansville, December 1972, from a 35-year-old female teacher. Motif J2013.1, "White man made to believe that he is a negro." See Dance, p. 97, for a version from Virginia, and Vance Randolph, *Hot Springs and Hell* (Hatboro, Pa.: Folklore Associates, 1965), p. 114, for an analogue from the Ozarks. Randolph provides an informative note, tracing this tale to a fifteenth-century manuscript, on pp. 243–44.

191. Collected in Evansville, November 1973, from a 21-year-old housewife and student. Type 1278, "Marking the Place on the Boat." Motif J1922.1, "Marking the place on the boat." Clements E5.6.2, "Good Luck at Fishing."

192. Collected in Evansville, November 1973, from a 22-year-old male student and part-time janitor. Type 1349D*, "What Is the Joke?" Baughman J2131.1(a), "Stranger puts hand on a stone, lets numskull hit it as hard as he likes. Man removes his hand; numskull hits the stone."

193. Collected in March 1974 from a 20-year-old female student from Seymour. Clements E7.8, "The Polack and the Mule."

194. Collected in Aurora, February 1970, from a 20-year-old male student. Baughman J2259*(m), "Fool considers traveling on beam of light." Clements E7.13, "The Beam of Light."

195. Collected in Indianapolis, February 1974, from a 30-year-old male carpenter. Baughman J2259*(k), "Fool discards about half the nails . . . He explains that those nails are for the opposite wall (or that they have their heads on wrong)." Clements E14.4, "Nails on the Wrong End." See Orso, pp. 124–25, for a version from Greece.

196. Collected in Shelbyville, April 1974, from a 21-year-old female student. Motif J2721, "Why he couldn't see."

197. Collected in Evansville, October 1973, from an 18-year-old male student and part-time stock clerk. Clements E5.2.2, "Instant Replay."

198. Collected in Princeton, May 1969, from a 33-year-old male computer technician. Clements E5.2.3, "The Football Game."

199. Collected in Evansville, October 1973, from an 18-year-old male student. Clements E14.14, "The Reckless Polack." Cf. Clements H2.6, "The Ignorant Polack on His Honeymoon."

200. Collected in North Vernon, August 1969, from a 20-year-old male student and part-time factory worker. Baughman X691.5.1*, "Men of three nationalities out walking come to skunk hole." Clements G4.5, "The Pig Pen." Buehler, pp. 154–55, has a version.

201. Collected in May 1971 from a 20-year-old male student from Indianapolis. Clements G6.5, "The Quartermaster."

202. Collected in Fort Branch, April 1974, from a 49-year-old male dairy farmer. Clements G6.7, "The Outhouse."

203. Collected in Evansville, April 1970, from a 54-year-old male fire inspector. Motif J1745, "Absurd ignorance of sex." Clements H2.0, "Ignorance of Sexual Matters." Cf. Legman I, p. 132.

204. Collected in Evansville, February 1970, from a 19-year-old female student. Clements I1.3, "The Polish King."

205. Collected in Evansville, October 1973, from a 22-year-old male student and part-time janitor. Clements M1.11, "The Polish National Guard Troop."

206. Collected in Cloverland, December 1971, from a 21-year-old male student. Hoffmann X737.1, "Too old to do otherwise." See Randolph, pp. 44–45, for a version.

207. Collected in Evansville, November 1973, from an 18-year-old male student. Motif J2174, "Foolish demands before death."

208. Collected in Evansville, October 1973, from an 18-year-old male student. Clements L5.15, "The Airplane." For versions, see Buehler, pp. 150–53, and Orso, pp. 50–51.

209. Collected in Evansville, October 1973, from a 22-year-old male student and part-time janitor. Clements L4.7, "The Fare to Poland."

210. Collected in Austin, March 1974, from a 12-year-old female student.

A version of this tale can be found in F. Ray Johnson, ed., *Oral Folk Humor from the Carolina and Virginia Flatlands* (Murfreesboro, N.C.: Johnson Publishing Co., 1980), pp. 69–70.

211. Collected in Patricksburg, April 1973, from a 62-year-old male farmer. Motif J1759.3, "Numskull thinks fireflies are mosquitoes carrying lanterns to find victims." Baughman X621*, "Jokes about the Irish."

212. Collected in Mitchell, December 1970, from a 79-year-old male retired stone mill worker. Motif J1761, "Animal thought to be object." Baughman X621*, "Jokes about the Irish." Vance Randolph reports a short version of this tale in *Hot Springs and Hell* (Hatboro, Pa.: Folklore Associates, 1965), p. 152.

213. Collected in Mitchell, December 1970, from a 79-year-old male retired stone mill worker. Type 1319A, "The Watch Mistaken for the Devil's Eye." Baughman J1772.21*, "Watch is taken for sea tick." Baughman X621*, "Jokes about the Irish."

214. Collected in Mitchell, December 1970, from a 79-year-old male retired stone mill worker. Type 1250, "Bringing Water from the Well." Motifs J1791.3.3, "Moon's reflection thought to be gold in water"; J2133.5, "Men hang down in a chain until top man spits on his hands. They all fall." Baughman X621*, "Jokes about the Irish."

215. Collected in Mitchell, December 1970, from a 79-year-old male retired stone mill worker. Type 1290B*, "Sleeping on a Feather." Motif J2213.9, "Numskull finds that one feather makes a hard pillow, thinks a sackful would be unbearable." Baughman X621*, "Jokes about the Irish." This international tale goes back to at least 1512, when it was published in Strasbourg by Heinrich Bebel in *Facetiae*. The story is still told in Germany, Ireland, Lithuania, and Poland. See Ranke, pp. 44, 143.

216. Collected in Terre Haute, May 1971, from a 23-year-old male bricklayer. Baughman X621*, "Jokes about the Irish." Cf. Motif K1687, "The easier job."

217. Collected in Gary, December 1969, from a 53-year-old male steel mill supervisor. Type 1626, "Dream Bread." Motif K444, "Dream bread: the most wonderful dream." Baughman X621*, "Jokes about the Irish." For a discussion of this international folktale, see Paul F. Baum, "The Three Dreams or 'Dream Bread' Story," *Journal of American Folklore*, 30 (1917): 378–410.

218. Collected in Vincennes, December 1968, from a 65-year-old white cleaning lady. Type 1791, "The Sexton Carries the Parson." Motif X424, "The devil in the cemetery." This is a typical American version of this international tale. See Baughman, p. 47.

219. Collected in Mitchell, December 1970, from a 79-year-old white male retired stone mill worker. Type 1676C, "Voices from Graveyard." Cf. Type 1532, "The Voice from the Grave." Motif K1974, "Living man at the grave pretends to be dead man speaking."

220. Collected in April 1983 from a 21-year-old white male student from Knightstown. Motif F547.3.1, "Long penis." Buehler, p. 56, has a version of this tale about two Texans.

221. Collected in Hammond, November 1968, from a 26-year-old white male steel worker. Baughman X665*, "Jokes about Negroes." Motif F547.3.1, "Long penis."

222. Collected in December 1971 from a 19-year-old white female student from Anderson. Cf. Baughman X691.2.1*, "Unusual sexual capacity of Negro."

223. Collected in August 1969 from a 20-year-old white female student from Clarksville. Baughman X665*, "Jokes about Negroes." Jan Harold Brunvand refers to other jokes about black astronauts in "The Study of Contemporary Folklore: Jokes," *Fabula*, 13 (1972): 8.

224. Collected in November 1968 from a 20-year-old white female student from Washington. Baughman X665*, "Jokes about Negroes."

225. Collected in Washington, December 1971, from a 21-year-old white male student. Richard M. Dorson prints a version of this tale in *Folklore: Selected Essays* (Bloomington: Indiana University Press, 1972), pp. 90–91. Also see Legman II, p. 478.

226. Collected in March 1969 from a 21-year-old white female student from Kokomo. Baughman X665*, "Jokes about Negroes." This joke also is told about a Pole and a black. Cf. Clements M, "Polacks and Other Ethnic Groups," M1.0, "Negroes."

227. Collected in Terre Haute, August 1969, from a 22-year-old black female student. Richard M. Dorson has a version in *American Negro Folktales* (Greenwich, Conn.: Fawcett, 1967), pp. 174–75. For another version, see Dance, p. 153. Tale 259 is a variant.

228. Collected in Indianapolis, March 1981, from a 48-year-old white male teacher. Baughman X665*, "Jokes about Negroes." Cf. Dance, "The Last Thing I Remember," p. 175.

229. Collected in Washington, April 1974, from a 25-year-old white male student. Baughman X665*, "Jokes about Negroes."

230. Collected in Terre Haute, July 1968, from a 23-year-old white male student. Legman II, p. 126, reports a version of this tale about a piccolo player in the Dinktown band.

231. Collected in Indianapolis, February 1981, from a 48-year-old white male teacher. Legman II, pp. 148–49, has a version dealing with a man with a wooden leg who wants to rent a cheap costume for a masquerade ball. When the one-legged customer objects to the price of several costumes, the costumer suggests, "How about a costume for only 35¢? All you need is a can of molasses and some red paint. You undress naked and pour the molasses all over you, and then the red paint. Then you stick your wooden leg up your ass, and go as a jelly apple." Also see Legman II, p. 633.

232. Collected in Hammond, January 1970, from a 21-year-old male student. Clements C6.10, "The Three Babies."

233. Collected in April 1969 from a 21-year-old female student from Kokomo. Clements E3.10.3, "The Polish Rocket."

234. Collected in Indianapolis, November 1971, from a 17-year-old male student. Clements E4.2, "The Battlefield."

235. Collected in Indianapolis, August 1971, from a 22-year-old male student. Clements E5.3, "The Polack at the Indianapolis 500."

236. Collected in Fort Wayne, November 1971, from an 8-year-old male student, who learned the tale from his uncle, a factory worker. Clements E5.6.3, "Polacks and Ice Fishing."

237. Collected in Terre Haute, March 1982, from a 21-year-old male deputy sheriff. Clements E5.7.1, "The Polish Tracker."

238. Collected in Terre Haute, August 1968, from a 20-year-old male student. Clements E5.7.2, "Game."

239. Collected in Terre Haute, December 1969, from a 30-year-old male printer. Clements E5.7.3, "The Lost Polish Hunters."

240. Collected in Elnora, March 1972, from a 23-year-old male welder. Clements E6.4, "The Polack's New Car."

241. Collected in Terre Haute, December 1969, from a 30-year-old male fireman. Clements E6.5, "The Flagpole Measurement."

242. Collected in Jasper, December 1967, from a 20-year-old female student. Motif J2213, "Illogical use of numbers." Clements E6.7, "The Pizza."

243. Collected in December 1967 from a 21-year-old male student from West Lafayette. Clements E7.2, "Why It Takes a Polack Four Hours to Wash a Basement Window."

244. Collected in December 1967 from a 23-year-old male student from Connersville. Baughman J2722, "Telling their horses apart." Clements E7.12, "Polacks and Horses."

245. Collected in Crawfordsville, December 1971, from a 25-year-old male teacher. Clements E14.18, "The Stolen Camel."

246. Collected in Terre Haute, March 1982, from a 28-year-old male police officer. Cf. Clements G1.0, "Baths and Hygiene," ff. A version of this tale, though not a Polish joke, is in Legman II, p. 408. The punch line is: "he's just a coal-miner that goes home for lunch."

247. Collected in March 1969 from a 24-year-old female nurse from Princeton. Clements G6.3, "The Polack and the Frog."

248. Collected in Montezuma, April 1979, from a 22-year-old female student. Cf. Clements F2.0, "Foolish Actions Resulting from Literalness."

249. Collected in Terre Haute, November 1980, from a 31-year-old male caseworker. Hoffmann X722.1.1, "Not good enough for her kinfolks, not good enough for us." See Randolph, pp. 80–81, and Legman I, p. 460, for versions.

250. Collected in Hammond, November 1968, from a 26-year-old male steel worker. Clements H2.1, "Rape by a Polack."

251. Collected in Terre Haute, March 1968, from a 20-year-old male student. Clements H2.10, "The Nude Polack on the Street Corner."

252. Collected in Crawfordsville, November 1981, from a 42-year-old male electric shop foreman. For a version of this joke, see Legman I, p. 69.

253. Collected in Terre Haute, December 1978, from a 42-year-old male fireman. Motif J1772, "One object thought to be another." Cf. Hoffmann J1772.16, "Water closet thought to be basin for washing feet."

254. Collected in November 1970 from a 20-year-old female student from Lynnville. Motif X610, "Jokes concerning Jews."

255. Collected in Terre Haute, May 1969, from a 20-year-old female student. Legman II, p. 235, has a version of this joke from New York, 1938. His version concerns the Brooklyn way, not Jewish way, but amounts to the same thing since the protagonist is called "Hymie" and his version was told in Yiddish.

256. Collected in April 1974 from a 21-year-old male student from Kokomo. Baughman K231.13, "Two men decide to leave sum of money on coffin of friend. One puts on his share in cash. The other makes out a check for the total amount, takes cash left by the other." For versions, see Cray, p. 336; Dance, pp. 154–55: Ranke, pp. 90, 155.

257. Collected in Evansville, April 1971, from a 31-year-old housewife. Versions appear in Dance, p. 158, and Richard M. Dorson, "Jewish-American Dialect Stories on Tape," in *Studies in Biblical and Jewish Folklore,* ed. Raphael Patai, Francis Lee Utley, and Dov Noy (Bloomington: Indiana University Press, 1960), pp. 152–53.

258. Collected in Terre Haute, March 1971, from a 71-year-old male retired supermarket owner and operator. Type 1331, "The Covetous and the Envious." Motif J2074, "Twice the wish to the enemy." Cf. tale 163.

259. Collected in Roselawn, May 1969, from a 21-year-old female student. Versions appear in Dance, p. 153; Richard M. Dorson, *American Negro Folktales* (Greenwich, Conn.: Fawcett, 1967), pp. 174–75; and Phyllis Potter, "St. Peter Jokes," *Southwest Folklore,* 3 (Spring 1979): 50. Tale 227 also is a version.

260. Collected in May 1971, from a 21-year-old male student from Kokomo. For a version of this tale, see Richard M. Dorson, "More Jewish Dialect Stories," *Midwest Folklore,* 10 (Fall 1960): 140–41.

261. Collected in December 1968 from a 21-year-old female student from Martinsville. A version appears in Cray, pp. 338–39.

262. Collected in Evansville, December 1969, from a 46-year-old male appraiser for a savings company. Buehler, p. 164, gives a version.

263. Collected in May 1971 from a 21-year-old male student from Greenfield. For versions, see Buehler, pp. 6–7; Cray, p. 341; and Richard M. Dorson, "Jewish-American Dialect Stories on Tape," in *Studies in Biblical and Jewish Folklore,* ed. Raphael Patai, Francis Lee Utley, and Dov Noy (Bloomington: Indiana University Press, 1960), pp. 145–46.

264. Collected in July 1969 from a 22-year-old female student from Hobart. Versions appear in Buehler, pp. 73–74; Cray, p. 340; Legman I, p. 418; Legman II, p. 765; and Richard M. Dorson, "More Jewish Dialect Stories," *Midwest Folklore,* 10 (Fall 1960): 142–43.

265. Collected in Evansville, December 1969, from a 17-year-old student. See Cray, p. 344, and Richard M. Dorson, "Jewish American Dialect Stories on Tape," in *Studies in Biblical and Jewish Folklore,* ed. Raphael Patai, Francis Lee Utley, and Dov Noy (Bloomington: Indiana University Press, 1960), p. 164. Cf. Type 1831, "The Parson and Sexton at Mass."

266. Collected in Terre Haute, April 1973, from a 23-year-old male unskilled laborer. Motif X610, "Jokes concerning Jews."

267. Collected in Rosedale, March 1973, from a 30-year-old male lab technician. This is a humorous treatment of Motif D476.3.4, "Meat miraculously turned into fish on a feast day." For a discussion of a fifteenth-century analogue of this tale, see Shirley Marchalonis, "Three Medieval Tales and Their Modern American Analogues," in *Readings in American Folklore,* ed. Jan Harold Brunvand (New York: Norton, 1979), pp. 270–72. A version is in Alan Dundes, "A Study of Ethnic Slurs: The Jew and the Polack in the United States," *Journal of American Folklore,* 84 (April–June 1971): 196–97.

268. Collected in Harrisburg, November 1980, from a 55-year-old male soil conservationist. For a version, see Cray, p. 333.

269. Collected in Brook, April 1981, from a 22-year-old female student. Motif X410, "Jokes on parsons."

270. Collected in Terre Haute, July 1968, from a 58-year-old male bartender. A version appears in Dance, pp. 67–68.

271. Collected in Seelyville, April 1970, from a 37-year-old male mechanic. Motif J1264, "Repartee concerning clerical incontinence."

272. Collected in April 1981 from a 20-year-old female student from Linton. Motif J 1264, "Repartee concerning clerical incontinence."

273. Collected in Princeton, March 1969, from a 22-year-old female nurse. Two versions of this tale are in Phyllis Potter, "St. Peter Jokes," *Southwest Folklore*, 3 (Spring 1979): 54–55. Cf. Type 1738C*, "Chalk Marks on Heaven's Stairs"; Type 1848, "A Pebble for each Sin"; Baughman J2466.1(a), "Man meets St. Peter at pearly gates. St. Peter orders him to make a chalk mark on the stairs for each sin he has committed."

274. Collected in May 1971 from a 20-year-old male student from South Bend. For a version, see Buehler, pp. 108–09.

275. Collected in Washington, December 1970, from a 21-year-old female student. Legman II, p. 777, prints a version of this joke collected in New York in 1965. Another version appears in Carol A. Mitchell, "The Sexual Perspective in the Appreciation and Interpretation of Jokes," *Western Folklore*, 36 (October 1977): 328.

276. Collected in Terre Haute, January 1974, from a 22-year-old female student. Motif J 1264, "Repartee concerning clerical incontinence."

277. Collected in Elnora, March 1972, from a 23-year-old male welder. See Legman II, p. 716, for a version.

278. Collected in Burney, April 1974, from a male informant. Age and occupation withheld. Hoffmann K1363.1, "Putting the key to heaven in the lock (the Pope in Rome)." Versions appear in Dance, pp. 58–59; Legman I, p. 552; Buehler, pp. 72–73, 109–10.

279. Collected in May 1971 from a 20-year-old male student from South Bend. Legman II, pp. 551–52, has a version, though it's about three stenographers and a hole in the boss's condom.

280. Collected in Burney, February 1974, from a 20-year-old male farmer. Hoffmann J1738.9.3, "Apprehension about penance." See Legman II, p. 134, and Orso, p. 109.

281. Collected in May 1971 from a 19-year-old female student from Greencastle. Motif J 1263, "Repartee concerning clerical abuses."

282. Collected in March 1969 from a 22-year-old female student from Richmond. Motifs J 1260, "Repartee based on church or clergy," and J 1805.1, "Similar sounding words mistaken for each other." A variant of this tale appears in Phyllis Potter, "St. Peter Jokes," *Southwest Folklore*, 3 (Spring 1979): 47–48.

283. Collected in May 1971 from a 21-year-old female student from Indianapolis. For a variant of this tale, see Legman II, p. 764.

284. Collected in May 1971 from a 19-year-old female student from Greencastle. Legman II, p. 576, gives a version of this tale.

285. Collected in Bloomington, March 1974, from a 21-year-old male foreman. A version about baby oil and sulphuric (or carbolic) acid instead of holy water and turpentine is in Legman II, p. 487.

286. Collected in Mount Vernon, May 1971, from a 40-year-old housewife. The informant is Lutheran. Motif J 1260, "Repartee based on church or clergy."

287. Collected in Westfield, November 1979, from a 49-year-old male carpenter. Hoffmann X749.5.4.1.1, "The Isle of Man: double entendre story developed around everyone's having an ass (donkey)." See Legman II, p. 817.

288. Collected in Indianapolis, February 1970, from a 20-year-old male student. Fragmentary versions appear in Buehler, p. 23, and Legman I, p. 158. For fuller versions, see Carol A. Mitchell, "The Sexual Perspective in the Appreciation and Interpretation of Jokes," *Western Folklore,* 36 (October 1977): 327; and Phyllis Potter, "St. Peter Jokes," *Southwest Folklore,* 3 (Spring 1979): 40. Cf. Motif X455.1, "Parson takes a drink of liquor during the sermon."

289. Collected in Terre Haute, November 1978, from a 45-year-old male jewelry store manager. Versions appear in Dance, p. 53, and Vance Randolph, *Hot Springs and Hell* (Hatboro, Pa.: Folklore Associates, 1965), p. 146.

290. Collected in May 1969 from a 19-year-old female student. For a version of this tale, see Legman I, p. 75.

291. Collected in August 1969 from a 21-year-old female student from Gary. Cf. Hoffmann K1339.6.2, "That and a great deal more." Dance, pp. 57–58; Legman I, p. 419; Legman II, p. 766; and Orso, pp. 96–97.

292. Collected in Elnora, March 1972, from a 22-year-old male farmer. Motifs X410, "Jokes on parsons," and J1264, "Repartee concerning clerical incontinence."

293. Collected in Jasonville, April 1969, from a 37-year-old male minister. For versions, see Cray, p. 337, and Legman I, p. 362. Cray's version is about a rabbi, priest, and minister. Legman's version deals with nuns, though he says that sometimes the tale is about ministers' wives.

294. Collected in the 1930s, this tale is from the WPA files. Type 1832M*, "Priest's Words Repeated." Baughman J2498.1, "The imitative choir."

295. Collected in December 1971 from a 21-year-old female student from Indianapolis. Hoffmann X735.9.4, "Creator endows man with twenty years of sex life, but he manages to get ten years each from monkey, lion, and ass."

296. Collected in Washington, December 1970, from a 21-year-old female student. For versions of this tale, see Buehler, pp. 75–76; Legman I, p. 265; and Legman II, p. 775.

297. Collected in May 1971 from a 20-year-old male student from South Bend. Cf. Motif J2215.4, "Fool waits for God to provide."

298. Collected in May 1971 from a 21-year-old male student from Kokomo. Variants appear in Buehler, pp. 113–14; Dance, p. 75; and Legman II, p. 778.

299. Collected in April 1983 from a 21-year-old male student from Vincennes. This tale about basketball and Coach Knight has analogues about other sports and sports heroes. For example, a similar tale in the ISU Folklore Archives is about golf and Arnold Palmer. Cf. tale 351, "Jesus and Moses at Golf."

300. Collected in November 1972 from a 21-year-old male student from Seymour. For two versions of this tale, see Phyllis Potter, "St. Peter Jokes," *Southwest Folklore,* 3 (Spring 1979): 55–56. Baughman X597*, "Jokes about new arrival in heaven"; Motif A661.0.1.2, "St. Peter as porter of heaven."

301. Collected in the 1930s, this tale is from the WPA files. Cf. Type 1931, "The Woman Who Asked for News from Home."

302. Collected in October 1970 from a 19-year-old male student from Evansville. Brian Sutton-Smith has a version of this short tale in " 'Shut Up and Keep Digging': The Cruel Joke Series," *Midwest Folklore,* 10 (Spring 1960): 21.

303. Collected in November 1972 from a 20-year-old male student from

Orleans. The scripture quoted in this tale is from John 8:7, "He that is without sin among you, let him first cast a stone at her." For a version of this tale, see Legman II, p. 776.

304. Collected in May 1971 from a 24-year-old male student from Evansville. This and the following two tales are jocular handlings of Motif V211.2.3, "The Crucifixion."

305. Collected in Lebanon, April 1982, from a 21-year-old male student. This is a humorous treatment of Motif V211.2.3, "The Crucifixion."

306. Collected in November 1972 from a 20-year-old male student from Orleans. Motif V211.2.3, "The Crucifixion," is applied humorously in this tale.

307. Collected in May 1971 from a 19-year-old female student from Seymour. This is a humorous treatment of Motifs V211.2, "Christ on earth," and V211.2.1.2, "Christ disguised as beggar."

308. Collected in Jasper, January 1969, from a 53-year-old male labor representative. Baughman X583(a), "Lost traveler asks native how he can find his way back to civilization."

309. Collected in Vincennes, December 1970, from a 15-year-old female student. Buehler, pp. 120–21, has a version of this tale.

310. Collected in May 1971 from a 21-year-old male student from Linton. Baughman X583, "Jokes about travelers."

311. Collected in December 1971 from a 21-year-old female student from Aurora. Versions are in Dance, p. 127, and Legman I, p. 435.

312. Collected in Indianapolis, December 1972, from a 23-year-old male city government intern. Hoffmann X725.1.2, "You'll have to quit using my ass for a tally-board." Versions can be found in Dance, pp. 292–93; Legman I, p. 773; and Randolph, pp. 81–82.

313. Collected in Carmel, December 1979, from a 21-year-old male student. Type 1363*, "The Second Cat." For versions see Dance, pp. 85–86, and Orso, pp. 128–29.

314. Collected in Seymour, August 1969, from a 22-year-old male student. Versions of this tale appear in Legman I, pp. 124, 682.

315. Collected in Terre Haute, November 1972, from a 20-year-old housewife. Type 1689, "Thank God they Weren't Peaches." Motif J2563, "Thank God they weren't peaches!" Variants appear in Dance, p. 86; Legman II, pp. 157, 825; and Orso, pp. 153–54.

316. Collected in Indianapolis, December 1972, from a 23-year-old male city government intern. Hoffmann X724.5, "Seduction by traveling man."

317. Collected in Carthage, March 1983, from a 24-year-old male pool supervisor. Buehler, pp. 90–93, reports a long version dealing with southern hospitality. Short versions appear in Legman I, pp. 413, 737; and Legman II, p. 741.

318. Collected in Highland, May 1969, from a middle-aged male metallurgist. Exact age withheld. Cf. Motif K1569.8, "Husband discomfits paramour and wife by clever remark showing that he knows all."

319. Collected in Terre Haute, July 1970, from a 49-year-old male truck driver. Hoffmann X741, "Humor concerning necrophilia."

320. Collected in Terre Haute, November 1969, from a 20-year-old female student. A version of this joke about two traveling salesmen is in Legman I, p. 360.

321. Collected in Terre Haute, November 1980, from a 31-year-old male janitor. Hoffmann X716.6, "Smell of breaking wind." For a version, see Legman II, p. 890.

322. Collected in Brazil, November 1972, from a 20-year-old male furnace repairman. For a version of this tale, see Legman II, p. 827.

323. Collected in Terre Haute, March 1969, from a 25-year-old male student. Cf. Motif K2320, "Deception by frightening."

324. Collected in November 1972 from a 21-year-old female student from Loogootee. Motif J1430, "Repartee concerning doctors and patients." Cf. Motif X100, "Humor of disability."

325. Collected in Terre Haute, April 1974, from a 25-year-old male waiter. Cf. Motifs J1430, "Repartee concerning doctors and patients," and X100, "Humor of disability."

326. Collected in Terre Haute, February 1972, from a 16-year-old male student. Cf. Motifs J1430, "Repartee concerning doctors and patients," and X100, "Humor of disability."

327. Collected in December 1969 from an 18-year-old female student from Logansport. Motif X350, "Jokes on teachers." Dance, p. 210, reports a version from Virginia.

328. Collected in Terre Haute, December 1969, from a 36-year-old male fireman. Motif X350, "Jokes on teachers."

329. Collected in Scottsburg, January 1971, from a 40-year-old female photographer. For a discussion of "Tormenting the Teacher" and "Sex in the Schoolroom," see Legman I, pp. 65–76.

330. Collected in Scottsburg, December 1970, from a 45-year-old female advertising manager. Hoffmann J1805.5.1, "Word understood only in its sexual meaning." Cf. Motif J1805.1, "Similar sounding words mistaken for each other," and Legman I, pp. 65–76.

331. Collected in Terre Haute, April 1971, from a 22-year-old male student. See Legman I, pp. 72–76, for a discussion of "Sex in the Schoolroom."

332. Collected in Vincennes, November 1971, from a 40-year-old male welder. Legman II, p. 90, reports two versions, one from Ann Arbor, Michigan (1935), and the other from Paris (1954).

333. Collected in Mount Vernon, March 1970, from a 22-year-old male student. Motif J1805.1, "Similar sounding words mistaken for each other." Cf. Hoffmann, X455, "How many Peters in this room."

334. Collected in Washington, December 1967, from an 18-year-old female student. A Greek analogue (Orso, pp. 207–08) deals with an arranged marriage. A matchmaker finds two girls, a telephone operator and a schoolteacher, for a young man, who selects the schoolteacher, explaining, "After three minutes the telephone operator always tells you you're finished. But the schoolteacher always makes you do your work over and over again!"

335. Collected in July 1971 from a 20-year-old male student from Georgetown. Legman II, p. 248, reports a version of this tale collected in New York in 1946. Cf. Baughman N251.7, "Misfortune pursues farmer."

336. Collected in Brook, April 1981, from a 22-year-old female student. Cf. Motif J1805.1, "Similar sounding words mistaken for each other," and Hoffman J1805.5.1, "Word understood only in its sexual meaning."

337. Collected in Brazil, February 1970, from a 61-year-old male businessman. Motif K134, "Deceptive horse-sale." Vance Randolph has a version of this tale in *Hot Springs and Hell* (Hatboro, Pa.: Folklore Associates, 1965), p. 340.

338. Collected in Brazil, June 1971, from a 75-year-old male retired farmer. Cf. Motif J1430, "Repartee concerning doctors and patients."

339. Collected in Terre Haute, April 1974, from a 25-year-old male waiter. For a variant, see Dance, p. 193. Cf. Legman I, pp. 211–12.

340. Collected in Vincennes, December 1968, from a 63-year-old male florist. This appears as a Jewish joke in Richard M. Dorson, "Jewish-American Dialect Stories on Tape," in *Studies in Biblical and Jewish Folklore,* ed. Raphael Patai, Francis Lee Utley, and Dov Noy (Bloomington: Indiana University Press, 1960), pp. 133–34. Also see Legman I, pp. 421–22, for a variant.

341. Collected in Greensburg, April 1969, from a 47-year-old male construction worker. Motif J1533, "Absurdities concerning birth of animals."

342. Collected in July 1971 from a 20-year-old male student from Georgetown. Two versions appear in Dance, p. 55. Cf. Legman I, p. 177.

343. Collected in Indianapolis, December 1972, from a 23-year-old male city government intern. Hoffmann X717.3.1, "Boy urinates in snow in front of girl's house. Her father is irate when he sees that it spells her name and is in her handwriting." A version about Nixon is in Michael J. Preston, "A Year of Political Jokes (June 1973–June 1974); or, The Silent Majority Speaks Out," *Western Folklore,* 34 (July 1975): 240–41. For other versions, see Legman II, p. 851, and Randolph, pp. 5–6.

344. Collected in Clinton, November 1973, from a 50-year-old male carpenter. Cf. Motif J1430, "Repartee concerning doctors and patients," and Baughman X599.1*, "Jokes on politicians."

345. Collected in Terre Haute, December 1971, from a 19-year-old male student. Legman I, p. 254, prints a version collected in Washington, D.C., in 1951. Although this version is about a politician trying to seduce his secretary, Legman says the tale usually is told about the President of the United States. For versions dealing with the President, see Legman II, pp. 227, 746.

346. Collected in Linton, April 1979, from a 22-year-old male student. Baughman X599.1*, "Jokes on politicians."

347. Collected in Terre Haute, January 1970, from a 44-year-old male traffic manager. Golf jokes are popular in the contemporary oral tradition, although they don't appear in the standard indexes or in many collections. The callous golfer who puts the game above everything else is a familiar figure in golf jokes. Cf. tale 348.

348. Collected in Terre Haute, January 1970, from a 44-year-old male traffic manager. The fanatic golfer appears in several contemporary golf jokes. See note 365.

349. Collected in Fort Branch, December 1967, from a 20-year-old female student. Versions appear in Buehler, pp. 10–11, and Legman II, pp. 842, 918.

350. Collected in Terre Haute, January 1969, from a 44-year-old male traffic manager. This is a humorous treatment of Motif Q223.6, "Failure to observe holiness of Sabbath punished." See note 351.

351. Collected in West Terre Haute, November 1979, from a 22-year-old female secretary. For versions of this tale, see Phyllis Potter, "St. Peter Jokes,"

Southwest Folklore, 3 (Spring 1979): 46–47. Religious figures are not uncommon in contemporary jokes about golf and other sports. See note 299 and tales 264, 275, 299, and 350.

352. Collected in Terre Haute, August 1969, from a 20-year-old female student. For a version, see Buehler, p. 59. Buehler says this tale "would have no meaning to one who had never seen water thrown on dogs locked in the mating position. . . . This is the only shaggy dog story I know of which approaches obscenity." Since this shaggy dog story deals with golf, it appears in this section rather than with the other shaggy dog tales.